WORK PSYCHOLOGY AND ORGANIZATIONAL BEHAVIOUR

Managing the Individual at Work

Wendy Hollway

SAGE Publications
London • Newbury Park • New Delhi

SAGE Publications Ltd
6 Bonhill Street
London EC2A 4PU

SAGE Publications Inc
2455 Teller Road
Newbury Park, California 91320

SAGE Publications India Pvt Ltd
32, M-Block Market
Greater Kailash – I
New Delhi 110 048

British Library Cataloguing in Publication data

Hollway, Wendy
   Work psychology and organizational behaviour:
   Managing the individual at work.
   I. Title
   658.3

   ISBN 0-8039-8353-0
   ISBN 0-8039-8354-9 Pbk

Library of Congress catalog card number 91-60441

Typeset by AKM Associates (UK) Ltd, Southall, Middx.
Printed in Great Britain by Dotesios Ltd,
Trowbridge, Wiltshire

To Robin Lister

Contents

Acknowledgements

I would like to thank colleagues and students at the Department of Occupational Psychology, Birkbeck College, University of London.

1
Introduction

Economic psychotechnics may serve certain ends of commerce and industry but whether these are the best ones is not a care with which the psychologist has to be burdened. (Munsterberg 1913: 19)

1. My Background and Reasons for Writing this Book

For nearly ten years I taught aspects of work psychology [1] in a graduate department of occupational psychology at Birkbeck College, University of London (1978–87). During the last three years there, I taught a course called 'History of Industrial Psychology' and it was through researching that history that I realized how limited and partial my understanding of work psychology had been when it lacked a historical perspective. Students, practitioners and even teachers are often ignorant of the history, reflecting the assumption of so much psychology that historical study is irrelevant because scientific study invariably leads to progress, and better applications are therefore guaranteed. I hope this book will challenge this deep-seated assumption in the students and teachers, not only of industrial, occupational and organizational psychology, but of management, business administration, personnel management and industrial relations.

The historical perspective I have used is not the usual kind: not a history of the progress of ideas through the influential figures in the subject and the improvements in practice which are the result of application. It does not assume that work psychology was a coherent discipline resulting from an objective mode of enquiry which reveals facts about people at work. I start with the premiss that the psychology of work, like other applied social sciences, is a body of knowledge which has been produced rather than discovered. The emphasis on production allows one to raise questions about the conditions of its production; about the situations in which problems are defined, by whom, with whose interests incorporated. These conditions will affect the product. Industrial psychology would not have emerged when it did, in the way it did (if at all) without the late nineteenth-century growth of mechanized production and of the size of factories in North America and Europe. This may seem obvious but this premiss changes the way that history is written. The question is changed: what conditions have produced work psychology in its eighty-year history and with what effects?

The average psychologist, and particularly the average work psychologist, does not come across the post-structuralist theorists who helped to form my approach to the history of work psychology. There is a considerable intellectual and ideological distance separating these areas, and it is one which took me some time to travel. To explain how I came to be familiar with the work of Althusser, Foucault and psychoanalytic theorists (among others), I should go back a little further into my early career as a psychologist.

In 1968, when I started as an undergraduate psychology student at Sheffield University, radical ideas had begun to affect student culture and the more daring of my peers were demanding that R.D. Laing's work should be included on the course called 'Abnormal and Personality Psychology'. The undergraduate psychology course continued, however, in the orthodox experimental tradition; rigorous, scientific, not very applied and restricted in vision by its methods and theories. I can't have listened very well to the few lectures on industrial psychology, because I remember thinking that Hawthorne was someone who had conducted some famous experiments. I think I felt that industrial psychology was beneath my dignity: it certainly didn't coincide with my idealistic views on human liberation. I received a good honours degree, went on to do a teaching qualification and, since psychology teaching was expanding, I had no difficulty in finding a job in higher education.

For the next three years, I taught social psychology in a variety of applied, multi-disciplinary contexts. I became interested in group processes and started to facilitate experiential groups. In the mid-seventies I attended a six-week summer course at the National Training Laboratories in Bethel, Maine, USA, which had an international reputation for applying human relations principles to the management of groups. I then took a research job involved in research on group and organizational dynamics. I attended a 'Leicester Conference', organized by the Tavistock Institute of Human Relations, which used experiential methods to learn about authority and group and organizational relations from a psychoanalytic perspective. By the mid-seventies, feminism was high on the personal-political agenda for many women of my age and subculture. The steps from experiential groups to consciousness-raising groups and from critical feelings about psychology to critical social theory (including feminist theory) were not difficult in that context.

The experiential groups which I designed and led increasingly emphasized power relations and social differences, particularly gender and class. This emphasis was different from the typical human relations approach which, by the 1970s, focused on individual change without locating people's behaviour in their social positions and social relations. In understanding group dynamics, I still find it most useful to see power relations in terms of major dimensions of social difference such as class, gender and 'race'. In organizational contexts, these interact with the formal status provided by the hierarchy as well as interacting with each other.

I moved to London at the end of a three-year research contract at Bristol University and the first job I was offered was in occupational psychology. By that time, I wanted to stay in London. The department appeared progressive and humanistic and I would be able to use experiential methods to teach group dynamics. It was the time when human relations had infiltrated to the top of what would otherwise have been a rather conventional department in the FMJ–FJM tradition ('fitting the man to the job and fitting the job to the man'; see below, section 2). Human relations and experiential group methods were soon on the wane, but the department of occupational psychology continued to be democratically managed and open to new ideas. When my interests moved on, I was able to develop courses in 'applied psychology in the Third World', 'Discrimination and Equal Opportunities', and 'History of Industrial Psychology'. By the end of 1981 I had completed a PhD thesis on identity and gender difference (not based in the work place, but on domestic relations, Hollway 1982). It was through this work, and subsequent collaboration to produce a book with like-minded academics (Henriques et al. 1984), that I continued to develop the post-structuralist and feminist strand of my academic work. Because of the character of occupational psychology, it was difficult fully to reconcile these strands.

By the time I came to research the history of industrial psychology for the Birkbeck course, I was knowledgeable about applying the historical perspective of Michel Foucault to the production of social science. Essentially this perspective does not accept the premiss that knowledge can be value free. It understands the production of knowledge by analysing the relations between knowledge, power and practice. I approach work psychology in the same way in this book. I pose three questions. How did work psychology come to be what it is? What, therefore, is it? What effects does it have? Under the last question, a secondary theme emerges: has work psychology influenced the behaviour and self-understanding of individuals at work and if so how? This is a question which arises from post-structuralism's interest in theorizing the production of the individual subject and subjectivity within the relations of power, knowledge and practice. Post-structuralism comprehensively rejects, as I do, psychology's theory of the individual (see Henriques et al. 1984), but recognizes that neither structuralism, Foucault nor psychoanalysis has an adequate account of the production of subjectivity. I find it helpful to be empirical in addressing this abstract, theoretical question. In Henriques et al. (1984), I used my thesis data on gender difference and the production of identity in couple relationships. In my subsequent book (Hollway 1989), I applied that theory to gender difference in the production of psychology. In this book I take a detailed look at eighty years of work psychology, its relations with management practices and its production of discourses and practices about the individual at work.

2. Work Psychology and Other Labels

This book is about those areas of knowledge that focus on people in the workplace and that affect practice in work organizations. These areas cannot be subsumed under one title, because they reflect many different approaches which are often theoretically inconsistent and even contradictory. They include scientific management, industrial, occupational and social psychology, human factors, human relations and organizational behaviour. At the engineering end, ergonomics overlaps with industrial psychology. At the social end, industrial sociology overlaps with organizational behaviour. To the extent that these titles refer to knowledge about people at work, they come within my scope. My interest is not to describe the areas of knowledge in themselves but to explore the relation between them and workplace practices; that is to look at their effects and, conversely, how workplace practice feeds into the production of knowledge in work psychology. For this reason, the historical texts and case studies I examine are selected for their relevance to practice. This book does not focus on the classic texts of industrial psychology such as Munsterberg (1913) or Viteles (1933). It stays close to the workplace and to the practices in which psychological knowledge was involved. Whether the agent was a psychologist, a business administration academic, an internal or external consultant or change agent, is of minor importance.

Managers are the largest group who use work psychology: all the areas I have listed have been incorporated at some time or other into management training. Other practitioners who would probably have training in some of these areas are consultants, trainers and researchers who are employed by organizations to do the following:

help select employees;
devise appraisal systems;
design systems and methods of work organization;
instigate change in the organization;

advise on the introduction of new technology;
advise on 'manpower' planning and succession plans;
enhance safety;
enhance productivity;
cope with stress and conflict;
help to problem-solve;
improve decision-making and teamwork;
find out what employees think about their jobs and about the
    company;
negotiate pay and conditions;
counsel people when they lose their jobs;
advise people on what jobs suit them and how to create a favourable
    impression on application;
train managers to manage people and supervisors to supervise them
    in ways that will promote a climate favourable to the work of the
    organization.

The list is impressive in its diversity, but the items have in common that
they try to understand how people work, for the purpose of improving
this. The present-day *Journal of Occupational Psychology* (subtitled 'an
International Journal of Industrial and Organizational Psychology')
demonstrates that its chosen scope covers more or less the same
ground:

> The journal's domain is broad, covering industrial, organizational,
> engineering, vocational and personnel psychology, as well as behavioural
> aspects of industrial relations, ergonomics, human factors and industrial
> sociology. Interdisciplinary approaches are welcome. (Guide notes for
> referees)

It is cumbersome, when referring in general to these areas, to specify
all the subtitles but it is often misleading to use one only, since the
labels mean different things in different epochs and countries. Before
the Second World War 'industrial psychology' was the commonest
label, and when I am referring to that period it is usually the
appropriate title. However it had different emphases in the United
States and Britain. In the US it came to refer almost exclusively to
psychometric testing, whereas in Britain it included fatigue research,
working conditions and job design as well (all of which together were
also referred to as 'human factors'). In Britain in the 1950s, Professor
Alec Rodger encapsulated the definition of the field in the slogan
'Fitting the man to the job and the job to the man' (FMJ/FJM):

Fitting the man to the job
       through occupational *guidance*
                 personnel *selection*
                 training and development

fitting the job to the man
through *methods* design
  equipment design
  design and negotiation of *working conditions*
  and
  (physical and social) *rewards.*
(From an undated student handout issued by Alec Rodger in the 1970s)

By the 1950s the title in Britain had changed to 'occupational psychology' to reflect a move away from purely industrial work settings. In the United States this term has been used only to refer to knowledge in the field of vocational guidance (vocational psychology in the US). A focus on the individual at work has been characteristic of the history of these areas, from scientific management to human relations, and this theoretical focus has had distinct effects practice. Rodger's definition is now deemed by many to be too narrow because it does not address the question of organizations within which the 'man' works. (It has also helped to render women workers invisible, but has not been rejected for that reason.) Since the 1960s, the term organizational behaviour had become increasingly popular.

When I need a label for the general domain which is not historically or geographically specific, I use the term 'work psychology'. Its main disadvantage is that it suggests that the areas I shall be talking about fall within psychology, which is not true: sociologists and management theorists would claim parts of 'work psychology' too. None the less the term is faithful to my purpose because it signals the focus on individuals at work which, as I shall argue, dominates knowledge and practice in the field.

The American and British histories of work psychology are closely interrelated, but their differences provide a further way of under-standing how specific conditions have produced different emphases in psychological knowledge (for example the greater power of trade unions in Britain in the 1920s affected the treatment of scientific management and the orientation of British industrial psychology). The topics and cases on which I focus are about equally divided between Britain and the United States.

3. The Status of Knowledge

This book is about the relation between knowledge and practice in work psychology and its history provides evidence of the nature of this relationship. My interest is not simply academic. I believe that work psychology is blind to the conditions of its own production and their consequent effects and that this has far-reaching and unfortunate consequences for its quality and integrity.

There is virtually no debate about the status of the knowledge which makes up work psychology and this state of affairs is the result of the uncritical identification of work psychology with behavioural science, which in turn identifies with natural science. There is lively debate about the status of scientific knowledge in, for example, physics and also within the social sciences, but the issues have largely passed psychology and work psychology by. Science provides a justification for believing that there is no problem with the status of knowledge. It prescribes that the knowledge gained through scientific methods is unproblematically true and that scientists are potentially neutral agents in the process. It assumes that, if applied correctly, such knowledge would necessarily be progressive and that, if there were a problem of application, science and scientists would not be responsible. This position has characterized industrial psychology from its beginnings. For example, Munsterberg, whose book *Psychology and Industrial Efficiency* (1913) is considered the seminal text of industrial psychology, features in his introduction a discussion of the relation between any technical science (into which category he puts applied psychology) and the product. The question of responsibility is central:

> We must understand that every technical science says only: you must make use of this means, if you wish to reach this or that particular end. But no technical science can decide within its limits whether the end itself is really a desirable one . . . We must make the same discrimination in the psycho-technical field. The psychologist may point out the methods by which an involuntary confession can be secured from a defendant, but whether it is justifiable to extort involuntary confession is a problem which does not concern the psychologist . . . Economic psychotechnics may serve certain ends of commerce and industry but whether these are the best ones is not a care with which the psychologist has to be burdened. (Munsterberg 1913: 17, 18, 19)

If scientific knowledge is believed to be neutral and true, this argument is persuasive If not, the argument collapses. It is one of my major purposes in writing this book to demonstrate the ways in which knowledge concerned with people at work (what Munsterberg calls 'economic psychotechnics') is not objective or true in any simple sense. It is a historical product of interests and power relations in practice. Knowledge should not be separated from its effects. However this position is not, in the first instance, an ethical one. I start from the premiss that there is no such thing as knowledge in isolation from its conditions of production and reproduction. Knowledge cannot be separated from its effects. Moreover the relation between knowledge and practice is not a one-way cause–effect relationship. Managerial practices, themselves affected by work psychology, reciprocally affect the concepts and theories emerging from work psychology. This is what I mean by the inseparability of knowledge and practice and the way that they reciprocally produce and reproduce each other.[2]

4. Power, Knowledge, Practice

In this section I shall try to illustrate the usefulness of these concepts in breaking through the barriers that science has erected against understanding how work psychology is produced. As a brief example of the relations between power, knowledge and practice, I shall take the case of the concepts of motivation and job satisfaction in organizational behaviour (see especially chapters 5 and 7). Because of the long-standing dominance of science in the West, the term knowledge itself has come to have connotations of fact and certitude. In contrast I see knowledge and practice as produced within the same historical conditions. In this case they were conditions which faced employers and managers with a serious problem of ensuring that the labour force turned out products of competitive price and quality.

Motivation and job satisfaction are not phenomena that exist in some universal and timeless state, that awaited human relations science to discover and apply them. Both the concepts and the practices that confer on them some kind of material reality are a product of changes in the organization of work, which were themselves the result of the dominance of some interests over others; of owners (both private capitalists and the state) over labourers. Job satisfaction would have been an unthinkable concept in a feudal regime, where tied workers had few means of opposing the power of the landowners and monarch. Neither was it produced in the context of pre-industrial, self-employed craft workers whose control over work was a condition of their existence.

The problem of motivating an individual worker emerged in order to create sufficient satisfaction with the job to produce adequate work. Since the concentration of workers in large factories, with mechanization and with the emergence of a management hierarchy to determine and control work performance (see chapter 2 for details), jobs had been fragmented, routinized and control often entirely removed from the person who actually performed the work. Supervision of this alienating work (the same conditions produced the sociological concept of 'alienation') became correspondingly tight and harsh, but despite attempts at perfecting systems of control, notably those advocated by scientific management, workers did not conform to management demands on them. Enough resisted, individually, in informal groups, or through labour organizations, to present a problem. Given the existence of these forms of resistance, the failure of employers and management to exercise unadulterated power and the need to devise forms of control of work performance produced human relations management. Its specific practices depended on the idea that individual workers could be motivated – could be made to find sufficient satisfaction at work – to perform in ways that management wanted.

In principle, there could be an almost infinite number of ways of conceptualizing the problem of getting workers' commitment to production, and hence an array of possible approaches to its solution. The concepts of motivation and job satisfaction did not emerge simply from managerial problems; although their production in human relations form in organizational behaviour was specific to those problems, they also had preconditions in lay, psychological and industrial psychological knowledge. In general psychology, motivation was conceptualized in predominantly physiological terms and its transition to application in the context of job motivation owed more to psychoanalytic and lay use of the term motivation.

Knowledge is a word which is usually used in the singular and this reflects the aspirations to coherence and unity of scientific knowledge. Where theories are multiple, concepts inconsistent and facts incoherent, it is said to be due to the immature state of a discipline, rather than to the character of knowledge itself. The assumption that knowledge is unitary makes it virtually impossible to untangle the complex conditions and the multifarious powers that produce knowledge (or rather, to underline the point, that produce knowledges). Work psychology is a hotchpotch of different theoretical assumptions and concepts which, unsurprisingly, make for some inconsistent and conflicting precepts underpinning practice. The attempt to increase job satisfaction is a case in point. I have said that the dominant knowledge underpinning the attempt was the human relations emphasis on modifying the individual. But when individual workers were insufficiently moved by supervisors' attempts to be nice to them (see chapters 5 and 6 for a detailed treatment of this point), there was another tradition within industrial psychology which approached questions of job performance from the point of view of job design; a tradition emanating from engineering through scientific management and ergonomics. Paradoxically, during the 1950s, this tradition became incorporated into the human relations approach to motivation and job satisfaction through job redesign (see chapter 6).

On the periphery there was a Marxist theoretical tradition, which drew some power through its close identification with working-class, and therefore trade union, interests. It was premised on the principle that a conflict between owners of the means of production and those who provided labour power was inevitable under capitalism. This tradition had drawn attention to the deskilling of work in industrial capitalism (Braverman 1974). In this view, job satisfaction would depend on changes to the whole organization and control of work.

Here were different knowledges, with different political and financial implications. It was not scientific merit which determined the emergence of a human relations model of motivation and job satisfaction, but rather the play of powers amongst interested groups at the time. Amongst the employers and managers of Western industrial organizations, demechanization was out of the question. Moreover it would have been heretical to consider handing back control of the labour process to the labourers (later this position was modified). Particularly in the United States, employers did not like to deal directly with unions, especially on basic issues like the organization of work, which was considered a management prerogative. They feared that such dialogue would represent a concession to trade union power. Politically, the best target was the individual worker and epistemologically the preconditions for this focus were already well developed in the changes which were taking place in work psychology.

In Foucault's conception, power, like knowledge, is never singular or one-way, never homogeneous or monolithic. If machine-pacing, deskilling, piece rates and tight supervision had succeeded in achieving optimal productivity, motivation and job satisfaction would never have seen the light of day. As I have argued, they were a product of the play of different powers at a given time. But even this gives a picture of power which is too simply dichotomous. Amongst workers and amongst employers, the understanding of their interests, the forces imposing upon their actions and the powers and practices available to them, all varied enormously. In addition the state intervened in different ways; for example in Britain during the First World War it initiated the fatigue studies in munitions factories which launched British industrial psychology, at least temporarily, on a welfarist path. Finally psychologists, whether of the 'pure' or 'applied' variety, have their interests, which feed into the conditions within which particular knowledge emerges. In general, the belief in their own scientific status and neutrality gave them legitimacy and a simple answer to potentially troubling questions of responsibility. These dovetailed nicely with the interests of employers, who wanted their view of the problem resolved and not challenged. They also benefited from the reputation of work psychology as scientific, because it was therefore deemed to be above the politics of industrial conflict. Indeed it appeared to offer them something even better, because it claimed to solve such conflict of interest (see chapter 2).

In this book, consistent with Foucault's usage, I use power to mean a productive force, ever-present in relations of all kinds. It is in this sense that I speak of the role of power in producing knowledge. Since there is a tendency to understand power as a negative, coercive force, this is important. To say that power is productive is quite separate from making a judgement about the value of its effects, positive or negative. Ultimately the importance of using power–knowledge–practice relations as a central analytical tool is to produce a different knowledge about work psychology. Consistent with this approach, I am not seeking to produce 'objective' knowledge but, through a particular reading of history, to undermine what I regard as the illegitimate power of science to produce a sanitized version of what work psychology is and how it came to be that way.

5. The Book's Contents

The book is divided into two parts. The first, Factory Hands, is concerned with the conditions of emergence of a psychology of work in the early twentieth century. Chapter 2 discusses the emergence of management, problems of supervision, scientific management and its effects. Chapter 3 looks at the emergence of industrial psychology in Britain in the First World War and the founding of the National Institute of Industrial Psychology in 1921. It then details the issues surrounding the appointment of the first industrial psychologist at Rowntree's Cocoa Works and discusses the department's subsequent psychological work. Chapter 4 concerns the emergence of psychometrics in Britain and how it transformed industrial psychology during the twenties and thirties.

Meanwhile, in the United States, the Hawthorne research was ushering in a new era for work psychology. Part 2, The Sentimental Worker, documents the emergence and development of human relations at work to the 1980s. Chapter 5 starts at the Hawthorne plant and analyses the conditions of emergence of human relations within the industrial relations climate of American manufacturing organizations. With human relations, the object of work psychology changes from a mechanical, performance-orientated model of the person at work to one which treats employees as having sentiments and socio-emotional needs. In chapter 6 I continue the story of human relations in US organizations, looking at why and how the emphasis shifted from shop-floor workers to supervisors to middle managers and training became the dominant practice of human relations 'change agents'. I then trace a parallel development of human relations: interest in motivation, job satisfaction and job redesign. In both these areas, work psychology was now premised on the belief that the 'whole person' had to be engaged in the objectives of the organization, as opposed to just their performance-related skills. Despite attempts to extend the conceptual framework from the psychological to the organizational, a similar approach pervaded the organizational change technologies of the seventies and eighties. The ideas of interpersonal skills, democratic leadership style and participative small groups still held sway under the new banner of organizational behaviour. Chapter 7 examines two British case studies which illustrate, among other things, the differences and similarities between American and British approaches to organizational change. Chapter 8 returns to the US to consider the organizational culture approach as the latest popular manifestation of human relations. I take the case of deregulation in AT&T (where, in the subsidiary called Western Electric, human relations emerged through the Hawthorne research). Under the banner of organizational culture, consultants tackled the same old problem of ensuring commitment to the company's goals. This time they were faced with the problem of how to change those goals without losing the commitment. Organizational change strategies were heavily supplemented with marketing a new image in a kind of public relations for employees. Finally, chapter 9 tries to look into the future, using the lessons of history. It is not a prescriptive approach and certainly not idealistic. It asks, from the examples in this book, what can be said about the forces that will shape the future of knowledge and practice concerning the individual at work.

Notes

1. Throughout this book I have chosen the phrase 'work psychology' when I need a label which is not historically or geographically specific. It is uncommon in both Britain and the United States, where industrial, occupational and organizational psychology refer to the same area. Work psychology is the accepted title in most of Europe. The question of the most appropriate title has come up in the UK with regard to a recent proposal to change the name of the *Journal of Occupational Psychology*: 'Some [committee members] accepted that marketing considerations might favour a change to 'Work and Organisational Psychology', some were sceptical and called for more evidence, whilst others very much rejected the notion of surrendering a distinctive title for a coherent body of applied psychology in which there is a strong British tradition' (*The Psychologist*, August 1990: 375).

2. This theory of knowledge derives from the work of Michel Foucault. It can be summed up in a single phrase: the relations between knowledge, power and practice. Foucault has developed this approach through its application to the emergence of psychiatry, modern medicine, prisons and modern forms of sexuality. Donzelot has applied it to the family (1979). Nikolas Rose (see chapter 4) has applied it to the use of psychological measurement in British education (Rose 1985). I have used it to examine management practice in Zimbabwe (Hollway 1986).

PART ONE

FACTORY HANDS

2

Scientific Management and the Task Idea: Precursors of Industrial Psychology

The reduction of the workman to a living tool . . . must either demoralize [him] or . . . produce great resentment and result in serious difficulties between masters and men. (Cadbury 1914: 105)

1. Introduction

'Scientific management' in its widest sense refers to the attempts made to devise efficient systems of industrial production and organization. In its narrower sense, it refers to the specific principles advocated by the American engineer F.W. Taylor before the First World War. (Gantt and Emerson developed different emphases from Taylor but never challenged his position as the leading protagonist of scientific management.) Its first introduction is usually dated at 1909, when the Chief of the Ordnance Department of the United States 'began to introduce certain features of scientific management at the Watertown Arsenal in Massachusetts' (Muscio 1974: 227–8). These included motion study and premium payments. Taylor's aim was increased productivity and the elimination of waste through management control of the labour process: 'as to the importance of obtaining the maximum output of each man and each machine, it is only through the adoption of modern scientific management that this great problem can be finally solved' (Taylor 1967: 27).

The central method for achieving these goals was 'the task idea' which Taylor claimed was 'the most prominent single element in modern scientific management' (1967: 64). This meant that 'the task of every workman is fully planned out, and each man usually receives written instructions describing in the minutest detail the work which he is to accomplish, as well as the means to be used in doing it' (Cadbury 1914: 101).

In section 2 I describe the task idea and evidence about its effects in the US. In sections 3 and 4 I discuss the conditions for the emergence of scientific management in early twentieth-century US manufacturing industries, and the effect of stronger trade unions on its reception in Britain. Consistent with my emphasis on the conditions which produce widespread changes in knowledge and practice, I consider the international economic climate, the growth of the size of factories and of organized labour and the problems of old-style supervision as a means of regulating the workforce.

Section 5 is based on a contemporary American text (Hoxie 1915) which provides statements on the significance of scientific management from Taylor's own point of view (the management perspective) and from the point of view of organized labour. Hoxie's book reports on the results of an investigation into scientific management on behalf of the US Commission on Industrial Relations in 1914. The investigation was called as a result of potentially serious industrial unrest resulting from the application of scientific management. The existence of Hoxie's report is testimony to the strength of resistance to scientific management in the US, in conditions which were hostile to the growth of organized labour (see section 3). Hoxie, the special investigator, saw his purpose as 'to determine what, if anything, can be done to harmonize the relations of scientific management and labor' (Hoxie 1915: 1) and for this he deemed it necessary to investigate scientific management in practice. In section 5 I quote extensively from Hoxie's text. In sections 6 and 7 I use this text to explore two interrelated themes: the use of science by management to claim legitimacy; and targeting the individual as a strategy for industrial relations. I conclude by discussing the political implications of taking up Taylor's position that the theory and practice of scientific management were independent of each other.

In section 8 I consider the differences in forms of regulation which were used in Britain. I use a 1914 text by Edward Cadbury, owner and director of Cadbury's chocolate firm, which was both highly successful and reputed to be one of the most advanced in respect of workers' welfare. In 1913 he gave a paper at the Sociological Society which was discussed by several well-known industrialists, trade unionists and academics. The paper and replies (Cadbury 1914) provide an interesting insight into the industrial and political context into which scientific management was introduced in Britain (see also chapter 3).

2. The Task Idea

The task idea is the principle that the task of each worker should be determined in advance by management, which specifies not only what must be done but – in the minutest detail – how it should be done. Taylor's attachment to the task idea derived first from his pre-occupation with 'soldiering'. For example:

The writer was much interested recently in hearing one small but experienced golf caddy boy of twelve explaining to a green caddy, who had shown special energy and interest, the necessity of going slow and lagging behind his man when he came up to the ball, showing him that since they were paid by the hour, the faster they went the less money they got, and finally telling him that if he went too fast the other boys would give him a licking. . . .

The greater part of the systematic soldiering . . . is done by men with the deliberate object of keeping their employers ignorant of how fast work can be done. So universal is soldiering for this purpose that hardly a competent workman can be found in a large establishment, whether he works by the day or on piece work, contract work, or under any of the ordinary systems, who does not devote a considerable part of his time studying just how slow he can work and still convince his employer that he is going at a good pace. (Taylor 1967: 21)

The task idea is significant for the emergence of management and for industrial psychology in two ways: it transferred control from the workforce to management and its object was the individual worker. In both respects it was a reflection of changes in industrial practice which were already gathering momentum. The task idea, like scientific management more generally, was not generated in the theoretical realm and subsequently applied by managers. The task idea was powerful because it collected and systematized what was already happening in many manufacturing industries. Taylor himself argued this: 'The theory, or philosophy, of scientific management is just beginning to be understood, whereas the management itself has been a gradual evolution, extending over a period of nearly thirty years' (Taylor 1967: 27–8).

Scientific management claimed that, through the task idea, industry would become more productive and trouble-free as it 'gathers up, systematizes and systematically transmits to the workers all the traditional craft knowledge and skill which is being lost and destroyed under current industrial methods' (Hoxie 1915: 10). In effect this was a transfer of control from workers to management and was a significant part of the creation of management. To set the task, and to control it, management had to transfer all the specific knowledge and skill required to do particular jobs into its own hands. As the American trade unions asserted in their charges against scientific management, the knowledge held by management was transmitted only 'piecemeal'; that is jobs were reduced in scope and skill, and craft workers could increasingly be treated – and paid – as unskilled. Thus through devising new methods of management control, scientific management contributed to the 'degradation of work' (Braverman 1974), which has characterized industrial production.

Hoxie's conclusions in the report into scientific management emphasize this point:

There can be little doubt that scientific management tends, in practice, to weaken the power of the individual worker as against the employer . . . As we have seen it gathers up and transfers to the management the traditional craft knowledge and transmits this again to the workers only piecemeal as it is needed in the performance of the particular job or task. It tends, in practice, to confine each worker to a particular task or small cycle of tasks. It thus narrows his outlook and skill and the experience and training which are necessary to do the work. He is, therefore, more easily displaced. Moreover, the changing methods and conditions of work and the setting of tasks by time study with its assumption always of scientific accuracy put the individual worker at a disadvantage in any attempt to question the justice of the demands made upon him; and the assumed payment of wages in exact proportion to efficiency, with the opportunities of exceptional reward held out if he will but make the task, tends to put upon him the responsibility for wage results of which he complains. There are no simple, definite, recognized and permanent standards of work and earnings to which he can appeal. The onus of proof is upon him and the standards of judgement are set up by the employer, covered by the mantle of scientific accuracy. The unskilled worker, especially, under scientific management, loses what little chance of success as an individual he may elsewhere have in any contest with the employer, and scientific management, from the viewpoint of competitive power, tends to relegate workers to the condition of the unskilled. (Hoxie 1915: 104)

The task idea is significant for a second major reason: it provided an industrial relations strategy which changed the focus from workers *en masse* to workers as individuals. American trade unions claimed that scientific management 'has refused to deal with workers except as individuals' (Hoxie 1915: 18; see also section 4, OL3). This shift of focus to regulation of the individual worker was an essential condition of the emergence of industrial psychology,[1] as well as being a political tool to counter increasing organization of labour into trade unions.

3. Conditions for the Emergence of Management

In 1880 the United States lagged behind Britain, Germany and France in industrialization, and between 1880 and 1910 it underwent the most rapid economic expansion of any industrialized country for a comparable period of time (Bendix 1956: 254). This was accompanied by ruthless practices towards workers which were not successfully restrained by unionization. In 1897, American trade unions had 487,000 members and seven years later this had increased 2.0727 million, an increment which was accompanied by considerable violence (Bendix 1956: 265; Hoxie 1921). This initially impressive growth must be offset by a recognition of the large numbers of immigrants, from rural America and from Europe, who were obliged to accept work under any conditions. For example, in Detroit in 1911, 22,000 manual workers arrived to work in the expanding car industry (Beynon 1984: 33). Many companies were successful in resisting the unionization of their workforce. In the late 1920s when the famous research in the Hawthorne works of the General Electric Company in Chicago was begun (see chapter 5), General Electric was a non-union company.

In Britain, in response to the dire working conditions of the nineteenth century, trade unions grew strongly. In 1914 there were 4 million union members (a quarter of the workforce). By 1918, this number had increased to 6.5 million. (Stevenson 1984: 54). The relative strength of trade unions in the two nations was an important factor in the take-up of scientific management, in regard to both its extent and its emphasis. In the eyes of progressive British employers liked Edward Cadbury and Seebohm Rowntree (see chapter 3), the sorts of exploitation which were attributed to scientific management in the United States would court industrial unrest and possibly revolution in Britain:

> the reduction of the workman to a living tool, with differential bonus schemes to induce him to expend his last ounce of energy, while initiative and judgement and freedom of movement are eliminated, in the long run must either demoralise the workman, or more likely in England, produce great resentment and result in serious differences between masters and men. (Cadbury 1914: 105)

Had it not been for Taylor, something very similar would still have happened: attempts at 'rationalization' and the search for new systems were gradually coming up with related practices in all the rapidly industrializing countries. As Cadbury remarked, most of Taylor's suggestions were not new. Beynon's (1984: ch.1) history of Ford's shows the effects of new machinery and the assembly line around the time that Taylor was working. Hobsbawn comments that 'innocent of Taylorism, the Bristol Boot and Shoe employers, who devised the team system around 1890, applied his principles' (1968). Roll (1968) in his history of the London firm of Boulton and Watt, who manufactured steam engines, argued that the general principles of specialization and systematization were in evidence in their reorganizations as early as 1830: 'The presence of experimentation in scientific management shows that these are not exactly a product of the era of mass production but were apparent from the very beginning of machine industry' (Roll 1968: 271).

Roll instances two developments, 'an intense preoccupation with problems of time study' and payment by results. These resulted from 'a higher degree of specialization of functions with its consequent gradation of workmen by the greater use of machinery and by the standardization attained in the variety of production' (1968: 268–9).

Changes in practice had already begun. What Taylor contributed was a 'scientific' rationale for the changes through his claim that work could be controlled according to 'the rule of fact and law'. It was an idea which was ripe for application, available and powerful because of the success and legitimacy of nineteenth-century natural science.

The corollary is that, on the one hand, all the ills of industrialization cannot be blamed on scientific management; on the other, those who formulate, disseminate and apply the ideas are part of the historical process and cannot fairly argue that they are exempt from responsibility. Put another way, it means that Taylorism was not a set of ideas emanating simply from the mind of a great or innovative thinker. It was part of the wider historical processes which moved industrialization along the road of new management systems whose primary purpose was the control of the labour process. In turn, the same forces ushered into being the new industrial psychology and the existence of a large and powerful interest group of managers with forms of organization for sharing concerns and disseminating ideas during a period of continuing, or increasing, conflicts with labour and severe economic competition.

The effects of industrialization established the ground for management to emerge: increasingly the machinery developed for production necessitated the containment of labour in factories, rather than the old system of 'putting out'. These factories grew in size to the point where informal relations with the owner were no longer possible and bureaucratic procedures and modes of organization were devised. Partly governed by the new machinery and partly by the desire to limit workers' control over their work, jobs became narrow, specialized and stripped of the craft skill previously associated with them. Initially the struggle against organized labour was waged by employers, who likewise recognized that there was strength in corporate action. Bendix documents the development of policy at the 1903 meeting of the National Association of Manufacturers, where 'it was clearly recognized that a collective approach to the labor problem constituted a new departure' (Bendix 1956: 268):

> Whereas Social Darwinism had encouraged the view that the employer's authority was assured and that his management of labor posed no problem, the open-shop campaign prompted employers as a group for the first time to formulate principles of managerial policy. . . . These larger implications of the open-shop campaign are evident to some extent from its coincidence with the rise of scientific management and of industrial psychology. . . . But they emerge also from the concerted efforts of dealing with the labor problems. (Bendix 1956: 269)

The growth of management is synonymous with the emergence of new and systematized forms of control over the labour process. In the middle of the nineteenth century in the United States, there were no middle managers. Fifty years later, management was well established with its own training institutions and journals: 'Rarely in the history of the world has an institution grown to be so important and so pervasive in so short a period of time' (Chandler 1977: 4). In Great Britain, the ratio of administrative to production employees is indicative of a similar trend: it was 8.6 in 1907 and had risen to 20.0 by 1948 (Bendix 1956: 214). The deskilling of labour produced a new management class to deal with a problem of control which has been fundamental to the history of Western capitalism and of industrial psychology ever since.

4. Supervision

The new forms of production and organization produced dramatic increases in productivity, but at a considerable cost in the form of a proliferation of supervision (not to mention resistance and alienation). Until the deskilling of jobs, there was no systematic supervision of work. In the early factories, an employer may well have been accustomed to walk around the shop and 'belabour his men with his own walking stick' (Pollard 1968: 232), but in the first, textile, phase of industrialization in Britain:

> the workers were managed by a reliance upon the traditions of craftsman- ship and of the master–servant relationship. . . . Traditionally skilled work was performed at a leisurely pace or in spurts of great intensity, but always at the discretion of the individual worker. In modern industry work must be performed above all with regular intensity. (Bendix 1956: 203)

Before the advent of scientific management, 'overlookers' or 'supervisors' or 'foremen' were routinely employed to control workers. During the period of increasing division of labour and machine-paced work, and before the advent of human relations techniques aimed at locating control of employees in their own attitudes, supervision reached marathon proportions: at one point at Goodyear in the United States, there was one supervisor to every ten workers (Goldman and van Houten 1979: 124).

Mary Parker Follett (Metcalf and Urwick 1971: 162) gives an example from British coal mines several decades after the period I am discussing which testifies to the continued and successful resistance to work supervision. An overman, who was called in to testify whether or not a certain workman did his work properly, was questioned as follows:

> *Magistrate*: But isn't it your duty under the Mines Act to visit each working place twice a day?
> *Overman*: Yes.

Magistrate: Don't you do it?
Overman: Yes.
Magistrate: Then why didn't you ever see him work?
Overman: They always stop work when they see an overman coming and sit down and wait till he's gone – even take out their pipes, if it's a mine free from gas. They won't let anyone watch them.

Supervisory relations came to be one of the longest-running problems in industrial psychology: how to get supervisors and managers to treat workers in such a way as not to precipitate industrial unrest, sabotage or restriction of output. The question ushered in the whole human relations movement in organizations, with its emphasis on good interpersonal relations, motivation and job redesign (see chapters 5 and 6).

According to Foucault, the trend towards supervision as a means of disciplining the population applied more broadly than to work institutions. 'The exercise of discipline presupposes a mechanism which coerces by means of observation' (Foucault 1977: 120). In Western societies it displaced the older feudal order of punishment, becoming widespread during the nineteenth century when many new institutions emerged for regulating conduct: the asylum, the factory, the school, the prison and the barracks (for a discussion of industrial psychology's part, see chapter 4). Foucault sees a shift in the techniques of social regulation taking place during the second half of the eighteenth century in Europe from traditional to disciplinary modes of domination (Foucault 1977), both having the body as their object. According to him the 'disciplines' of the human sciences were a product of a further shift in disciplinary techniques away from direct coercion of bodies towards the production of normal subjects who will discipline themselves.

Scientific management was a forerunner of management principles which advocated the shift from the reign of arbitrary personal authority to the rule of law, procedure and science. It did not achieve the desired social regulation, but in Taylor's ideas of functional foremanship, rate setting and piece rates we see the seeds of themes which later, backed up by more developed knowledges in industrial psychology, went some way towards achieving self-regulation in workers. The concepts of motivation, job satisfaction, interpersonal skills for managers and the long-running attempt at democratic leadership style all testify to the shift from coercion of bodies to the attempted production of self-regulated individuals in managerial knowledge and practice.

Supervision and management are intimately connected: 'discipline is [not] simply an art of distributing bodies, of extracting time from them and accumulating it, but of composing forces to obtain an efficient machine' (Foucault 1977: 186). In the early days of industrialization, foremen or supervisors exercised control through the use of force and sanctions which were relatively arbitrary. The basic idea of 'functional foremanship' was that foremen should control workers through the precise planning, organization and coordination of their movements. It was these functions which called into being new levels of hierarchy specifically concerned with management and changed the job of the foreman. Initially an unskilled labourer could proceed all the way up this hierarchy, becoming an overlooker, foreman and manager. Gradually the promotion patterns in industrial organizations changed from a continuous hierarchy to an arrangement where managers were recruited from a separate class who had access to further education and training. This both reflected and reproduced a situation in which the perspective and values of workers and management were increasingly differentiated and these differences were structured into the organization.[2]

5. Claims about Scientific Management

Hoxie provides an illuminating summary of the claims of scientific management, which he then juxtaposes with organized labour's objections to scientific management. His account is closely based on testimony from Taylor and the trade unions. In this section I quote exclusively from his summary (Hoxie 1915: 8–11, 15–19).

T1. Taylor: The General Definition of Scientific Management
Scientific management is a system devised by industrial engineers for the purpose of subserving the common interests of employers, workmen, and society at large, through the elimination of avoidable wastes, the general improvement of the processes and methods of production, and the just and scientific distribution of the product.

T2. Taylor: Fundamental Principles of Scientific Management
Scientific management rests on the fundamental economic principles that harmony of interests exists between employers and workers, and that high general wages and better general conditions of employment can be secured through low labor cost.

T3. Taylor: The Relation of Scientific Management to Fact and Law
Scientific management attempts to substitute in the relations between employers and workers the government of fact and law for the rule of force and opinion. It substitutes exact knowledge for guesswork and seeks to establish a code of natural laws equally binding upon employers and workmen.

T4. Taylor: The Scientific and Democratic Character of
Scientific Management
Scientific management is thus at once scientific and democratic. In time and motion study it has discovered and developed an accurate scientific method by which the great mass of laws governing the easiest and most productive movements of men are registered. These laws constitute a great code which, for the first time in industry, completely controls the acts of the management as well of those of the workmen.

It pays men rather than positions and through its methods of payment makes possible the rewarding of each workman on the basis of his efficiency. It makes possible the scientific selection of workmen, ie, the mutual adaptation of the task and the worker, and is a practical system of vocational guidance and training.

It analyzes the operations of industry into their natural parts, makes careful studies of fatigue and sets the task on the basis of a large number of performances by men of different capacities with due and scientific allowance for the human factor and legitimate delays.

It assigns to each workman a definite and by him accomplishable task, institutes rational rest periods, and modes of recreation during the working hours, eliminates pace setters, standardizes performance, and guards the workers against over-speeding and exhaustion, nervously and physically.

It substitutes the rule of law for the arbitrary decisions of foremen, employers, and unions and treats each worker as an independent personality.

Scientific management thus democratizes industry. It gives a voice to both parties and substitutes joint obedience of employers and workers to fact and law for obedience to personal authority. No such democracy has ever existed in industry before. Every protest of every workman must be handled by those on management side, and the right or wrong of the complaint must be settled not by the opinion, either of the management or the workman, but by the great code of laws which has been developed and which must satisfy both sides. It gives the worker in the end equal voice with the employer; both can refer only to the arbitrament of science and fact.

T5. Taylor: Scientific Management and Productive Efficiency
Scientific management improves and standardizes the industrial organization and equipment, betters the training of the workmen and increases their skill and efficiency. It rationalizes the management, improves the methods of planning, routing and accounting, furnishes the best machinery, tools and materials, eliminates avoidable wastes and standardizes the methods of work.

It gathers up, systematizes and systematically transmits to the workers all the traditional craft knowledge and skill which is being lost and destroyed under current industrial methods.

It employs in the shop a corps of competent specialists whose duty is to instruct and train the workers, and to assist them whenever difficulties arise in connection with the work.

It trains the men in the easiest and best methods of work, and brings the workmen into close and helpful touch with the management.

It removes from each worker the responsibility for the work of others, and prevents the more efficient from being held back and demoralized by the inefficient.

It increases the productive output, and improves the quality of the product.

T6. Taylor: Scientific Management and Labor Welfare

Scientific management, through its accurate scientific methods, and the laws which it has discovered and established, its improvement of organization and equipment, and its democratic spirit:

Sets each workman to the highest task for which his physical and intellectual capacity fits him, and tends to prevent the degradation and displacement of skilled labor. It rewards the men for helpful suggestions and improvements in the methods of work, and provides immediate inspection and immediate rewards for increased or improved output.

It requires the workers to perform, not one operation merely, but several operations or tasks.

It trains the workmen mechanically, as they were never trained before, opens the way for all workmen to become 'first class men', and opens up opportunities for the advancement and promotion of the workers.

It stimulates and energizes them intellectually, and promotes their self-reliance and individuality.

It insures just treatment of individual workers, and pay to each in proportion to his efficiency.

It guarantees the worker against the arbitrary alteration of the task, arbitrary rate cutting, and limitation of earnings.

It raises wages and shortens the hours of labor.

It increases the security and continuity of employment.

It lessens the rigors of shop discipline.

It promotes friendly feelings and relations between the management and the men, and among the workers of the shop or group.

It renders collective bargaining and trade unionism unnecessary as means of protection to the workmen.

It tends to prevent strikes and industrial warfare and to remove the cause of social unrest.

OL1. Organized Labor: The General Definition of Scientific Management

Organized labor understands by the term 'scientific management', certain well-defined 'efficiency systems' which have been recently devised by individuals and small groups under the leadership of men like Frederick W. Taylor, H.L. Gantt and Harrington Emerson, by whom this term has been preempted. Organized labor makes a clear distinction between 'scientific management' thus defined and 'science in management'. It does not oppose savings of waste and increase of output resulting from improved machinery and truly efficient management. It stands, therefore, definitely committed to 'science in management', and its objections are directed solely against systems devised by the so-called 'scientific management' cult.

OL2. Organized Labor: Scientific Management in its Relation to Labor Welfare

'Scientific Management' thus defined is a device employed for the purpose of increasing production and profits; and tends to eliminate consideration for the character, rights and welfare of the employees.

It looks upon the worker as a mere instrument of production and reduces him to a semi-automatic attachment to the machine or tool.

In spirit and in essence, it is a cunningly devised speeding-up and sweating system, which puts a premium upon muscle and speed rather than brains, forces individuals to become 'rushers' and 'speeders'; stimulates and drives the workers up to the limit of nervous and physical exhaustion and over-speeds and over-strains them; shows a constant tendency to increase the intensity and extent of the task; tends to displace all but the fastest workers; indicates a purpose to extract the last ounce of energy from the workers; and holds that if the task can be performed it is not too great.

It intensifies the modern tendency toward specialization of the work and the task; is destructive of mechanical education and skill; splits up the work into a series of minute tasks tending to confine the workers to the continuous performance of one of these tasks; tends to eliminate skilled crafts; deprives the worker of the opportunity of learning a trade; degrades the skilled workers to the condition of the less skilled; displaces skilled workers and forces them into competition with the less skilled and narrows the competitive field and weakens the bargaining strength of the workers through specialization of the task and the destruction of craft skill.

It displaces day work and day wage by task work and the piece-rate, premium and bonus systems of payment.

It tends to set the task on the basis of 'stunt' records of the strongest and swiftest workers without due allowance for the human element or legitimate delays, so that only a few of the strongest and most active workers are capable of accomplishing it, and has devised and established modes of payment, usually arranged so that it is greatly to the advantage of the employer to prevent the workers from equaling or exceeding the task, and which usually result in giving the worker less than the regular rate of pay for his extra exertion, and only a portion and usually the smaller portion of the product which his extra exertion has created.

It establishes a rigid standard of wages regardless of the progressive increase in the cost of living, and tends to make it permanent at its present low level; puts a limit upon the amount of wages which any man can earn; offers no guarantee against rate cutting; is itself a systematic rate-cutting device; tends to lower the wages of many immediately and permanently, and means in the long run more work for the same or less pay.

It tends to lengthen the hours of labor; shortens the future of service; lessens the certainty and continuity of employment; and leads to over-production and the increase of unemployment.

It condemns the worker to a monotonous routine; tends to deprive him of thought, initiative, sense of achievement and joy in his work; dwarfs and represses him intellectually, tends to destroy his individuality and inventive genius; increases the danger of industrial accidents; tends to undermine the worker's health, shortens his period of industrial activity and earning power, and brings on premature old age.

It puts into the hands of employers at large an immense mass of information and methods which may be used unscrupulously to the detriment of the workers, creates the possibility of systematic black-listing, and offers no guarantee against the abuse of its professed principles and practices.

OL3. Organized Labor: Scientific Management in its
Relation to Industrial Democracy
'Scientific Management' is undemocratic; it is a reversion to industrial autocracy which forces workers to depend upon the employers' conception of fairness and limits the democratic safeguards of the workers.

It tends to gather up and transfer to the management all the traditional knowledge, the judgement and the skill of the workers and monopolizes the initiative and skill of the workers in connection with the work.

It allows the workman ordinarily no voice in hiring or discharge, the setting of the task, the determination of the wage rate or the general conditions of employment.

It greatly intensifies unnecessary managerial dictation and discipline; tends to prevent the presentation and denies the consideration of grievances; and tends to increase the number of shop offenses and the amount of docking and fining.

It introduces the spirit of mutual suspicion and contest among the men, and thus destroys the solidarity and cooperative spirit of the group.

It has refused to deal with the workers except as individuals.

It is incompatible with and destructive of unionism; destroys all the protective rules established by unions and discriminates against union men.

It is incompatible with and destructive of collective bargaining.

OL4. Organized Labor: The Unscientific Character of Scientific Management

'Scientific Management' in its relations to labor is unscientific.

It does not take all the elements into consideration but deals with human beings as it does with inanimate machines.

It violates the fundamental principles of human nature by ignoring habits, temperament, and traditions of work and tends to minimize the acquired skill of the workers.

It greatly increases the number of 'unproductive workers', i.e., those engaged in clerical work, and often squeezes out of the workers vast overhead charges.

It is unscientific and unfair in its determination of the task and furnishes no just or scientific basis for calculating the wage rate.

It concerns itself almost wholly with the problem of production, disregarding in general the vital problem of distribution, and violates and indefinitely postpones the application of the fundamental principle of justice to distribution.

It is based on the principle of the survival of the fittest and tends to disregard the physical welfare of the workers.

OL5. Organized Labor: The Inefficiency of Scientific Management

'Scientific Management' is fundamentally inefficient.

It does not tend to develop general and long-time economic efficiency.

It tends to emphasize quantity of product at the expense of quality, and to reduce the quality of the work and output.

It is incapable of extensive application.

It is a theoretical conception already proven a failure in practice.

OL6. Organized Labor: Scientific Management and
Industrial Unrest
'Scientific management' intensifies the conditions of industrial unrest.

It libels the character of the workmen, and its methods are evidence of suspicion and direct question of the honesty and fairness of the workers.

It fails to satisfy the workers under it, but, on the contrary, is regarded by them with extreme distaste.

It pits workman against workman; displaces harmony and co-operation among the working group by mutual suspicion and controversy, and increases the antagonism between the workers and their employers.

It increases the points of friction and offers no guarantee against industrial warfare and is conducive to strikes.

6. Science, Management and Industrial Relations

The most striking feature of the two sets of claims is that they are diametrically opposed in what they claim are the results of scientific management. This is the case with the effect on industrial relations (in particular regarding democratic safeguards) and the effect on the workers' relation to work (in particular regarding pay, speeding up, and welfare). This difference must largely be attributed to the difference between rhetoric and practice.

In the controversies which followed the use of scientific management in United States industry, Taylor always maintained a rigid distinction between his principles and their application: 'the best mechanism for applying these general principles should in no way be confused with the principles themselves' (Taylor 1967: 29). Hoxie's position, in contrast, was that:

> scientific management, in its relations to labor, must be judged, not merely by theories and claims but mainly by what it proves to be in its actual operation. Mr Taylor . . . has intimated that if any principle of scientific management which he has laid down be violated, scientific management ceases to exist . . . . It is what it is in fact, and not what the ideals or theories of its advocates or opponents would have it to be. . . . Like all other things which affect humanity, it must therefore be judged by actual results and tendencies. (Hoxie 1915: 4–5)

It is not surprising that Taylor was against this initial definition which was crucial in permitting the findings of Hoxie's Commission (see section 1). The distinction between scientific management theory and practice (or at least between the ideal practice, which would be a perfect reflection of the theory, and existing practice) protects Taylor from any responsibility for the negative effects of what he was advocating (he does not disclaim responsibility for what he considered positive effects).

Hoxie's position, though forcefully and plausibly stated, is not typical of applied social scientists. Taylor's position is backed up by the norms of science, which insists on the separation of science (even applied science) from its applications. As I argued in chapter 1, this position characterized the field of industrial psychology at its beginnings and remains largely unchallenged. Once Hoxie bases his enquiry on the position that scientific management must be judged according to what it proves to be in operation, his job becomes more complicated, No simple cause and effect can be attributed, so it is not possible to sort out what has been caused by scientific management and what 'would exist without it' (Hoxie 1915: 6). Science has always liked to point with exactitude to the relation between its theories and applications and has tended to posit an orderly world where effects are simple and controllable. If Hoxie had observed this distinction, he would have been obliged to exonerate scientific management for the effects he recorded in his conclusions (see section 1). In contrast he concluded: 'It is a common assumption that scientific management shops, in organization and methods, conform closely to the ideal and models presented by the leaders. This assumption is completely shattered by first-hand study of the facts' (Hoxie 1915: 25–6).

When Hoxie goes into the detail of what usually happens in practice, it becomes clear that power lies with the employers and that they have a short-term and ruthless view of what is in their interests. So: 'the management usually wants to see quicker returns than can be secured by the slow process of systematic and thoroughgoing reorganization and the expert is usually forced to yield to the demand for immediate results that can be measured in cash terms' (Hoxie 1915: 29).

Let me briefly deconstruct Taylor's discourse. The place of 'common interests' and harmony consistent with low labor costs is primary in the claims of scientific management (T1 and T2). The means through which harmony can be achieved is 'the rule of fact and law', in other words, science. In Taylor's discourse (consistent with the wider status of natural science at the time), science functions as the neutral arbiter, outside the interests both of management and labour. According to Searle, the essence of 'efficiency' after the turn of the century was one that embodied a 'technocratic' approach: 'Technocracy . . . celebrates science as a kind of self-sustaining force which provides objectively valid solutions to social and political problems, quite independently of the wishes and beliefs of the majority' (Searle 1971: 260).

The appeal to science places power relations outside the 'great code of laws'. This also gives the laws their democratic character, since they are 'natural' laws and management too must observe them: 'It substitutes joint obedience of employers and workers to fact and law for obedience to personal authority' (T4). Such democracy had not 'ever existed in industry before' (T4). But was it democratic? Although the 'great code of laws' must satisfy both sides, and although science is supposedly the neutral arbiter, 'every protest of every workman must be handled by those on management side' (in other words, it is not to be taken to the unions). As organized labor says (OL3): scientific management is incompatible with and destructive of unionism and collective bargaining; destroys rules protective of workers and discriminates against union men. This science is owned by management, not by workers. If we go along with Taylor in placing science outside industrial relations, we would have to believe that its neutrality is not tainted by the circumstances of control. However in Foucault's terms, the connections between power and knowledge are clearly in evidence. Organized labour had no doubts about these connections in claiming that scientific management was 'a reversion to industrial autocracy which forces workers to depend upon the employers' conception of fairness and limits the democratic safeguards of the workers' (OL3).

Since scientific management depended on its claim to scientificity, its opponents were obliged to challenge that claim. It is testimony to the power of the discourse of science at the time that organized labour did not challenge the nature of science itself, but accepted that it was outside social interest. Organized labour in the United States took the position that they were not against 'science in management' only against certain efficiency systems which had pre-empted the term (OL1). They cite several instances where scientific management is unscientific (OL4) and point out that it is based on a particular theory, that of survival of the fittest.[3] They were not against savings of waste or increase in output resulting from improved machinery and truly efficient management (OL1). This distinction is the same as that which Myers drew on behalf of British industrial psychology in his criticism of the efficiency experts (see chapter 3).

The harsh authoritarianism of supervisors had been a major cause of unrest and it was undoubtedly one of Taylor's chief aims to mitigate this without diminishing managerial control. At Ford's for example, 'the plants were run by the iron hand and arbitrary justice of the foreman' (Beynon 1984: 33). These relations did not change overnight as a result of Taylor's ideas about 'functional foremanship':

> Often the new officials perform merely or mainly delegated duties, the old time foreman retaining practically all or a great part of his former directive and arbitrary authority. This seems to be the case particularly where labor is directly concerned. . . . The results are such as to weaken materially the claims that scientific management treats each workman as an independent personality and that it substitutes joint obedience to fact and law for obedience to personal authority. (Hoxie 1915: 31)

The task idea defined management's responsibility; it distinguished management from supervision. Where supervisors used surveillance and discipline to regulate performance, managers regulated performance through minute control of the task. This would not have been possible under the old craft system of work, but new technology controlled jobs and provided management with the conditions to 'gather up, systematize and systematically transmit to the workers all the traditional craft knowledge and skill which is being lost and destroyed under current industrial methods' (T5). Organized labor saw this deskilling as part of the same process of the introduction of efficiency systems (OL2). For them, scientific management 'tends to gather up and transfer to management all the traditional knowledge, the judgement and the skill of the workers and monopolizes the initiative and skill of the workers in connection with the work' (OL3). According to Hoxie's conclusion, the knowledge was transmitted back to the workers 'piecemeal, as it is needed in the performance of a particular job or task' (Hoxie 1915: 104).

Most of the rest of the claims by organized labour revolve around the negative effects that efficiency systems had on the workers, their pay, their relations to the job, the quality of the product and on harmony in the workplace, both between workers and foremen and amongst workers (OL2, OL6). They point to the considerable increase in numbers of 'unproductive' workers which came with the regulative strategies of the new management. This suggests that overall profitability might have been less of a concern than the short-term preoccupation with control over the labour force. Similarly, organized labour contradicts Taylor in claiming that, while quantity may well increase, quality suffers (OL5). The wider goals of manufacturing were being subordinated to regulation. Regulation was the new management's *raison d'être*.

7. Scientific Management and the Individual

Although performances were standardized, scientific management could claim to treat 'each worker as an independent personality'. Was this not a contradiction in terms? It was made possible by the measurement of individual performance against a standardized instrument, in this case the standard task.[4] However, it is not the 'individual personality' which is being treated by management, but aspects of performance directly related to output which are given by the technology and defined by management: according to organized labour, scientific management was unscientific in treating human beings like 'inanimate machines'; this 'violates the fundamental principles of human nature by ignoring habits, temperament, and traditions of work' (OL4). These were some of the inadequacies of scientific management which industrial psychology, in the name of science, set itself to correct.

In T4, three examples are given of the areas in which science has produced natural laws to dictate good practice, laws which are binding on both management and workers. The first is time and motion study, 'an accurate scientific method by which the great mass of laws governing the easiest and most productive movements of men are registered'. In practice, as Hoxie concluded on the basis of considerable first-hand evidence, time-study systems for setting rates had little to do with science (Hoxie 1915: 61–87). The second is performance-based pay, which had become possible where production was sufficiently mechanized to count work by the piece. The third is 'the scientific selection of workmen', 'vocational guidance' and 'training', all of which appear to be categorized as 'practices which promote the mutual adaptation of the task and the worker'. It is significant that this definition is almost identical to the way that Professor Alec Rodger was later to define British occupational psychology; fitting the man to the job and the job to the man (see chapter 1). In practice, scientific management achieved nothing in this area. It was industrial psychology that did so. All of these new practices depend on the task idea and to this extent industrial psychology could not have emerged without the task idea being very widespread in practice. This permitted new technologies which targeted the individual, and hence brought into being industrial psychology. 'Competent specialists' would subsequently control the workers' relation to this knowledge and through it their performance. Through time and motion study, selection and training, industrial psychologists became intimately involved in this process (see chapter 3). These new forms of regulating the individual worker created the space for industrial psychology.

8. Scientific Management and Self-Regulation

In Britain, Cadbury welcomed some of the ideas which were associated with scientific management:

> Although one may criticise some of the principles underlying Taylor's system of task work, there are many suggestions of his which as time goes on will have to be much more widely adopted, although probably they are not altogether new. Amongst these are the careful and accurate teaching of the workers, instead of their being left to find out the methods from their fellow workmen as best they can . . .; the study of the right kind of tool for any particular piece of work, which is obviously a most important problem; and the selection of the workers best suited to any particular task. (Cadbury 1914: 100)

Cadbury's description of the Card Box Department at Bournville illustrates the educative approach to improving performance. It was a department which employed over 500 of the 'more intelligent' girls. Scientific management principles in the more general sense were put into operation: 'in this department, as in others, we give the most careful attention to the planning out of the workrooms, and the procuring of the most up-to-date machinery, as the higher the wages the more important becomes the question of labour-saving machinery' (Cadbury 1914: 112). Special trade classes in card-box making for these apprentices included substituting 'right methods of working . . . for wrong methods which the girls had picked up' (1914: 113). Also there were lectures on the manufacture and properties of paper and cardboard and even a visit to a local paper manufacturer. 'Therefore the course is truly educational, not merely a training in manual dexterity and time-saving devices, and it aims at giving students an interest in, and a knowledge of, the materials which they have to use' (1914: 113).

Of course control of the labour process was still in the hands of owners and managers, but cooperation of workers was sought by a wider educative approach integrated into skills training concerned with a whole product, by using an apprenticeship system and by fixing rates through consultation and collective bargaining. 'Such methods . . . will obtain efficiency without making the worker merely an animated tool' (Cadbury 1914: 114). Cadbury is therefore critical of scientific management to the extent that it was based on '*enforced* standardization of methods, *enforced* adoption of the best implements and working conditions, and *enforced* co-operation' (Cadbury is quoting from Taylor and adding the emphasis: 1914: 102).

Cadbury gives an account of works discipline which is an example of a partial movement from punishment to reform:

> In the early days of the firm we adopted the usual methods of fines and deductions, but experience showed that it was in no way reformative . . . and so we adopted the record system – ie each girl has a record card and on this any offence is entered in the same way that any special merit is. Each month one of the directors interviews the alleged offenders. The whole system is designed to be reformative, so we have no fixed rules as to punishment. In dealing with these offenders actual punishment beyond a caution is not often necessary. (Cadbury 1914: 110)

Devinat, reporting a survey of scientific management in Europe for the International Labour Organization, summarized the English position as follows:

> During the [First World War and post-war] period similar circumstances led in England to the rapid development of the 'Welfare' movement, which aimed at furthering the physical and general welfare of the workers, and which was closely bound up from the outset with the application, after adequate study, of scientific management methods. (Devinat 1927: 20)

Industrial psychology in Britain emerged in close cooperation with this welfare movement, that is with progressive employers who had learned that it was necessary not to antagonize organized workers. For example, Myers asserted:

> There can be no doubt that Labour is rightly opposed in this country to the introduction of the early American methods of scientific management. It was at first conducted there with far too little regard of the workers' standpoint. The organization of Labour in America is still far behind that in this country. (Myers 1920: 175)

The three areas of scientific management which, according to Cadbury, 'will have to be much more widely adopted' are the three areas which become the province of industrial psychology: training workers in 'better' methods (based on time and motion study); design of tools (which was part of the approach to improving working conditions and reducing fatigue) and selection. In chapter 3 I shall examine these practices in British industrial psychology in the period until the Second World War.

Notes

1. It is because scientific management was the first discourse systematically to target the individual worker that industrial psychology claims Taylor as its forefather and sometimes as its founding father.

2. By 1954 in Britain (after the new Education Act had extended public education) Urwick, an influential management thinker, could argue that: 'It is doubtful if the promoted-ranker type of manager can continue to measure up to what British business will require, even if there are enough of him. And with the democratization of educational opportunity which has occurred over the last decade it is obvious that there will be less first class ability starting on the shop-floor' (quoted in Child 1969: 143).

3. The idea of the survival of the fittest was popular at the turn of the century in both the US and UK. It derived its legitimacy from Social Darwinism, which extended the Darwinian notion of natural fitness from biology to society. In these terms, those who failed to survive and make good in the industrial climate of competition and self-interest were naturally unfitted. Therefore it was acceptable that they should be weeded out. This idea was popular among American employers. Its application to the employment context is illustrated in a popular contemporary book entitled *A Message to Garcia*, whose author is sympathizing with the hard life of employers whose 'help' does nothing but loaf when his back is turned. Bendix quotes the following passage: 'In every store and factory, there is a constant weeding out process going on. No matter how good times are, this sorting out continues, only if times are harder and work is scarce, the sorting is done finer – but out, and forever out, the incompetent and unworthy go . . . . It is the survival of the fittest. Self-interest prompts every employer to keep the best' (quoted in Bendix 1956: 264–5).

4. The principle is identical to psychometric measurement in other fields of applied psychology, such as educational, where intellectual performance could be compared across individuals by the use of a standard IQ test (see chapter 4).

3
Human Factors

Experience has shown that vocational selection and motion study cannot be begun without the full knowledge and consent and cooperation of all concerned. (Myers 1920: 179)

1. Introduction

Industrialization, the introduction of machines, scientific management and labour resistance set the scene for the emergence of industrial psychology. Treating workers as hands, or as extensions to the machines, was creating problems of control for employers and the new class of managers. Industrial psychology was suspected by unions of being involved in 'speeding up'. In Britain it negotiated this difficulty, which threatened its aspirations to achieve a solid base in industry, by distancing itself from scientific management and efficiency engineering. At the same time it had to be engaged in work which contributed to efficiency, since this was the basis on which it could sell its services to employers and management. Both its initial fatigue and working conditions research and the subsequent central involvement in selection emphasized workers' welfare.

In Britain, early industrialization and its attendant exploitation of labour resulted in government intervention into factory conditions before the end of the nineteenth century. In section 2 I discuss the welfare tradition in British industry and how it was a precondition for British industrial psychology. The First World War produced conditions in which employers, workers and government united to increase output. Researchers used experimental methods associated with psychology and physiology to produce studies on the relations between fatigue, hours of work and output which were the paradigm for human factors industrial psychology. In sections 3 and 4 I discuss these studies and the conditions of emergence of the new industrial psychology in Britain. In section 5 I describe the National Institute of Industrial Psychology, which represented the field in Britain. Section 6 discusses in detail the work of the first industrial psychologist employed in British industry, at Rowntree's Cocoa Works. The experience of Rowntree's profoundly influenced the position taken by early industrial psychologists such as Myers (quoted above). The Rowntree's example also provides new evidence of the sensitivity of industrial psychology, connected as it was with time and method study. I finish, in section 7, by contrasting British and American industrial psychology after the First World War.

2. Fatigue

The problem of fatigue became prominent in British industry during the First World War. The Health of Munitions Workers Committee (HMWC)[1] was renowned for managing to improve the productivity of workers in the wartime munitions factories at the same time as reducing hours of work and introducing improvements in working conditions. Psychologists were able to take much of the credit for this noteworthy achievement – advancing the goals of efficiency and welfare simultaneously – and it was on the basis of this reputation that psychology claimed a useful place in British industry. The National Institute of Industrial Psychology (NIIP), established in 1921, inherited the reputation of the Industrial Fatigue Research Board (IFRB: the successor to the HMWC), which was set up at the end of the war on the invitation of the Home Office.[2]

During the eighteenth and nineteenth centuries, industrial workers worked for long hours and no attention was paid to the relation of hours to productivity. Workers were regarded as 'hands', and from this perspective, employers assumed that the more hours they were put to work, the more they would produce. There was evidence to the contrary. May Smith cites a report from the Inspector of Factories dated 1845. It 'gives the results of reducing the hours of work in a Lancashire mill from 12 hours to 11, and to the surprise of all concerned the output was quite as good'. Despite the fact that 'several other mill owners followed his example', there was 'no general realization of the value of reform' (Smith 1952: 19). It took the conditions of war, and also the reputation of science, to produce a wider acceptance of the principle that longer hours did not necessarily mean greater output.

Trade union organization, industrial unrest and government response in the form of legislation on hours and working conditions, had succeeded in reducing working hours dramatically by the First World War. Then, in conditions of national emergency, 'an increase in the output of munitions became of primary importance. To this end hours of labour [for men] were increased, 70–90 hours a week being common and over 90 hours not infrequent' (IHRB 1940, quoted in Hearnshaw and Winterbourn 1945). The IHRB pointed to 'the fallacy of believing that one gets a similar output each hour of the day, irrespective of where the hour comes in the working day'. Studies showed that increased hours beyond a certain point were detrimental, indeed they could decrease output: 'In one investigation concerned with the heavy work of sizing fuse bodies, reducing the hours worked from 58.2 per week to 51.2 resulted in an increased total output of 22 percent. The hourly output increased from 100 to 139' (Hearnshaw and Winterbourn 1945: 22).

The findings of the wartime fatigue studies can be summarized as follows:

> An extension of the usual hours of work does not – except for short periods during an emergency – give a proportional increase of output; on the contrary it causes the rate of output to fall off with increasing rapidity.
>
> After a continuous period of overtime, improvement in output rate does not take place for some time after the re-introduction of shorter hours.
>
> An unbroken spell of four and a half to five hours is generally too long. Man must rest even at work. (IHRB 1940, quoted in Hearnshaw and Winterbourn 1945: 22, 24)

Because the HMWC was part of the Ministry of Munitions, central control could ensure that the results of the fatigue studies could be put into practice. Seebohm Rowntree played an influential part in these reforms and their subsequent wider dissemination (see section 4).

The results of the fatigue research, and other related findings, for example an optimal illumination in factories, were largely due to psychologists working within the methodological framework of experimental psychology; that is laboratory work where variables are carefully controlled and the data from large numbers of individual 'subjects' are pooled to produce averages which can be compared between different conditions. The conditions of industrial jobs made performance easy to measure in this way, since jobs were broken down into small parts and highly repetitive. Variables such as hours worked, number and timing of rest pauses and changes in illumination could all be controlled for experimental purposes.[3] Moreover when psychology had broken with its philosophical roots and allied itself with natural science, it had adopted a psycho-physical model of human perform-ance: 'industrial psychology does not attempt to draw any distinctive line between psychology and physiology' (Myers 1926: 12). This paradigm was effective in the area of fatigue research, where the object of change was often working conditions in an attempt to improve workers' health and performance.

Fatigue research represented a happy union between the often opposed forces of efficiency and welfare: not only did productivity increase, but workers undoubtedly benefited. This union was especially welcome to government and employers after the war when trade unions were powerful and expressed strong criticism of working conditions. The fact that the IFRB included representation from the trade unions reflects the strength of the labour movement in this period.[4] The terms of reference of the IFRB reflect the theme of reconciliation between welfare and efficiency: 'To consider and investigate the relations of hours of labour and other conditions of employment, including methods of work, to the production of fatigue, having regard both to industrial efficiency and to the preservation of health among workers' (Myers 1926: 15).

The question of fatigue united concerns which were already of political importance: national efficiency, the health of the labouring classes and, because of trade union demands, working conditions in factories.

3. Welfare Work

In chapter 2 I argued that industrial psychology was indebted to scientific management for its emergence. In Britain, the tradition of welfare work was also influential. The fatigue research conducted during the war was conceived in the context of women being recruited into work which had previously been thought too difficult and heavy for them (many men having left to fight the war). Six thousand women were employed in munitions factories alone (Niven 1967: 42). In 1916 the HMWC, under Seebohm Rowntree, recommended that welfare workers be appointed to all factories where women were employed (which was the great majority, since it was wartime). Later that year this recommendation was incorporated into an Act, which extended the provision to men. By the end of the war there were approximately 1,000 welfare workers employed in British factories (Niven 1967: 42).

This movement from women's welfare to men's characterized much of government and employer welfare intervention, yet the history has been written as if workers were all male, or at least all the same. In the nineteenth century, women social workers were employed by humanitarian factory owners to visit sick employees and extend charity to their families. During a period when there was no sickness benefit, workers and their families could quickly become destitute in times of sickness. In 1896 Rowntree's employed the first social worker with a more radical brief, which was to take charge of women in the factory (who at the time numbered about 500) and 'watch over their health and behaviour' (Niven 1967: 21). This concentration on women and girls characterized the early days of welfare work. In 1874 the Women's Protective and Provident League had been formed to protect the interests of women factory workers and in 1906 there was a public outcry over girls' and women's 'sweated labour' which was a significant influence in forcing the government, in 1909, to legislate on minimum standards for women factory workers.[5]

Although it was commonly assumed that women needed welfare

protection because of their greater sensibilities, government comment and the concerns of the day with fitness (see section 4) make it plausible to argue that women were a target of intervention because of the fears of decline in the health (and numbers) of the next generation of workers if women's health was damaged by factory work. The dominant attitude at the time was that the trade unions would look after the interests of men. (They took up the cause of women workers only in parts of Lancashire.) Legislation and public concern meant that welfare workers increased from fewer than six in 1906 to between 60 and 70 in 1914 (Niven 1967: 21). Almost all of these were employed to look after women and girls, although Rowntree's (again the pioneer) employed three men under the labour manager to do similar work.

I shall explore the political considerations which surrounded industrial psychology's new role in efficiency and welfare through the perspective of Seebohm Rowntree, whose connections with business, welfare and government made him an influential figure in this period.

4. Welfare, Efficiency and Seebohm Rowntree

Rowntree's horizons were not limited to the survival and profitability of his company, Rowntree's Cocoa Works, nor even to the towns-people of York, for whose destiny he felt so responsible.[6] He had a national perspective and saw industry as a national service (Child 1969: 46). He was close to government. Rowntree's work in the Ministry of Munitions during the war familiarized him with appalling industrial conditions and widespread resistance. He was influential in recommendations on worker participation, organized a meeting in 1917 between leading employers and trade unionists (Child 1969: 44) and initiated the professionalization of welfare work (later to become personnel management) (Child 1964; Fox 1966a; Niven 1967). He looked to managers and welfare supervisors 'to introduce the new outlook, the new spirit and the new understanding which will ultimately make serious strife impossible between capital and labour' (Rowntree 1979: 11).

Rowntree's understanding of industrial welfare can best be captured by quoting from his brief when appointed Director of the Welfare Department for the Ministry of Munitions in 1916 (a brief which he had created for himself as part of his insistence on having sufficient powers to carry through sweeping changes):

> Welfare is by no means an isolated series of activities which may or may not be appended to a business organization. It is rather a method of factory administration in which careful regard is paid to the well-being of the workers in all the multitudes of factory conditions which affect them. (quoted in Briggs 1961: 118).

In order to understand why British employers like Rowntree were concerned to unite efficiency and rationalization with industrial welfare, and in order to understand why they needed to retain the cooperation of the workforce in this endeavour, we need to examine the economic, political and social context of employment in Britain in the period after the First World War. That war was an important watershed in the British economy. From a position of imperial dominance and control of the world trade routes, after the war Britain found that it had lost pre-eminence and with it some of the massive profits from the colonies on which the economy had depended (Hobsbawm 1968).

Industrial efficiency became of widespread concern. 'National efficiency' was one of the dominant ideologies of the second half of the nineteenth century (White 1901; Searle 1971) and its proponents were not limited in their interests to the business sphere. Since the Boer War, fears were abroad about the degeneration of the physical stock of the nation. The labouring classes were so unhealthy as a result of inadequate diet and housing, and long hours spent in factories (60 hours a week from ten years of age before the turn of the century), that they were quite unfit to fight:

> In the Manchester district, 11,000 men offered themselves for war service between the start of hostilities in October 1899 and July 1900. Of this number 8,000 were found to be physically unfit to carry a rifle and stand the fatigue of discipline. Of the 3,000 who were accepted only 1,200 attained the moderate standard of the muscular power and chest measurement required by the military authorities. In other words, two out of every three men willing to bear arms in the Manchester district are virtually invalids. (White 1901: 102–3)

'It is estimated that even in 1910 one third of all wage-earners lived in absolute poverty' (Niven 1967: 28).

Seebohm Rowntree's early interest in nutrition, which led to his famous survey of poverty in York, was couched in terms of 'physical efficiency'. However, because of the humanistic beliefs of the Rowntree employers which were being articulated at a time of growth in trade unionism, this practice of efficiency was tempered by the democratic process and a commitment to the welfare of workers. Industrial welfare (the successor to the 'industrial betterment' practised by Seebohm's father Joseph) was central to Seebohm Rowntree's philosophy and religion (Child 1964). Quaker employers like Rowntree and Cadbury were in the vanguard of making improvements in factory working conditions and welfare. Like industrial psychologists, they maintained that such changes were sound business sense as well as being humanitarian (Rowntree 1979: 148; Cadbury 1979: xvii).

Victorian complacence had begun to be shattered by the outbreaks of industrial unrest which were already acute before the war. It is with this concern, in 1921, that Rowntree introduces his book *The Human Factor in Business*:

> In pre-war days Labour Unrest was one of the most serious problems confronting the country. In 1913, 11,491,000 working days were lost through strikes and lock-outs. The situation was steadily growing worse, when the contending forces in this country united in defence against a foreign foe. Now however, it has broken out again with redoubled force. (Rowntree 1979: v)

From this Rowntree concludes that 'there are certain conditions which must be secured for workers' and they include decent wages, working conditions and security, and 'a status for the workers suitable to men in a free country in the twentieth century' (1979: vii). Rowntree believed that the majority of men in the workforce 'would have no objection to the continuance of the present system (which he called 'capitalistic') if the conditions of workers could be improved' Rowntree 1979: 129). As for women workers: 'although they are anxious for better working conditions, [they] have no desire to control them' (1979: 130).

5. The National Institute of Industrial Psychology

Charles Myers was responsible for founding the NIIP, which was established in 1921. Until the outbreak of war, he was an experimental psychologist and came to know about industrial psychology 'through a chance remark' (Myers 1970: 10). From treating shell-shocked soldiers in France, his leisure time during the last year of the war was spent 'devising tests, and supervising their application, for the better selection of men suited to hydrophone work, in which they had to listen in order to locate enemy submarines' (Myers 1970: 10). He returned to his position as head of the Psychological Laboratory at Cambridge and with H.J. Welch, Director of Harrison's and Crosfield's, who was to become its chairman, set up the NIIP, soon after leaving academic life to work full-time for the NIIP. The NIIP was an independent, self-financing organization, supported by politicians and progressive employers, such as Rowntree. In ten years the institute grew from 2 to 50 staff (Myers 1970: 11).

At one of its early fund-raising events in London, the aims of the Institute were summarized in a speech as:

> to assist employers in finding the best way to do each piece of work by the aid of scientific knowledge and scientific methods; and in addition to finding the best way to do each piece of work, we also want to help the employer to find the best job for each worker. (*JNIIP* [1922] 1(2): 60)

The speech goes on to mention fatigue research, motion study, vocational selection and vocational training:

> It will help to increase output. But in addition to this, and perhaps more important, we know that it will reduce fatigue and it will add, we think, directly or indirectly to the happiness and well-being of the workers of all classes. [*Cheers.*]
>
> It is because of these things that we feel that we can appeal to every class for support of the Institute. We appeal to the workers in our endeavour to reduce fatigue, by finding the job most suitable for his particular qualities, and by the application of scientific methods to the study of the work which he has to carry out. . . . We shall not only improve his chances of enjoyable leisure and happiness, but also by increasing output without additional effort we hope to make it possible to increase his wages. We can appeal to the employer merely on selfish grounds, because if, as has been proved over and over again, scientific methods do increase output per unit per worker, then this must mean increase of profit; and if these scientific methods also reduce unnecessary fatigue, this must mean better health to the employee and a better quality of work for the employer. We appeal also to the socialist and the philanthropist, because we are helping to strike directly at some of the root causes of illness and poverty, of unhappiness, and even of crime. (*JNIIP* [1922] 1(2): 60)

Industrial psychology had high hopes and made big claims and in the post-war climate, there was considerable support for these.[7] At a similar public relations and fund-raising dinner in 1925, a Labour MP said 'I have no hesitation in admitting [the NIIP's] strict impartiality so far as employer and employee is concerned' (NIIP speeches 1925: 7).

In the 1922 journal of the NIIP, the work of the first year was summarized under two headings: investigations and research; and vocational guidance and selection. Under the first heading came work in the experimental tradition, largely into working conditions.

In a paint and varnish manufacturers:

- recommendations were made regarding the arrangement of machinery to avoid unnecessary stooping, which greatly reduced fatigue. The most suitable weight of tool was determined and rest pauses were introduced, also resulting in reduced fatigue.
- an improved type of chair was introduced, which reduced fatigue but a sufficient period had not elapsed to witness any improvement in output.
- improved ventilation conditions were recommended in a soldering department and screens to protect workers from heat from stoves were introduced.
- a new method of payment was recommended, though the firm could not adopt it at the time due to working half-time.

In a London sweet manufacturers:

– an entirely new bench was designed; chocolates came in a form more convenient for handling; seating was improved.

The workers 'stated that they felt less fatigued at the close of each day under the improved methods, despite an average 35% increase of output' (*JNIIP* [1922] 1(2): 51). The firm was so satisfied that it asked the Institute to prepare selection tests.

A week's survey of 'a large firm of sweet makers at York' was carried out. The average efficiency of an experimental group of 'inefficient girls' was improved by nearly 27 per cent. Novices were then trained, with similar results. New investigations had begun: in a Lancashire colliery; in connection with chocolate dipping; and into the cause of breakages.

Under the heading vocational guidance and selection, the report talks about new developments in the work of Cyril Burt, Psychologist to the London County Council, into selective tests for typists and shorthand writers. Although handicapped by lack of funds, 'Mr Burt is preparing to extend his work to other occupations – to accountancy, dressmaking, designing etc' (*JNIIP* [1922] 1(2): 53). At such an early stage in the Institute's history, this area was still in its infancy, and the dominance of fatigue in the Institute's work is evident. However, the NIIP became increasingly dependent upon work based on psychometric measurement, which employers wanted to improve selection. There was a retreat from working conditions research, maybe partly because legislation and the factories inspectorate covered these areas, but also because of the move towards the individual as the object of strategies of regulation. The forces that produced these moves can best be seen through a detailed consideration of the work of the Psychological Department at Rowntree's.

6. Industrial Psychology at Rowntree's

The first psychologist in British industry was employed in Rowntree's Cocoa Works in 1922. Before this date, industrial psychologists later connected to the NIIP did several pieces of work for Rowntree's. The company therefore illustrates both internal and external work by psychologists. Industrial psychology's use of time and motion study, its emphasis on selection and the developing interest in the feelings of employees at work must be understood in the light of the industrial relations climate at Rowntree's.

In the opinion of Seebohm Rowntree, if workers were 'simply taken into consultation' (Rowntree 1979: 142) it would not meet their demands. He recommended the course of 'consulting the workers on all matters directly affecting them, and extending as rapidly as experience shows to be prudent the sphere of their real responsibility' (1979: 143). Consultation could be achieved by 'the development of a scheme for joint control of working conditions in the individual factory' (1979: 133). At the Cocoa Works, this was achieved through the Central Works Council, the representative committee of workers and administrative staff.

The idea of employing a psychologist was discussed between Seebohm Rowntree and Charles Myers in 1919. When, after his meeting with Myers, Seebohm Rowntree reported back to the Central Works Council (CWC), he said that Myers had outlined three uses for psychology:

> to give expert advice from the psychological point of view in regard to the selection of applicants for work, so that as far as possible each one selected should be given the work for which he or she was most fitted; by means of test and observation, to detect waste effort on the part of individual workers; to study the question of industrial fatigue.[8]

In the event, the first two uses came to dominate the activities of the department. Agreement was not reached with the Central Works Council until 1920. An appointment was not made until 1922. Subsequently, the Psychological Department was renamed 'Selection and Training'. As I shall show from archival material, during this whole period, the appointment of a works psychologist and the activities of his department were contentious issues.

The Psychologist and Efficiency

Why did Rowntree's employees resist industrial psychology? For the workers, psychology was tarred with the same brush as efficiency engineering (see Muscio 1974: 35ff.)[9] Myers refers to this problem for the nascent industrial psychology when he comments:

> it was obvious that the workers were straightway prejudiced against it by such terms as 'efficiency' and 'scientific management'. By improvement in efficiency they feared speeding-up and the dismissal of their less competent comrades. The mention of scientific management made them suspect that all their craft knowledge would pass from them into the hands of their employers and that they would be degraded to the position of servile mechanisms. (Myers 1926: 26)

From this quotation it can be seen that the industrial relations effects of scientific management were not confined to America. Knowledge of scientific management, efficiency systems and 'speeding up' was widespread amongst workers and, given their organization and power through trade unions, industrial psychology was conditioned by its need to differentiate their work from scientific management from the very beginning.

Myers strongly opposed the efficiency engineers (Myers 1926, 1923). For example in discussing the difficulty of gaining the cooperation of employers – more difficult than employees according to Myers – he comments 'He may have already suffered at the hands of some efficiency expert who, after spending a few hours in the works has written a verbose, relatively useless report and has charged a correspondingly high fee' (1926: 36). The theoretical key to Myers' criticism was that psychology did not make the same mistake as engineering in assuming that there was 'one best way' to do a job. He used the new individual differences perspective to argue against it:

> there is no one best way . . . for mental and bodily differences between workers are such that it is impossible to train, or to expect, each worker to perform the same operations in identically the same way . . . it may also be harmful to the worker because it tends to discourage inititative. (Myers 1926: 27)

Yet if psychologists were to be given a position in industry, they had to contribute to 'efficiency'. Myers distinguished the psychologist's intervention from that of the efficiency engineer in the following way:

> it was sought not to press the worker from behind, but to ease the difficulties which may confront him. It has aimed at removing the obstacles which prevent the worker from giving his best to the work and it has almost invariably succeeded in increasing output by this method. (1926: 28)

A report by Farmer and Eyre (1922) provides an example of this approach. They were part of an NIIP team, headed by Muscio, who worked on contract for Rowntree's before it established a Psychological Department. Muscio and his team conducted psychological work in the Cream & Almond Packing Rooms, the Card Box Mill, the Sawmill and the Offices (Central Works Council Minutes [CWCM] August 1921). We can therefore reasonably assume that the anonymous company reported on by Farmer and Eyre was Rowntree's. Farmer and Eyre begin their report with the following summary: 'Under the new method here described, output increased by over 35% and the workers were unanimous in their appreciation of a considerable saving of fatigue at the end of the day, spontaneously expressing to the investigators their gratitude' (1922: 12).

Their methods were typical of the scientific, psycho-physiological approach of early British industrial psychology. Despite the fact that their report conforms to the canons of scientific reporting in its sparseness, Farmer and Eyre do choose to highlight in their introduction the potential abuses of the time-study method (thus referring by implication to efficiency engineering):

> It is obvious that such data as are obtained in this investigation are liable to

be abused by anyone who regards the human body purely from the mechanical standpoint; he may commit errors in his suggested improvements which will only lead to false economy, through his neglect to take into account the various physiological and psychological factors involved. (1922: 12)

The basis of the method was to time workers' performance of standard operations. This was done initially, whereupon it 'appeared that a considerable amount of effort was wasted by the workers in discriminating between different chocolates and in endeavouring to overcome mental states of indecision by voluntary effort'. In this way mental as well as physical state was taken into consideration in 'deciding to treat the problem as one of fatigue and to do everything that was possible to relieve the strain put upon workers'. The fatigue aspect of the research is closely tied to the time and motion study aspect except that it is based on the output curve at different times of day. Gains in output are derived not from a speeding up in hourly output throughout the day, but in marked improvement in what had previously been a steep downward curve in the afternoon's work output graph (Farmer and Eyre 1922: 14).

Although it is clear that this perspective was distinct from an efficiency perspective that treated the worker as a machine which had to be speeded up, the fact of the stop-watch alone creates links between their practice and 'speeding up'. It was the stop-watch that was feared when the Psychological Department was set up.

After much delay and negotiation with the CWC, a psychologist named Moorrees was appointed at Rowntree's Cocoa Works in 1922.[10] By 1923, Moorrees had two assistants working for him. However, much of the work was done in tandem with either the Employment or the Time Study Department (the former for selection work, the latter for work to do with improvement of methods). It was the latter connection which continued to be contentious.

Time and Motion Study
In 1933 Moorrees (the psychologist) and Northcott (the labour manager) published a pair of articles on industrial psychology at Rowntree's. In the introductory quotation to his article, Moorrees states that there must be 'no confusion as to the true scope and object of psychology' if it is to overcome workers' resistance. Moorrees does not elaborate on what this is, but it is reasonable to assume that he is referring to its hard-fought distinction from scientific management and efficiency engineering. No doubt he would have claimed for industrial psychology the same virtues that the NIIP stressed in its fund-raising speeches (see section 5). In fact a great deal of confusion is evident from a study of the Central Works Council Minutes after 1922,

when Moorrees was eventually appointed. In 1923 the CWC Minutes, under the heading 'time study and alteration of piece rates' record that 'the methods [of the Psychological Department] were such as should secure the confidence of the workers if they were understood', and continue 'at present there was misunderstanding and the Psychological Department was being blamed for matters which were outside its control' (CWCM March 1923). It is likely that the matters referred to are time and motion study activities because a minute two years later refers to workers' confusion about the fact that the psychological and time study sections were 'entirely separate' (CWCM March 1925).

The obliqueness of these statements is probably in danger of perpetuating the confusion. The point of quoting them here is to illustrate the industrial relations sensitivity surrounding every statement and every action of the Psychological Department. Were the psychological and time study sections 'entirely separate' or not, and what difference did it make? The following evidence leads me to conclude that in practice the Psychological Department (or section, as it is sometimes called in the minutes) had to work closely with time study because 'better working methods' were ultimately defined in terms of workers' greater productivity, due to increases in speed which were sustained over time. However, the acceptability of the Psychological Department hinged on it being perceived as quite different and separate from any activities associated with speeding up, since these linked its reputation with that of scientific management and efficiency engineering.

From the Psychological Regulations that were drawn up in 1931, we learn that these activities were only formally separate: 'Responsibility for Motion Study research rests with the Time Study Department subject to the following arrangements made in the interests of the Psychological Department.' What follows in the regulations indicates that the Psychological Department was at liberty to make motion study arrangements that suited it, including the provision that it could use its own staff rather than those of the Time Study Department. The Psychological Department was in charge of training workers in the new methods and time study was required to establish 'learning curves', so that the time allowance for retraining could be set. These learning curves and learning allowances were set by the Psychological Department. As Myers points out: 'movement study is intimately associated with time study – because often its value can only be expressed in terms of a comparison of the times taken to carry out an operation before and after the results of movement study have been applied' (Myers 1926: 80). None the less, Moorrees omits to mention the time-study aspect of the work (Northcott 1933).

When the Chairman, Hawksby, made the annual report to the CWC on behalf of the Psychological Committee, its adoption was carried despite an earlier reference to 'considerable doubt about psychological work throughout the factory' (CWCM December 1923). The same annual report refers to an agreement (in May 1923) with the trade unions for basing standard outputs on time studies, acknowledging the department's responsibility by saying 'the psychological department were always willing to hear objections and rectify any errors'. There is no doubt that the department was involved in setting new rates.

To what extent were the wishes of individual workers protected, when they were affected by the changes that were made to their work by psychological measurement and time and motion study? The Psychological Committee had received complaints about 'the transfer of older girls' (CWCM December 1923) and it is safe to assume that continuing complaints of this nature led to the safeguards which were written into the Psychological Regulations. For clerical work:

> where any fresh method is, after motion study, arrived at by the Psychological Department, it shall not be obligatory on any individual to adopt such a new method, provided that in such case the output and efficiency shall not be less than that obtainable under the new method. (Psychological Regulations 1931: 2)

For factory work, the guarantees are weaker:

> Where any new method has been devised, it shall in general be used, with agreed time allowance for training, but the management will not unreasonably insist upon its adoption in those individual instances where the method in use is demonstrably more efficient, or where age and experience indicate a habit too firmly established to be altered with advantage. (1931: 5)

These guarantees recollect the dangers of scientific management. However, in Rowntree's Cocoa Works, as a result of a combination of Rowntree's humanism and the control won by organized labour, the new methods were not imposed on established workers in a mechanistic fashion. These constraints did not apply to selection.

Selection
Northcott documents the benefits for efficiency in the new psychometric methods of selection, claiming that 'it has been proved to be right in approximately 95% of instances' (Northcott 1933: 168). Yet it seems that workers' representatives did not mount criticism or opposition to psychological measurement for selection purposes and in this respect it was a much more useful technology than converting workers to new methods at new speeds. The chief shop steward in his role as chairman and workers' representative of the Psychological Committee summed up his annual report by making the familiar double claim – efficiency and welfare: 'he spoke of the usefulness of

psychological work generally and how essential it was in order to achieve greater efficiency and a higher standard of life for the workers'. He continued 'that much useful work had been done with regard to vocational selection' (CWCM December 1923). Vocational selection functions as the foil for the politically sensitive aspects of the department's work.

Labour Research

The field of 'labour research' involved activities which were aimed at personalizing management's relations with employees as individuals:

> I contend that no workers can continue to feel mere cogs in a machine when persistent steps are taken to show an individual interest in them and they are made to feel it is worthwhile explaining to them the intricacies of their organization and how they serve and are served by it. (Moorrees 1933: 166)

The way this is done appears similar to the educational approach described by Cadbury (see chapter 2, section 8). Moorrees' example is the procedure used when a section became a 'storm centre' and 'routine that was once accepted is questioned, adjustments necessary in the interests of production are refused recognition, and some small event may easily lead to a situation of mild mob hysteria':

> The procedure recommended is similar to that of Elton Mayo in America, but not so definite. Instead of the investigator conducting a set 'interview', she simply works with the workers to try and find out what recommendations could be made as regards room conditions or methods of notifying how much work has been done at regular intervals; she organizes factory tours for them, where the work of other departments is explained to them and how it links up with the work of their own department. She meets them afterwards socially and initiates a discussion of their experiences. (Moorrees 1933: 166)

Labour research was seen by Moorrees as 'equally important with selection, and perhaps from certain points of view more important' (1933: 165). Its importance is indicated by the way he introduces labour research, after having discussed the areas mentioned above:

> Were what I have detailed to you the only activities of our Department, we might well run the risk of the criticism being levelled at us that, apart from an adventitious benefit to the worker – in that our tests select the right person for the right job – our Department is merely a dehumanized function devoted to material ends. (1933: 165)

In contrast to the department's selection work, labour research claimed to 'take an individual interest' in the worker. This clearly coincides with Rowntree's views on the importance of dealing with individuals. His arguments regarding the 'welfare spirit' (1920: 5) revolved round the idea of the 'human element': 'There is a growing need for some relationship between the management and the workers which is more intimate, more personal, more flexible than anything that can be achieved merely through improvement of labour's material environment' (Rowntree 1920: 5).

The need for 'taking an individual interest' in the worker was necessary because the 'instinctive emotional equipment of the individual' (the worker, that is) means that a 'small event may lead to a situation of mild mob hysteria' (Moorrees 1933: 165). Moorrees was evidently familiar with Elton Mayo's work at Hawthorne and we shall see how the Hawthorne research formalized the view of the worker as an individual of emotionality and potential irrationality (chapter 5). Here, the effect of that approach is evident: by seeing workers' objections to rationalization as illogical, he is better able to override them: 'The ground must be very carefully prepared for the introduction of psychological methods, for at times like these [that is times of 'rationalization'], factory people are not much inclined to think logically, and the psychologist will find great difficulty in overcoming resistance there' (Moorrees 1933: 159–60).

Industrial Psychology by Another Name
During the 1930s, Rowntree's psychological department was renamed 'selection and training'. In this way the company which had represented British industrial psychology's high hopes to become institutionalized in industrial concerns chose to give psychology a lower profile in its activities. This move is consistent with the subsequent trend. Selection and training increasingly became established in companies in their own right. I could find no account of the reasons for Rowntree's decision (nor of the exact date), but I surmise that it reflects how politically sensitive industrial psychology remained in industrial relations, because of its associations with speeding up.

Instead consultants, notably from the NIIP, continued to provide advice to companies on their selection and training methods.[11]. For example, early in the life of the Psychological Department, Muscio and Brooke, reporting on their work at Rowntree's, claim that 'the efficiency of workers is improved by nearly 27% after a suitable course of training' (1922: 68). This same piece of work is referred to in section 4, where the sample was referred to as a group of 'inefficient girls'. There the report goes on to say that novices were trained with similar results. The greatest achievements in efficiency, according to this study, were as a result of selection and training combined.

In the 1920s at Rowntree's, training came under work study, which, along with selection, were industrial psychology's two major contributions to management. At the beginning, training involved the established workforce in learning new methods and to this extent it was connected with scientific management. In order to avoid its associations with speeding up, training was often subsumed under the consideration of fatigue, which, it was claimed, was improved by training in better methods. None the less, in order to measure learning curves and the effectiveness of training, the stop-watch was used (see section 5) and that was the tangible symbol of speeding up.

Training and selection testing have tended to shadow each other in the sense that training is dominant in conditions of full employment and selection when there is considerable unemployment.[12] Yet in 1925 and 1926, when Rowntree's was obliged to engage applicants irrespective of test results because of a shortage of labour, they applied psychological tests to placement, with the result that 'the misfits have nevertheless been halved' (Moorrees 1933: 168).

7. Conclusions

When industrial psychology emerged in Britain after the First World War, psychology was at a turning point. Until that time it was a small discipline which had allied itself to the methods of natural science in its development of an experimental method to study aspects of performance. The psycho-physiological model of the individual and the experimental method were well suited to research on industrial performance. The results of the fatigue research were dramatic because they showed scientifically that changes in working conditions could improve both welfare and efficiency. The welfare emphasis was necessary in the contemporary British industrial relations climate. In addition, the focus on fatigue provided a base for industrial psychology to distinguish itself from industrial engineering and scientific management, whose exploitative effects were widely recognized by British workers. The distinction rested on the claim that where industrial engineering used a model of worker as machine, industrial psychology based its claim on its understanding of the human factor, notably the differences between individuals.

Hardly had industrial psychology become established than its focus shifted, and this shift is exemplified in the emphasis on selection at Rowntree's and the politics within which it was practised. Still, there has been a continuous tradition in British occupational psychology based on the human factors approach. It has been characterized by the experimental method, a psycho-physiological approach to the individual, and a humanistic concern with working conditions. In the 1970s this was manifest in the 'Quality of Working Life' movement (White and Jessup 1979; Tynan 1980). In the 1980s, emphasis in British occupational psychology on stress at work reflected the same tradition.

Since the 1960s in Britain, training has been a huge area outside the province of industrial psychology. Psychologists felt that laboratory studies had a contribution to make, for example to establish whether 'spaced practice' was more effective than 'massed practice' (Tiffin and McCormick 1966) or the importance of 'knowledge of results'. In industrial training attention was also paid to wider issues such as job analysis.

Training took on a new meaning when human relations principles were applied to the training of supervisors and managers (see chapter 6). This involved training in social aspects of work performance. In this context, a division developed; 'training' tended to apply to shop-floor workers and 'development' to managers. This 'development' distinction was differentiated from the early training emphasis which was aimed at training workers in mechanized jobs to adopt better (and faster) methods. 'Development' emphasized that training was not just something done on courses. Management jobs involved the whole individual.

Human factors was a largely British phenomenon, for the political reasons which I have discussed in this chapter. In the US the excesses of scientific management precipitated the human relations movement (see chapter 5). In the US from the First World War onwards industrial psychology existed in parallel with efficiency engineering and was largely confined to the development of psychometric tests. The contrast between British and American industrial psychology was recognized in the following statements, reproduced in the NIIP journal.

> Great Britain appears to have more interest in her employees than we have on this side, where workmen, while understanding that they are producing more, are receiving more and their employers have lost sight of the dehumanizing effects of intensively efficiencyized methods of production.
>
> The Taylor system was introduced in the United States by main strength. It is being maintained to-day through the same sort of fear. The lessons of fear, hold the pace or lose your job, upon which were based the introduction of scientific management, maintain in every shop in the United States wherein the Taylor or Gantt system of production is in operation.
>
> The method of handling certain employees in Great Britain is entirely different from what it is in the United States. . . . There is a disposition to consider the employee as well as the day's product. (*JNIIP* 1924–5: 303–4)

Notes

1. The Health of Munitions Workers Committee came under the Ministry of Munitions. At the end of the war it became the Industrial Fatigue Research Board and later the Industrial Health Research Board, under the Medical Research Council.

2. Relations between the NIIP and the IFRB were 'intimate and harmonious' (Myers 1926: 17). They exchanged researchers when the need arose and collaborated in joint research. The only difference was as a result of their financial status. The Board was funded by the government through the Medical Research Council and studied 'general

problems of common interest to all industries' (Myers 1926: 18). The NIIP was self-financing and carried out investigations at the request of specific firms. The Institute was also concerned to spread popular knowledge of its research and to indicate its value by lectures to employers, managers and workers, as well as by publications (Myers 1926: 18).

3. This is what industrial psychologists were doing at the Hawthorne works, where failure to control these variables was a factor in precipitating the shift to a human relations model. See chapter 5.

4. In the mid-twenties there was a downturn in the British economy. With the consequent labour surplus, trade union power declined. Working conditions research became a minor part of the work of industrial psychology.

5. May Smith, an investigator at the NIIP, puts industrial psychology in the perspective of 'the rapid expansion of industry during the early 19th century' when 'the labour not only of adults but even of very young children was ruthlessly exploited in England' (Smith 1952: 17). She quotes from a report on factory children's labour produced in 1832 which provides evidence of 'the appalling conditions under which young children were forced to work' (1952: 17). A father, giving evidence to the committee, testified that during the 'brisk season' (about six weeks), they had to be woken at 2 a.m. to be shaken from sleep and dressed in order to be at the factory by 3 a.m. They worked until 10 p.m. or half past. During those 19 hours of labour, they had 15 minutes for breakfast, 30 minutes for dinner and 15 minutes for drinking. The report concluded 'and these disgraceful hours are only part of the inhuman story' (Smith 1952: 17–18).

6. In 1921 the Cocoa Works in York employed over 7,000 people. Approximately 80 per cent of female school-leavers in York applied for jobs there (Rowntree 1920: 5).

7. The second annual meeting of the NIIP was a grand affair where men with titles from parliament and industry gave speeches saying how important industrial psychology could be (*JNIIP* [1923] 1(7): 261–74).

8. This and subsequent quotations are taken from the Minutes of the Central Works Council (CWCM), preserved in the archives. I am grateful to archivists at Rowntree Mackintosh for their help.

9. 'Efficiency engineering' was a development from scientific management by industrial engineers. It referred primarily to methods of devising the most economical way to perform the movements in tasks which were determined by machinery, and then ensuring that workers used these methods.

10. Rowntree met Myers in 1919 to discuss the appointment. When this meeting was reported to the CWC, they wanted more information and Myers gave an evening lecture which was open to all. Soon after, Rowntree was obliged to give certain 'pledges' concerning the psychologist's appointment which were never recorded in the CWC minutes but must have been given orally. From the context, the pledges may have consisted of guarantees against unemployment which might otherwise result from the psychologist's activities. Alternatively or additionally they may have been to reassure workers about not 'speeding up'. No decision was made. Another lecture was given, this time by Professor Pear. A plebiscite followed, after which the proposal to appoint a psychologist went through with some abstentions. The workers' side was asked 'to elect three representatives to serve on the committee which shall select and supervise the activities of the psychologist' (CWC Minutes 16 February 1920). The sensitivity of the issue led to a preference for an internal candidate, but he declined 'in view of the inevitable risk involved in connection with an appointment which must be of a more or less experimental nature' (CWC Minutes 16 October 1920). A compromise was achieved

by appointing J.S. Rowntree Junior as technical head of the Psychological Department. He appears to have been actively interested; in 1923 he published an article on the scope of vocational selection in industry in the *Journal of the NIIP*.

11. It may also reflect the fact that external consultants, with the support of top management, have more power to implement changes than inhouse psychologists, who are more subject to the internal politics of the organization.

12. In Britain in 1964, the Industrial Training Act, no doubt influenced by the situation of full employment, provided for the setting up of industrial training boards. Training became as popular as selection once had been. Rodger warned against the fashion of seeing training as the 'key' to manpower problems, rather than treating it in the context of the wider FMJ–FJM framework (Rodger n.d.). In 1990s Britain training women for re-entry to the workforce is salient because of the impending shortage of skilled personnel.

4
Fitting the Worker to the Job: The Use of Psychometric Tests for Selection

It is the duty of the community . . . before it leaves [the child] to guide him into the career for which his measure of intelligence has marked him out. (Burt 1924: 71)

1. Introduction

From the First World War to the present day, the use of psychometric tests in an attempt to fit the worker to the job has dominated industrial psychology. The specific field is sometimes referred to as personnel psychology (more commonly in the US) or vocational psychology. Whereas personnel psychology reflects the point of view of the employer interested in selection, placement and promotion, vocational psychology has been applied to both this and to the individual, often school-leaver, deciding on the kind of work she or he would like to do. In this chapter I discuss the reasons for this development and the conditions which made it possible. The conditions I identify include the dominant themes in social thought and scientific investigation which were the precursors of the new psychology of individual differences, whose method was psychometric testing. They also include the requirements for a new social technology to administer a population which was increasingly located in institutions. These conditions created a role for a new applied psychology. Wartime produced the technology of mass psychometric selection where before there had existed the knowledge conditions but only the beginnings of a practice.

I start by describing some of the developments around the time of the First World War which illustrate how important the new psychometricswas judged to be in applied psychology. Then I discuss what was going on in general psychology at the time, in particular the turn-of-the-century rise of Social Darwinism which provided the discursive framework for the new psychology of individual differences. I argue that, as well as being confined by Social Darwinist assumptions, psychometrics was limited in its model of the person by its narrow utilitarian goals of measuring a person's fit for specific work. I discuss these themes through the work of two figures in British industrial psychology who represented the new developments. Cyril Burt was the key figure in pioneering psychometric testing in Britain, both within industrial psychology and outside it. Bernard Muscio did some early work for Rowntree's, which introduced the use of psychometric tests for selection, and later worked for the NIIP. In 1916 he gave a series of lectures on industrial psychology which illustrate his particular enthusiasm for 'selection of workers on the basis of natural fitness' (Muscio 1974, title of lecture 3), a phrase which illustrates the way that vocational selection was incorporated into the discourse of Social Darwinism, especially the idea of efficiency and fit. I show how the notion of natural aptitudes was used within Social Darwinist discourse. The concept of 'natural aptitudes' means that performance is seen as determined by static, inherited traits. The subsequent adaptation of this view to include learning, skill and interest did little to change its effects. The use of psychometrics to measure work-related performance or ability reduces the person to a few unidimensional actions and excludes experience, multiple and dynamic potential and the variety of circumstances which can lead to prowess, satisfaction and change in one area or another.

2. Wartime Selection

I have already mentioned that Myers devised a test to select hydrophone operators towards the end of the First World War. When the United States entered the war in 1917, an urgent mobilization of personnel was required which involved not only recruiting but placing men in a wide variety of specialisms and ranks with very little time for training. This is a perfect scenario for the use of psychological tests that treat large numbers at a time in a consistent way, yet provide a measure on the basis of which *individuals* can be placed. Testing was being pioneered before the war. For example a psychologist called Scott offered a testing service to industry; one of his clients was the Western Electric Company (Rose 1975: 92). But in 1917 the scale of activities changed. The army's Committee for Psychology was established for placing recruits; it used tests for identifying a range from subnormals to officer material, and eventually dealt with two million men. Michael Rose concludes that 'applied psychology thus achieved much favourable publicity, massive development funds and full respectability' (1975: 92). The US army selection exercise largely used the 'Army Alpha', a general test of ability.[1] In Britain, the NIIP's subsequent work emphasized the design of tests based on specific jobs needs. In Britain, Myers wrote of the important part played by the war: 'the more scientific development of vocational selection was greatly favoured by the recent war. In Great Britain tests were then devised and applied to select for example air pilots and hydrophone operators' (1926: 114–15).

After the war the same method was followed by the NIIP to develop selection tests for 'engineers, weavers, embroiderers, dressmakers, packers, chocolate and biscuit makers, box makers, solderers, clerical workers, invoice machine operators, retail saleswomen, etc.' (1926: 116).

In the United States, as in Britain, the experience and reputation that psychology had gained in the war was being applied in the industrial sphere. In 1922, the journal of the NIIP carried an item which began by declaring that: 'the United States have just established a Corporation of the most renowned American psychologists, similar in object and in constitution to the NIIP of the United Kingdom' (*JNIIP* [1922] 1: 76).[2]

The *New York Times* of 17 February 1922 announced the new Psychological Corporation whose aim was described as 'the application of psychology to business'. It too referred to the 'impetus . . . applied psychology received during the war when intelligence and other tests were designed to determine the fitness of soldiers' (*JNIIP* [1922] 1: 76). The *New York Times* article continued: 'Some of the backers of the Psychological Corporation believe that it would be possible to increase by $70,000,000,000 the national wealth each year by properly fitting every man, women and child to the kind of work each could best perform' (*JNIIP* [1922] 1: 76).

It is clear from this extract that financial, and therefore business, interest revolved round the new psychometric psychology which had been applied to soldier selection. None the less, the list of directors represents a broad church within psychology. There are names which are renowned for their part in test development, such as Terman and Cattell (who was the only one to give the Corporation as his institutional affiliation, rather than a university or college). Walter Dill Scott has already been mentioned for work which preceded the war. Yet names like John B. Watson, Edward Thorndike, E.B. Titchener, William McDougall and Stanley Hall remind us that other areas of psychology as diverse as behaviourism, experimental psychology and personality theory saw scope for the application of psychology 'to educational, business, administrative and other problems' (*JNIIP* [1922] 1: 77). Yet the charter pays particular attention to selection:

> The problem of selection for general intelligence and for special aptitudes or training is one in which psychology can be of great service at the present time. If standard tests are developed to be used everywhere, both among employees in groups and with individuals seeking employment or advancement, the Corporation can give useful employment to many psychologists and probably earn sufficient income to carry on its work, and by research improve and standardize the tests. (*JNIIP* [1922] 1: 77–8)

The attraction of many of the most prestigious American psychologists to a business corporation based on psychological measurement is a clear reminder that the history of applied psychology is not one of disinterested academics in their ivory towers. Psychometrics, with its unique cocktail of 'scientific' measurement, mass regulation and the claim of enhanced productivity for business and the nation, looked set to strengthen psychology, and the interests of psychologists, in an unprecedented way.

3. Individual Differences in Mind

The psychology of individual differences was recognized as quite distinct from laboratory psychology by all those involved, as can be seen from Munsterberg's claim that 'a complete change can be traced in our science' (1913: 10) and Burt's assertion of a 'new, advanced and separate branch' which he called 'individual differences in mind' (1924: 67). The relation of the psychology of individual differences to psychometrics was symbiotic. Where psychometrics provided the method, individual differences was the theory. The theory did not develop prior to the method; if anything, the reverse. Viteles, whose textbook on industrial psychology succeeded Munsterberg's as the classic American text in the 1930s, summed up the interest of the new psychology as follows:

> Industrial psychology is interested in the individual – in his reactions to a specific situation. The growth of industrial psychology has been associated with the development of psychology interested not in general tendencies, but in problems of a single individual and in the nature and extent of the variation of his response from the reactions of other individuals. (Viteles 1933: 29)

The new psychology of individual differences took over from fatigue that place in industrial psychology which claimed to meet the needs of welfare and efficiency at the same time.

The psychology of individual differences used different methods to laboratory psychology:

> Individual differences have been an annoyance rather than a challenge to the experimeter. His goal is to control behavior, and variation within treatments is proof that he has not succeeded. Individual variation is cast into that outer darkness known as 'error variance'. . . . The correlational psychologist is in love with just those variables that the experimenter left home to forget. He regards individual and group variables as important effects of biological and social causes. . . . Just as individual variation is a source of embarrassment to the experimenter, so treatment variation attenuates the results of the correlator. His goal is to predict variation within a treatment. (Cronbach 1957: 674)

From this it is evident that 'correlational psychology' (including the psychology of individual differences) had a different focus and a different method. It also had different effects in industrial practice which, according to Cronbach, brought engineering psychology and personnel psychology into 'active conflict':

> The program of applied experimental psychology is to modify treatments so as to obtain the highest average performance when all persons are treated alike – a search, that is, for 'the one best way'. The program of applied correlational psychology is to raise average performance by treating persons differently – different job assignments, different therapies, different disciplinary methods. The correlationist is utterly antagonistic to a doctrine of 'the one best way'. . . . The ideal of the engineering psychologist, I am told, is to simplify jobs so that every individual in the working population will be able to perform them satisfactorily, ie so that differentiation of treatment will be unnecessary. (Cronbach 1957: 678)

Differentiation of treatment is the key phrase in understanding the popularity of the new psychology of individual differences. Generalized treatment based on averages was not adequate to the more subtle modes of regulation which appeared to be called for in twentieth-century institutions. As we have seen in the case of Rowntree's, workers expected (and had the power to demand) more. Whether psychometrics and the psychology of individual differences lived up to its promise is a fascinating question, which I shall come back to later, but certainly it claimed to be able to differentiate the treatment according to the individual.

4. Conditions of Emergence for the New Psychology

Discussing the late nineteenth and early twentieth centuries, Nikolas Rose (1985) analyses the two psychologies from a perspective that emphasizes the role for a differential psychology in administration. He argues that it was the needs of administration which required the new method of psychological measurement and new knowledge or theory to underpin it:

> From Gustav Fechner's psychophysics to Edward Titchener's textbook of experimental psychology, psychological measurement operated upon the model of the experiment. . . . (I)ts object was the formulation of the general laws of experience. To be adequate to the task it was now set, measurement would have to leave the closed space of the body and the artificial territory of the laboratory. It would have to relinquish the quest for indexical measures in search of distributional rankings. It would have to concern itself . . . with the classifications of the behaviours and abilities of individuals in respect to social norms. And it would have as its object not . . . that which is common to all humans, but differences amongst individuals within a population. Only then would a psychology of measurement be able to

establish itself in the space which had opened up for it in the apparatus of social administration. (Rose 1985: 113–14)

Rose locates the emergence of a psychology of measurement in a broader sociopolitical context than the factory, as is suggested by his use of the term 'the apparatus of social administration'. He argues that there was a 'symbiosis' of science and administration at the time when administration became dependent upon classification. At that point 'the question of diagnosis' became crucial and that 'depended upon a knowledge and technique to enable individuals to be properly evaluated, and a class of agents and system of administration to carry out the job' (Rose 1985: 109). The knowledge was statistical; the technique was measurement of individual differences through psychological tests; the agents were psychologists. It is not therefore a coincidence that the branches of applied psychology – 'the psychology of war, of education, of industry, of mental disorder, deficiency and crime' (Burt 1924: 67) – are based on groups who were accessible through institutions (barracks, school, factory, asylum, prison). These both provided the populations to measure and required the technology to distinguish potential inmates from the rest of the population, and some inmates from others. Both the areas of applied psychology and the institutions took as their object groups within the population which posed an administrative problem for efficiency or ones where social differentiation already existed.[3]

The first such group, according to Rose (1985: 106), was the feeble-minded. A British report in 1910 on the 'Care and Control of the Feebleminded', illustrated a change in strategy from penalty to prevention. This change depended on a technology which could identify the feeble-minded, irrespective of what they had done, purely on the grounds of who they were. Where before psychology based its measures on performance, psychometric tests claimed to provide the technology to measure 'mental functions by mental symptoms' (Burt 1924: 68). In other words, this new brand of applied psychologist claimed to be able to *measure the mind*.

The tests were dependent on developments in statistics which had the power to distinguish between the normal and abnormal: 'its conception of normal and abnormal mental functioning would be constructed from the point of view of a theory populations, averages and correlations, not from a conception of the psyche itself' (Rose 1985: 123). However, the new psychology was not a pure theoretical invention, conjured up in response to a sudden shift in the modes of administration or regulation. Changes in dominant social theory were already reflecting the priorities of administration. The psychology of individual differences was closely allied to Social Darwinism and specifically to eugenics, which has spawned the statistics on which psychometrics was based.

Darwinism had enabled theory in terms of populations rather than individual organisms. The new statistics depended upon ideas such as eugenics which were derived from Social Darwinism; that is the application of Darwinist biology to society. Turn-of-the century Social Darwinism was concerned with maintaining the fitness of the race, genetic inheritance and national efficiency (see chapter 3, section 3). Galton's science of eugenics was 'the science of improving stock which takes cognisance of all influences that tend . . . to give the more suitable races or strains of blood a better chance of prevailing speedily over the less suitable than they otherwise would have had' (Francis Galton 1883, quoted in Rose 1985: 63). Eugenics, according to Rose, 'gave a new political salience to the question of individual differences' (1985: 63).[4]

The theoretical and political principle of eugenics, which has underpinned the psychology of individual differences from its inception, is that individual differences are largely determined by genetic inheritance. When it is assumed that people's performance is genetically determined, no attempt need be made to change it. Rather, people are grouped, placed and regulated according to a one-off measure of performance. It is a conservative doctrine with conservative effects: the technology maintained, legitimized and made more efficient existing systems of social differentiation.

Galton used new concepts in statistics to develop, and 'prove', his eugenic theory. He could proclaim as early as 1883: 'There is no bodily or mental attribute of any race of individuals that cannot be . . . gripped and consolidated into an ogive with a smooth outline and thence forward be treated in discussion as a single object' (quoted in Rose 1985: 69). Rose summarizes:

> This thesis of continuity and regularity delivered up the variability of the population to the regularity of scientific knowledge [but] it was the norm which allowed the formulation of the laws of this variation and hence the organisation of all features of human ability within a single conceptual space. For the relationship between average and deviation was the foundation of the theory of normal distribution and the basis of the power of the normal curve. (1985: 69)

With such a tool, mental powers (and their absence in the form of feeble-mindedness) could be diagnosed in whole populations, an idea which Burt enthusiastically embraced. In a 1952 lecture on 'The Contributions of Psychology to Social Problems', Burt began by remarking how, when British Psychology made the transition from being a branch of philosophy, it was effected 'through the influence of those who were primarily biologists, particularly the earlier advocates of evolutionary doctrines' (Burt 1953: 2). He challenged Adam Smith's argument that differences in ability were the effect of the division of labour by claiming that Galton 'was the first to adduce convincing evidence against this'.

The psychology of individual differences was not based on a theory of the psyche. Rather it derived from a statistical theory of population distribution based on the normal curve. For Burt, once the psychologist has 'measured all measurable capacities' this added up to a 'skeleton of mind' (1924: 74). Cronbach disagrees: 'a naive operationalism enthroned theory of test performance in the place of theory of mental processes. And premature enthusiasm exalted a few measurements chosen almost by accident from the tester's stock as the ruling forces of the mental universe' (Cronbach 1957: 675).

Myers, who later embraced the use of selection testing within the NIIP, was critical of mental measurement as a science. Myers was still at the psychological laboratory at Cambridge (and therefore still firmly identified as an experimental psychologist) when, in 1911, he published a paper called 'The Pitfalls of Mental Tests', which argued that 'the wholesale collection of measurement is apt to give us only a very blurred and often inaccurate picture of the factors which really underlie the problem under investigation' (1911: 196). While recognizing that classification in order to place an individual as suitable or unsuitable can be usefully applied *en masse*, he stressed that such tests are 'tests of production', not mental tests. He underscores the difference between practical utility and theoretical understanding when he says 'a man's productivity, of course, is what we want to ascertain in everyday life . . . from this aspect mass experiments have some value. But this aspect cannot properly be called psychological' (Myers 1911: 196). Only a decade later, it would have been almost unthinkable to challenge the place of measurement of individual differences in psychology: applied psychology had emerged and grown on the basis of this technology.

5. Mental Measurment: 'A Plan for Every Man'

In Britain, Cyril Burt is the most prominent representative of the psychology of individual differences. He exemplifies the links with eugenics, with administration and the relation between educational and occupational testing which characterized the developing area of vocational selection in British industrial psychology. In this section I shall therefore use his case to illustrate these connections. Sir Cyril Burt gained great notoriety after his death because of the way he falsified data in his studies of identical twins which set out to prove the genetic determination of intelligence.[5] For my purposes this is regrettable, because it makes it easy to dismiss what Burt stood for as an exception. On the contrary (and without implying that his kind of cheating was widespread), I use his example because his position epitomizes the expression of the emerging psychology of individual differences and the social, political and knowledge conditions within which this occurred in Britain in the early twentieth century.

While he is known primarily as an educational psychologist (the first educational psychologist in Britain ever employed as such, by the London County Council in 1912), Burt also worked closely with industrial psychology, establishing the NIIP's vocational guidance department in 1920 and then being head of it from 1922 to 1924 (Welch and Myers 1932: 115). As Burt later saw it, around the time of the First World War 'the practical psychologist turned his attention from the tasks of educational guidance to those of vocational guidance and selection' (1953: 35). In vocational guidance, the measurement of general intelligence in children and the interests of employers to 'fit the man to the job' came together. Burt claimed:

> it is the duty of the community, first, to ascertain what is the mental level of each individual child; then to give the education most appropriate to his level; and lastly, before it leaves him, to guide him into the career for which his measure of intelligence has marked him out. (Burt 1924: 71)

Evidently Burt identified completely with the regulatory aims of educational administration and employers (here called the community). Bartlett (1955: 210), a prominent experimental psychologist who trained under Myers at Cambridge, satirized the testers emerging from the First World War

> chanting in unaccustomed harmony the words of the old jingle
> God has a Plan for Every Man
> And he has one for You.

For 'God', read any psychologist who claimed to measure the mind.

According to Burt, one of Galton's chief objectives was 'an anthropometric survey of the British Isles which should include mental as well as physical qualities' (Burt 1953: 17). Burt was in a position to provide information deriving from the mass measurement of mental differences. Eight years after a subcommittee of the British Association was formed for this purpose, 'the appointment of an educational psychologist by the London County Council made it possible for such surveys to be carried out among large samples of the general school population' (Burt 1953: 17). Burt cites this survey (1924: 70) as proof of the enormous range of innate individual differences in the childhood population.

Burt claimed (1924: 70–1) that the results of the measurement of general intelligence not only corresponded well with the existing forms of classifying the school population, but could also justify the sorts of jobs which less intelligent adults should find themselves in:

> Since variations in intelligence are so wide and so continuous, it becomes convenient to divide the entire population into about six or eight separate classes or layers. A classification of this kind, worked out empirically, for children, is already implicitly embodied in the organisation of our various schools. A second classification can be drawn up, on an analogous basis, for adults, and will be found, in the main, to reflect the amount of difficulty and responsibility entailed by their several occupations. (Burt 1924: 70–1)

For Burt, intelligence tests provided scientific evidence that children had been correctly classified according to their innate abilities. I find it more plausible to see it the other way round. In Burt's view, mental measurement served to legitimate (and make more efficient) the social administration that was already taking place: it was now based on 'proof' of innate differences in ability.

The coincidence that Burt emphasized between the results of mental tests on one hand and school and work achievement on the other does illustrate the congruity which was established between statistical norms and administrative or social norms. The concept of normal was undergoing a massive transformation as a result of its new construction within statistics and its new importance to administration: 'The whole project of individual psychology depended upon . . . a congruity between norms of healthy mental functioning, norms of social demand and expectation, and statistical norms of the distribution of variations in a population' (Rose 1985: 218).

Special abilities turn out to mirror the criteria of school performance: 'arithmetical, manual (drawing, writing, probably handwork of simpler kinds), verbal (reading, and spelling), literary (composition in one's own tongue), linguistic (learning foreign languages), artistic, and musical' (Burt 1924: 72). The congruity is hardly surprising since the tests originated in those designed to measure classroom performance.[6] Similarly tests for school-leavers construed vocation in terms of those skills required for factory jobs: 'the vocational psychologist must work backward from the measurement of acquired dexterities in every trade to the measurement of related capacities' (1924: 73).

6. Vocational Guidance

'The impartial idea at the basis of selection for vocations is the reduction to the minimum of certain forms of waste' (Muscio 1974: 104). This statement incorporates the premiss on which is based the technology of individual measurement for work; an idealized notion of a world of industrial harmony and productivity resulting from a neat fit between individuals and jobs. The idea of fit is applied solely to the individual in this discourse.[7] The complementary idea of 'misfits'[8] became the term for those who, by virtue of being in the wrong job, did not match up to the new methods and speeds which were introduced into production. The effect of the term 'misfit', contained as it was in a discourse referring to what was natural and unchangeable, was to justify as inevitable, even humane, the removal of misfits from the jobs concerned. This was not always possible, as I have shown at Rowntree's, where the Psychological Department accepted restrictions imposed by the Central Works Council. I also showed that it was less politically contentious to shift the emphasis of fitting workers to jobs to the selection of new employees, that is of school-leavers. This principle partly explains the emphasis on vocational guidance. Muscio, for example, acknowledged that the ideal system could not be applied straightaway by removing misfits from jobs in which they were established (1974: 147). Vocational guidance for school-leavers was of particular interest to industrial psychologists because, if everybody's natural aptitudes could be measured, it would solve for the future work generation the waste incurred by people who 'spend their lives in work other than that for which they are most fitted' (Muscio 1974: 106). For this reason, he was especially interested in vocational guidance for school-leavers.

Muscio had ambitious plans for fitting school-leavers to jobs. He imagined a large vocational laboratory for girls and boys about to become wage earners which would be under the control of psychologists and connected with both schools and industry (Muscio 1974: 149ff.). Here school-leavers' 'capacities' would be tested to reveal the jobs for which individuals were naturally fitted. However, the capacities would be based on those for which tests had been devised. Industrial psychologists devised either 'analogous' tests – tests to simulate specific jobs – or 'analytic' ones; an analytic test 'depends on abstracting the various qualities required for success in a given occupation' (Myers 1926: 114). Both types were used for adolescent vocational guidance as well as selection. They are based on the particular needs of the division of labour where many jobs require no more than finger dexterity and a capacity for monotonous repetition. For example Muscio discusses the need to select women for a particular job which required them only to pick up exactly twelve pencils and transfer them from one hand to the other (Muscio 1974: 106). The talents of the individual become defined by the constructs of the industrial psychologist: as a result of vocational testing, an individual's 'natural capacity' would, for example, be reduced to speed, finger dexterity and hand–eye coordination.[9] The nature of the tests themselves, while claiming to measure individual ability, are devised within the requirements of a machine-based manufacturing industry.

Psychology makes claims to institute a perfectly ordered world where the psychologist (in the name of the people themselves) has the expertise to place people in particular work. Although the psychologist gives 'advice' (Muscio 1974: 151), the discourse proceeds on the assumption that advice will be followed. If, as was the case, psychologists believed themselves to be neutral technicians, revealing what was already inherent in the individual's genetic make-up for their greater good, the distinction between the psychologist's choice and that of the client would not have been salient. With 'scientific' advice coming from an 'expert', the school-leaver would have little space to formulate alternative preferences. The status of science and the power of the expert was such that it is unsurprising if lay people (for whom all of this was very new) believed what they were told about themselves and, on the basis of what they believed to be true, 'chose' the vocation that was being advised. Myers recommended: 'if vocational guidance is to be successful the applicant should be made to feel that he is himself finally choosing his vocation' (1926: 114).

Industrial psychologists applied the notion of 'vocation' to every job (for example Muscio 1974; Myers 1920, 1926; Burt 1924) though in practice their vocational tests were applied almost entirely to mechanized jobs. The connotations of the high-status, professional 'calling' are in this way transferred to all jobs, however routine, and since the idea of vocation is inserted into a Social Darwinist discourse of natural fitness, even these jobs are assigned qualities of appropriateness and natural justice. After discussing the case of the job which requires women to pick up exactly twelve pencils and transfer them from one hand to the other, day in, day out, Muscio concludes 'It seems likely, also, that, even in conditions of industry such as exist at present, selection of workers will increase the number of operatives who find an interest in their work' (1974: 107). J.S. Rowntree states that vocational selection would be able 'to reduce to an almost negligible number the cases in which work is felt to be monotonous'. He saw automatic machinery as suiting 'the lowest grade of worker' (1923: 245). Worries about the inhumanity of deskilled jobs and the dangers of monotony are just evident in these statements, but they surface only to be quieted by the assurance that selection ensures that appropriate individuals (the 'lowest grade of worker') occupy these jobs and for them, there is no problem.

At this point, the discourse left little room for a distinction between interest and abilities, though it was developed later in vocational guidance. Muscio (1974: 149) does briefly mention the possibility that interests and natural abilities or talent might not coincide. The conceptual separation of interests and abilities was still in its infancy and not easy to emphasize within a discourse whose rationale was mass administration for the purposes of efficiency. Myers cites an example of a telephonist who scored highly on tests but whose supervisor ranked her low (1926: 121). He interprets the discrepancy in terms of 'interest', but abandons an analysis of the implications for testing in favour of a reassertion that, despite such factors, the use of tests in another case (Rowntree's) were of such practical utility that 'this firm estimates that the introduction of vocational tests . . . has saved it many thousands of pounds per annum' (1926: 122). By the early 1970s, Alec Rodger is taking the position that

> What matters is that we should recognise that being 'good' at something and 'liking' it are, for the psychologist, to be distinguished. If they are found to 'go together', that is fine; but often they do not and many mistakes are made in assessing people because it is rashly assumed that an individual who likes a particular task will be good at performing it. (Birkbeck College, Department of Occupational Psychology, undated notes)

For employees the problem is more likely to be the reverse; that, while they may be good at performing it, they do not like it. In Muscio's ideal world there might be no need to distinguish the interests of the new recruit from the interests of the employer, or, therefore, vocational guidance from vocational selection. The latter distinction does remain unclear in the industrial psychologist's discourse. Myers' chapter entitled 'Vocational Guidance' (1926: ch. 4) illustrates the elision of the two terms: despite its title, the main emphasis of the chapter is on vocational selection, and its discussion moves between the two in such a way as almost to obliterate the distinction. He defines the difference clearly enough:

> By 'vocational guidance' is meant the advice given to the applicant, based on systematic examination of his mental and bodily condition, as to the occupations for which he is fitted and unfitted. 'Vocational selection' on the other hand, is the process of choosing by such examination those applicants who are best fitted for the existing vacancies in any one occupation. (Myers 1926: 108)

The distinction hinges on who is the client – employer or potential employee – and it is just this point which industrial psychology tended to blur because it was committed to claiming that the interests of employer and employee were complementary. Never is it admitted that the nature of industrial capitalism, technology and the division of labour might mean that few individuals could find a vocation in endless repetition.[10] Industrial psychologists and employers believed that the measurement of individual differences was a technology which could surmount the problems posed for industrial capitalism by the unpredictability of workers' commitment to deskilled factory labour.

Notes

1. The 'Army Alpha' test was a development of the intelligence test, which was designed for the purpose of diagnosing poor educational peformance.

2. The main difference, apart from size, was that the US corporation consisted entirely of psychologists, whereas the NIIP included 'representatives not only of psychology but also of physiology, education and medicine' (*JNIIP* [1922]: 76).

3. In both Burt and Munsterberg, there is a significant slippage in the discourse of individual differences from individual to social group. Burt talks about variations largely in terms of social groups: 'The variations have attracted [the psychologist studying individual differences] more than the averages; and the mental disparities between childhood and age, between race and race, between one sex and the other, and between each unique individual and the rest have formed their chosen topic' (Burt 1924: 67). Munsterberg likewise claims: 'in practical life we never have to do with what is common to all human beings, even when we are to influence large masses; we have to deal with personalities whose mental life is characterized by particular traits of nationality, or race, or vocation, or sex, or age or special interests' (1913: 9).

While the method depended on individual measurement, the results of this measurement *en masse* were used to compare social groups, notably those of class, race and sex which were already the subject of social differentiation.

4. Cronbach (1957: 672) notes the use of the label 'genetic psychology' at the turn of the century to refer to what I am calling the psychology of individual differences.

5. See the *Bulletin* of the British Psychological Society 33, supplement 1980.

6. The first 'intelligence' test – that devised by Binet and Simon in France – was constructed as an administrative device. The authors stressed that its criteria were not theoretical but educational. Because of its power to treat large numbers, the device was soon extended to the measurement of normal performance as well. By 1908 its title had changed from 'new methods for the diagnosis of the intellectual level of the abnormal' to 'the development of intelligence among children' (Rose 1985: 128).

7. At this stage there is no formalized notion of unfit jobs (but see chapter 6).

8. For example Burt says 'The worst misfits arise, not from forcing round pegs into square holes, but from placing large pegs in little holes and small pegs in holes too big for them to fill' (1924: 71). Muscio points out: 'considering the altogether planless manner in which industrial vocations are now ordinarily entered upon, it is only likely that, distributed through society as a whole, there are numerous vocational misfits such as I have suggested' (1974: 106). Northcott, the Labour Manager at Rowntree's (1933: 168) says: 'the misfits have been practically halved'.

9. Women were (and are) believed to have greater natural finger dexterity. Elson and Pearson (1981) demonstrate that this belief still justifies the gendered division of labour in the new Third World electronics and textile jobs.

10. J.S. Rowntree (Seebohm's son and the technical head of the department) commented in his paper on this subject that 'a cocoa and chocolate factory is in the fortunate position of being able to place almost every worker in the job for which he is best qualified' (1933: 245). Seebohm Rowntree welcomed a suggestion by the workers' side that the boys on the box-nailing machines should be replaced by girls 'on the grounds that it was a blind-alley occupation' (Rowntree 1979: 139). Women's 'nature' commonly provides the justification for situating them in dead-end, and often monotonous jobs.

PART TWO

THE SENTIMENTAL WORKER

5
Hawthorne and the Emergence of Human Relations

In matters pertaining to collaboration, the sentiments and their interactions are very important. (Roethlisberger 1949: 39)

dimly the experimenters perceived a new method of human control. (Roethlisberger 1949: 16)

1. Introduction

Over a period of thirty years, beginning in the 1930s, 'human relations' became the dominant paradigm within which the management of people in organizations was understood and its practices modified. In its most popular and well-established sense, human relations 'is simply a catch-all term for describing the way in which the people who comprise an organization think about and deal with each other' (Gellerman 1966: 1). More precisely, it refers to a social-psychological paradigm for understanding the individual at work and to recommendations for management practice which stem from this approach. It is no more the exclusive property of psychology than of sociology or management theory.[1] Though arguably the peak of its dominance passed in the sixties or seventies, its assumptions are still so widespread that it is difficult to distance ourselves from them; we take them for granted.

This is important because, as I shall argue, human relations has dominated the understanding of organizational behaviour. The result has been a preoccupation with the characteristics of individuals in interpersonal relations, particularly the relations between managers and subordinates, as exemplified in the interest in 'leadership style'. This preoccupation has virtually excluded other approaches. In his book on British management thought, John Child argues that:

At the time of its greatest influence, human relations led much of British management thought towards an extreme analysis in terms of organizational solidarity, an almost exclusive emphasis on social motivations, and on the

role of personal leadership. It completely discounted the likely technological, financial, and socio-environmental constraints bearing upon any
viable managerial policy. (Child 1969: 156)

The practice of planned change has taken place predominantly
according to these human relations emphases.

In part 2 of this book I document the emergence of, and developments within, human relations up to the 1980s and I examine what
conditions produced these. I start with the Hawthorne experiments,
which are generally recognized as the first example of a human
relations paradigm formalized into a scientific discourse.

Section 2 gives a brief description of the Hawthorne research,
attempting to set it in the wider historical context of management and
work psychology. Section 3 introduces the 'sentimental worker',
formalized with the Hawthorne research, and its significance as a new
object of psychology and management which stresses the emotional
and social determinants of work behaviour. In section 4 I discuss the
conditions for the transition from scientific management to human
relations as the dominant approach to work regulation. Sections 5, 6
and 7 all consider aspects of the production of the sentimental worker;
its application in supervisory relations and training, its relation to the
counselling programme and to productivity. Finally, in section 8, I
examine the relations between the interviewing method, supervisory
training and the production of a new subject worker.

2. The Hawthorne Research

The famous studies were conducted at 'Hawthorne', a site of the
Western Electric Company situated in a Chicago suburb, in the second
half of the 1920s. They continued into the 1930s. Western Electric was
a wholly owned subsidiary of American Telephone and Telegraph
Company, AT&T. The original research by the National Research
Council, focusing on the relation of illumination and productivity,
began in 1924. The Relay Assembly Test Room was opened in April
1927. Here experimenters measured the effect on the productivity of
women workers of a great variety of changes in working conditions,
including illumination and rest pauses. Productivity increased under
all conditions, a result which was attributed to the improved social
relations. The extent to which this experiment became synonymous
with the Hawthorne studies is evident in the way that this phenomenon
is called the 'Hawthorne effect'. In 1928, Mayo (who was already
Associate Professor of Industrial Research at Harvard Business
School) went to the plant. Also in 1928, an internal Industrial Research
Division was set up to develop the interviewing programme. According
to Roethlisberger, one of the Harvard research team, in 1928, 'a new

era of personnel relations began': 'It was the first real attempt to get human data and to forge human tools to get them. In that year a novel idea was born; dimly the experimenters perceived a new method of human control' (Roethlisberger 1949: 16).

The counselling programme which developed from this research at the Hawthorne works continued until 1956. In 1931, observation began in the Bank Wiring Room (where restriction of output was first formally documented and investigated). The formal involvement of the Harvard team ended in 1932. I do not intend to describe the Hawthorne experiments here because there is a voluminous literature which does so (see especially Roethlisberger 1949: ch. 2; Landsberger 1968; Argyle 1953; Baritz 1965).

Many secondary accounts of the Hawthorne studies choose to focus almost exclusively on conclusions about the informal group (an emphasis for which Elton Mayo's philosophy was largely responsible). By the end of the 1940s, a typical opinion, however was that the Hawthorne research 'led to the now famous conclusions that work output is a function of the degree of work satisfaction which in turn depends upon the informal social pattern of the work group' (Bendix and Fisher 1949: 315)

The evidence on the relation between output and the informal group produced by the Hawthorne studies was conflicting. Early on, in the Relay Assembly Test Room, the women's productivity rose whatever changes were made to their conditions.[2] Yet the opposite conclusions derived from the fourth and final phase of the Hawthorne experiments in the Bank Wiring Observation Room. Here the men's solidarity contributed to an informal norm to limit output. Likert's work (see chapter 7) was based on the Hawthorne principle of the positive benefits of the small informal group. By the 1960s, however, in common with most other human relations work, the target of his intervention was managers, not lower-level employees, as in the initial Hawthorne studies.

Despite Mayo's values of communal ties, loyalty and solidarity which infused human relations and social psychology, the discovery of the influence of the small group did not lead primarily to changes in practice based on small groups for the majority of employees. For example, it did not become standard practice in factories to select workers, say on the basis of friendship, or to develop ways of encouraging them to relate well together. The line of argument developed was the concern with worker satisfaction. For this purpose, the individual employee in relation to management became the focus; the group becoming just background.

The training group was destined to become the most common form of small group in human relations practice and organizational

behaviour. (Later, when training turned into organizational development, the focus on the work group reappeared.) This group was the
antithesis of the informal work group: temporarily constituted of
strangers in isolation from the workplace and permanently under the
control of the trainer. The group was largely an administrative
convenience for dealing with individuals. It was such practical
exigencies, coupled with the politically preferred focus on the individual, which led to the trend in the social psychology of groups in which
the individual group member is the dominant object in both practice
and theory.

This reaffirmation of the emphasis on the individual is not
surprising, given the history of industrial psychology which we have
already traced, particularly in the US. Groups were experienced as a
risky object of regulation because of the power of organized groups:
the threat of unionization. The men's solidarity in the Bank Wiring
Observation Room demonstrated the power of the informal group,
and while this was a useful lesson, human relations psychology
concluded that it could be most effective if it offered strategies that
individualized the treatment of employees. The work group did,
however, later become the focus for the Tavistock approach to the
design of work, and the Quality of Working Life movement (see
chapter 7).

The Hawthorne studies combined two radical departures from
previous industrial psychology. The first involved a shift from the
psycho-physiological model of the worker to a socio-emotional one.
The second was a change in method from an experimental one whose
object was the body (or the interface between the body and the job), to
one whose object was attitudes as the intervening variable between
situation (working conditions) and response (output). Human relations
not only made possible the production of different kinds of information
for the first time in the workplace, but had a powerful effect on the
workers themselves. The Hawthorne interview programme discovered
that a sympathetic interview technique (see section 6) could not only
elicit new information which was valuable to management, but could
itself be instrumental in effecting a change in employees' attitudes.
Human relations training was later to be based on this insight. In
summary, Hawthorne is where the 'sentimental worker' came into
being as the object of social science.

3. The Sentimental Worker

I call the subject of this new knowledge 'the sentimental worker'
because it was at this time that the worker was formally discovered to
have sentiments (feelings or emotions as we would call them now) and

interpersonal needs. As Roethlisberger describes the conclusions of one set of studies (in the Relay Assembly Test Room): 'What all their experiments had dramatically and conclusively demonstrated was the importance of employee attitudes and sentiments' (1949: 15). According to Roethlisberger, the important characteristic of sentiments was that 'they cannot be modified by logic alone' (1949: 31). He described the early experimenters at Hawthorne as:

> carrying around in their heads the notion of 'economic man', a man primarily motivated by economic interest, whose logical capacities were being used in the service of this self-interest. Gradually and painfully the experimenters had been forced to abandon this conception of the worker and his behavior . . . they found that the behavior of workers could not be understood apart from their feelings or sentiments. (1949: 19)

Of course this knowledge was a feature of workplace relations before (see chapter 3, section 6). It was partly because the personalized and potentially humane treatment of the worker had largely been lost with the increasing size of factories and the change in technology that it had to be rediscovered. With the Hawthorne experiments the knowledge was produced by social science and therefore had more status and legitimacy. It was formalized and disseminated.

By far the most important source is the original one: *Management and the Worker* (1939/1970), written by Roethlisberger, one of the Harvard team of researchers, and Dickson, an employee in Hawthorne's personnel department. This book is extraordinary in its theoretical range and in its attention to detail in description of the research process. *Management and the Worker* represented a massive intellectual and practical shift. The fact that the ideas contained in the book are now part of our commonsense conceptions should not detract from, but should contribute to, an appreciation of the radical innovation that was achieved with the formalized production of the sentimental worker.

In summary, the new discourse which built up a picture of the sentimental worker saw his/her performance not as based on rational response to reality, but as being emotionally and irrationally affected by complex social and interpersonal factors, both outside and inside the workplace, both past and present. Emotion or sentiment was an important variable because it intervened between workers' experience (for example of supervision) and their job performance (see the case of worker W7, in section 7). It is not a discourse which developed first theoretically, later leading to application: the 'sentimental worker' was produced through interviewing and observation in the Hawthorne plant.[3] From the beginning, the research was bound up with management: how its interests produced a certain definition of the problem (the need for improved control of output without changing material conditions) and how knowledge in terms of the discourse of the sentimental worker led to certain practices and not others; for example counselling and interpersonal skills training, rather than the resolution of grievances.

4. From Scientific Management to Human Relations

The transition to human relations as the dominant discourse and practice of industrial psychology and management in the United States is usually understood as a radical break – a paradigm shift. This emphasis is the almost inevitable result of writing the history of industrial psychology as a history of ideas. In this tradition, the transition is viewed as one in which certain prominent researchers saw the theoretical and/or scientific inadequacy of previous principles, understood for the first time the importance of the human element, and drew on different intellectual traditions to create new paradigms, such as ones in which motivation, group cohesiveness and attitudes played the key role. The typical account of the Hawthorne research process reflects just this theory of scientific progress. For example describing the reasons for the transition from the early illumination studies at the Hawthorne plant, Mayo comments: 'The conditions of scientific experiment had apparently been fulfilled – experimental room, control room; changes introduced one at a time; all other conditions held steady. And the results were perplexing' (1949: 61).

The scientific progress account of the shift to human relations is not untrue; the human factor paradigm of the initial research did leave unanswered pressing questions about output. But it does not explain what it changed to, and why it did so at that time. It was not simply improved science that enabled movement in understanding. If scientific legitimacy had been the criterion for the subsequent influence of the Hawthorne experiments, it is probable that the human relations paradigm would have been dismissed in its infancy. Despite being 'the first major social science experiment' (Baritz 1965: 77), there has been plenty of retrospective criticism of the scientificity of the Hawthorne experiments (for example Argyle 1953; Carcy 1967).

In contrast to the scientific progress view, I account for the emergence of human relations in terms of the relation between power (in this case management interests and worker resistance) and knowledge. In this view, claims of scientificity play their part in legitimizing the take-up of human relations practices. However it does not rely on an idea of science promoting progress towards objective truth. The relation between social science knowledge, or discourse, and management practice is a continuous, two-way affair. Child illustrates the effects of management practice on discourse in his comments on the likely reasons for the predominance of the human relations paradigm in Britain:

> Interested academics and management writers with a keen eye to prevailing social problems . . . were quite aware of the numerous and complex causes of the industrial conflict then so much in evidence. These writers between them put forward a comprehensive list of causes such as fatigue, monotony, speeding-up, lack of worker autonomy on the shop floor, gross inequalities of economic reward in society, class-consciousness, the disparity between the ideal of political democracy and the absence of democracy in industry.
>
> On the other hand, we shall find that management thought tended increasingly to place its main hopes for worker motivation and the resolution of conflict not on an attempt to mitigate the factors just listed, but rather on the persuasive powers of personal managerial leadership. . . . It appeared most promising to concentrate attention on motivational techniques which managers could readily use. (Child 1969: 55)

These practical contingencies pre-existed the Hawthorne research and so management preferences were already developing along human relations lines: Child points out that one reason the British management movement so readily adopted 'Mayoism's practical human relations recommendations' (1969: 83) was that these were anticipated in British management thought 'at least as far back as the close of the first world war'. As already discussed, employee-centred considerations were central to the practice of enlightened British employers, and British management thought already reflected this interest. The Hawthorne studies then gave legitimacy to those employee-centred ideas in British management thought. Child concludes that: 'It is [Hawthorne's] apparent scientific backing which helps to explain why human relations held so much influence, not only over British management thought, but over some Labour leaders as well' (Child 1969: 155).

Why was the emphasis of the Hawthorne research so attractive to management? The fame of the Relay Assembly Test Room experiments lies in the perplexing but tantalizing discovery (from a management point of view) of the 'Hawthorne effect': namely that whatever experimental conditions were imposed on the women in the test room (illumination changes, differing wage systems, rest pauses, beverages, changes in the length of working day and even a return to previous conditions), output rose. It is not surprising that, as Baritz put it, 'the lure of the miraculous' took hold (1965: 49).

Managements were facing a widespread problem of control – of output restriction, absenteeism and labour turnover. 'Soldiering', as Taylor called restriction of output, was widely recognized as a problem. During and after the First World War, union membership had risen enormously, an increase for which scientific management was in part responsible (along with the labour shortage brought on by the war). Membership declined again during the 1920s. In that decade, according to Baritz, American employers had dealt with dissatisfaction – in a serious and well-organized attempt to keep unionism at bay – by comprehensive welfare provision within a framework of paternalistic control.[4] Yet in 1935 a researcher reported that one-third of all American workers were dissatisfied with their jobs (Baritz 1965: 125).

Resistance took different forms in different epochs. The famous limitation of output 'discovered' in the Bank Wiring Observation Room at the Hawthorne Works is an example of workers' strategy in a non-unionized (and anti-union) company during a period where lay-offs and unemployment were a threat. Despite the claims of scientific management to promote 'hearty cooperation' of employers and workers, and partly because of their experience of scientific management, workers saw a relationship between increased output and the scarcity of jobs: 'working slower than management wanted meant to the worker that his job would last longer' (Baritz 1965: 99). In such a context there was a growing recognition that 'men' were the most precious resource of the company:

> This growing attitude, translated into personnel policy, took several shapes. Though it was certainly not the only tendency, paternalism did become the most characteristic form of personnel programs. Management would take care of its workers in the hope that they would reciprocate with appreciation, loyalty, and harder and more efficient work. Welfare plans were invented to cover virtually every aspect of the worker's life, from the moment when he was hired by a centralized and 'scientific' employment department to his retirement years when he would benefit from a carefully constructed pension plan. Hundreds of such personnel programs emerged in this decade [1920s]. And the ranks of organized labor declined steadily. (Baritz 1965: 59–60)

Commentators as far apart politically as Braverman (famed for his Marxist analysis of deskilling and the labour process) and Drucker (the popular management writer) are of the opinion that scientific management was not superseded but was built into the technology of the production line. Drucker (quoted by Braverman 1974: 87) states that Taylorism 'is no longer the property of a faction, since its fundamental teachings have become the bedrock of all work design'. Braverman develops this by examining the role of management and related behavioural sciences once the technology is in place:

> Work itself is organized according to Taylorian principles, while personnel departments and academics have busied themselves with the selection, training, manipulation, pacification, and adjustment of 'manpower' to suit the work processes so organized. Taylorism dominates the world of production; the practitioners of 'human relations' and 'industrial psychology' are the maintenance crew for the human machinery. (1974: 87)

Applied behavioural science was faced with new situations to understand and for which to recommend strategies of regulation. Strategies based on scientific management were not working. For example, when Mayo was a consultant in a textile mill on the problem of labour turnover 'several firms of efficiency engineers had been consulted [and] . . . labour turnover had not dropped one point' (Mayo 1949: 52). Towards the end of their book, Roethlisberger and Dickson discuss the ways in which a counselling programme such as the one they pioneered can help: 'this kind of non-authoritative agency (the counselling programme) serves to control and to direct those human processes within the industrial structure which are not adequately controlled by the other agencies of management' (1970: 601).

Human relations represents the extension of a welfare strategy into production itself – a well-aimed but ultimately only partly successful attempt to enlist the cooperation of workers in the goals of the company without changing its structures or technology. The key ideas of the human relations approach became supervisory training in interpersonal skills and leadership to influence the morale and motivation, attitudes and feelings of their subordinates. What characterizes this cluster of ideas is that its focus is entirely at the psychological and interpersonal level. For example, an ex-counsellor at Hawthorne said that they were instructed to deal 'with attitudes towards problems, not the problems themselves' (Baritz 1965: 105). Jobs, technology and work performance ceased to be mentioned and pay and complaints only figured in order to assert that their significance was not real but symptomatic of workers' sentiments (see below). This is why human relations was taken up and, despite considerable evidence for its lack of success, this is why human relations is still important.

5. Defining the Problem and the Object of Change

A clinical analysis offers the possibility of exonerating supervisors' conduct, blaming workers and thus displacing responsibility for workers' 'poor' performance from the factory management.[5] Roethlisberger and Dickson were aware of the dangers of their reductionist analysis and also were inconsistent with regard to it: 'At the time, the investigators were primarily interested in the individual complainant and the particularities of his personal situation. . . . As a result they failed to see some of the more general uniformities which existed among employee complaints' (Roethlisberger and Dickson 1970: 358). In a separate chapter (chapter 16) they attempt to compensate for this emphasis but the accounts remain largely unintegrated with the dominant paradigm of the book. The authors' difficulties demonstrate the power of the theoretical framework (in this case the focus on the non-rational) to guide their conclusions in ways with which they are themselves uneasy.

It has been commented in a broadening area of social sciences that contemporary theory has a tendency to 'blame the victim'; that is, to advance explanations which seemingly locate responsibility in one group, which is consistently the group with less power and which does not produce the dominant knowledges (Hollway 1989: ch. 6). It is a phenomenon which is predictable in terms of Foucault's analysis of the relation between power and knowledge. This is indeed what happened in parts of the Hawthorne research. Thus Roethlisberger and Dickson claim that 'it was evident that the complaints of this type of person [that is the less rational] could not be taken seriously as criticisms of company policy and conditions' (1970: 313) and that 'comments on supervision, more than any other area could not be taken at their face value' (1970: 292). The authors are on sensitive political ground here and their account, although it places a considerable burden of responsibility on the worker, still contains several footnotes stating that what they say must not be taken as criticism of supervisors (1970: 292–3, 331–2). While the authors' intention is to leave it an open question whether particular supervisors were 'slave drivers, bullies' and so on (1970: 292n.) the effect of the analysis is to blame the interviewees' 'distortion', 'loss of contact with reality' etc. So this effect can be reproduced by others taking up the framework, irrespective of the authors' intentions, if it fits the exercise of power, and the use of knowledge by those with power in organizations.

In making such claims they are failing (because of their theoretical framework, but also inevitably because of their relation to management – the two are linked) to ask other questions. Why are comments on supervisors less 'rational' than comments in other areas? Why did a certain type of person make complaints about particular areas of company policy and conditions? The label 'irrational' enables them to dismiss the factual legitimacy of workers' accounts. Reading the four individual cases which are analysed in this clinical way (Roethlisberger and Dickson 1970: ch. 14) left me with the feeling that the reasons given by interviewees for long-term resentment of supervisors appeared justified. I shall take just one example here.

Mr Green's suspicions that his supervisor is responsible for threatening phone calls made to his home is seen as evidence of a paranoid psyche, and the concept of projection is used to account for his endownment of the supervisor with unpleasant attributes. But Mr Green's account of his supervisor's treatment of him suggests to me a reasonable response to a man who was making trouble for him. Mr Green's actions were on grounds entirely consistent with company policy; for example obeying doctor's orders in refusing to lift heavy weights after an operation for which the company took responsibility. Indeed Green was so reasonable that when the departmental chief 'bawled me out in front of all the men . . . so rough I think [it was] to get me to hit him', he was 'too wise to do that' and instead was 'nervous all over' (1970: 229). In the world of 1930s Chicago and Prohibition, it was commonplace for companies to persecute troublemakers as Communist-inspired and to spend enormous amounts on breaking trade union organization. It is not necessarily paranoid to suppose that a vindictive supervisor, who fears for his own position, would pass on to those specializing in intimidation the name of a man who was not entirely submissive.

Acceptance of this story was less palatable to the researchers than seeing Mr Green as paranoid. Western Electric was keen to maintain its image as a caring employer and the academics had their own reasons for wanting to believe this: they, like Mayo, were humanistic in their intentions and would not want their consciences troubled by doing work on behalf of a company that they saw as exploitative. The authors insist in various places how the interviewees trust and respect the company (for example, p. 284). Mayo's political philosophy meant that he was deeply committed to developing cooperation in modern industrial society, where he saw alienation as having taken root, and this led him to avoid any perspectives on the organization which admitted conflict as a fundamental feature (Bendix and Fisher 1949; Landsberger 1968; Koivisto 1953; Sheppard 1949). If the attitudes that led to conflict could be understood as pathological, within a clinical framework, these beliefs and loyalties to the company could remain unchallenged.

The effects of the economic depression continually appear in the case material in the form of shorter hours, relatives being laid off and fear of the sack leading employees to put up with appalling treatment. Yet the authors only treat this as a rational explanation of behaviour when, from 1931 on, they start a programme of interviewing *supervisors* and comment: 'It should be remembered that during the period that the supervisors were being interviewed, the employees were being subjected to stresses and strains of an unusual order' (Roethlisberger and Dickson 1970: 336). This indicates a greater reluctance to see supervisors in the light of a discourse which stresses irrationality.

The effect of the location of the problem of output in the individual worker – that is to shift the responsibility from conditions or supervisors – was not that Western Electric could avoid treating the problem, but it did recommend a completely different programme of treatment. The organization – its work conditions, payment systems, rate setting and so on – was displaced as the object of knowledge and practice. The psychological perspective came to dominate, producing individuals and their relations as the focus. Although the workers were the eventual object of adjustment, supervisors became the focus of human relations practices because of the important effect they had on workers' satisfaction:

> Virtually all managements and social scientists, as well as a few labor leaders, agreed that the foreman was the key figure in labor relations. The degree to which the worker was satisfied with his foreman was the degree to which he was satisfied with his job. (Baritz 1965: 182)

Roethlisberger and Dickson produced a distinction – between fact and non-fact – which enabled them to move from a perspective which sees employees' complaints concerning their work as facts or falsehoods, to a perspective which sees the importance of what workers say as residing in its 'emotional significance' (a category which was juxtaposed to 'objective information'). The specific area in which the concept of non-fact is taken up and developed further is, significantly, in the area of supervision: 'Comments on supervision, more than those in any other area, could not be taken at their face value' (1970: 292).

6. The Interviewing Method

A necessary element in producing the sentimental worker was the emergence of the new interviewing methods as a way of getting reliable information from the workforce. Moreover the principles of interviewing could 'be used by the personnel manager of a large industrial corporation in his daily activities as well as in the more formal industrial relations interviewing' (Roethlisberger and Dickson 1970: 286). The interviewing method provided information which was used by management in two ways. First, interviewers regularly submitted to management a general survey of employee morale. Secondly, the information was used in supervisory training (a scheme which pre-existed the research, but into which the research objectives fitted, objectives which eventually transformed supervisory training).

The benefits of the programme were seen to be even wider than that, however. Viteles' discussion of the Hawthorne studies (which he treats in the context of motivation) exemplifies the close relation that was seen between information, the interview method, satisfaction and supervision:

> [through the interview programme] employees' comments and opinions are brought back indirectly to supervisors whose consideration of them has led to a marked improvement in supervisory techniques. ... Those interviewed have had a chance to express themselves fully and to clear their minds of burdensome thoughts. As a result supervision becomes easier. Morale is improved because the employee who has been interviewed is convinced that

the management wants to better his surroundings and conditions of work. The company is obtaining first hand information as to the effect of such incentives to work as thrift plans, pensions, sick benefit plans, athletic activities, vacations etc. The management of Western Electric is convinced that it has progressed further in the knowledge of employee relationship during the short time that this plan has been in operation than in all of the previous years of the company's existence. (Viteles 1933: 573–4)

The interviewing programme at the Hawthorne works changed from being 'rather simple and incidental to the material which it was hoped such a technique could obtain' to one which 'could obtain with some accuracy the emotional significance to the worker of particular events and objects in his experience' (Roethlisberger and Dickson 1970: 270). The quality of trained personnel necessary for this (all derived from the ranks of supervisors) was only achieved after 'some 20,000 employee interviews have been taken' (1970: 270). The questionnaire method was already in use in industry, but previously it 'tended to elicit opinions on topics which the interviewer, rather than the employee, thought to be of importance' and the method lacked 'a sufficient context for interpreting the response' (1970: 271).

Five rules were produced to guide interviewers, rules which would do justice to a counselling training course in the 1980s:

1. The interviewer should listen to the speaker in a patient and friendly, but intelligently critical, manner.
2. The interviewer should not display any kind of authority.
3. The interviewer should not give advice or moral admonition.
4. The interviewer should not argue with the speaker.
5. The interviewer should talk or ask questions only under certain conditions. These were
— to help the person talk;
— to relieve any fears or anxieties on the part of the speaker which may be affecting his relation to the interviewer;
— to praise the interviewee for his reporting his thoughts and feelings accurately;
— to veer the discussion to some topic which has been omitted or neglected;
— to discuss implicit assumptions if this is advisable. (Roethlisberger and Dickson 1970: 287)

Rules of orientation elaborated the theoretical premises:

1. The interviewer should treat what is said in the interview as an item in a context:
(a) — the interviewer should not pay exclusive attention to the manifest content of the intercourse
(b) — the interviewer should not treat everything that is said as either fact or error
(c) — The interviewer should not treat everything that is said at the same psychological level.

2. The interviewer should listen not only to what a person wants to say but also for what he does not want to say or cannot say without help.

3. The interviewer should treat the mental contexts described in the preceding rule as indices and seek through them the personal reference that is being revealed.

4. The interviewer should remember that the interview is itself a social situation and that therefore the social relations existing between the interviewer and the interviewee is in part determining what is said.

5. The interviewer should see to it that the speaker's sentiments do not act on his own. (Roethlisberger and Dickson 1970: 272–3)

Chapter 13 of *Management and the Worker* largely consists of an elaboration of these principles and rules. In conclusion, Roethlisberger and Dickson express the opinion that several years' experience are necessary to develop these skills. They also point out that 'any successful executive, administrator or politician implicitly makes use of many of the rules of orientation which we have explicitly stated' (1970: 291).

Although they were influenced by psychoanalysis, and although they developed a distinctly clinical model, the researchers did not start with a model ready-made and borrowed from therapy.[6] They started with a questionnaire-type interview and gradually modified it. Their reason for the change was the questionnaire's failure to elicit 'the emotional significance' of experience in a way which was not predetermined by the interviewer (1970: 271). Without a clinical understanding they could not have intervened at the level of workers' attitudes to the job, rather than the job itself. The advantage of what became famous as the non-directive counselling method was discovered by industrial psychology at this point; 'an indirect type of interviewing was preferable if the spontaneous convictions of the worker were to be obtained' (1970. 271).[7] Above all it was important that the interview did not 'remain at the level of polite social conversation': what the interviewer wanted to emerge became defined as having its importance at a deeper level.

To produce this different information, the stance of the interviewer was crucial because the position a member of the company normally occupied would preclude most self-revelation. As one interviewee said; 'if you open your mouth out of turn, it can get you into a whole mess of trouble' (1970: 301). Such experiences would no doubt have established with employees the practice of saying as little as possible. It was the resultant serious lack of information which was a problem for management and this is why the method outlined here was taken up widely.[8]

A big change was required to transform the habitual supervisor's relation with an employee to that which the interviewers adopted (and remember they were largely Hawthorne supervisors). First it involved divesting the interviewer of power to use the information in a harmful way. This was done by using supervisors from elsewhere in the plant, as well as by rules of confidentiality. Second, the non-evaluative stance the interviewer took up made it different from any other relationship. Contrast the tone of Roethlisberger and Dickson's rules for interviewing with Mayo's worried account of typical supervisory practice and it can readily be seen what radical implications the new methods had for supervisory training:

> The fact that one man has been set in control of others has usually been taken to imply that he is expected to give orders and to have them obeyed. So supervision has frequently come to mean 'ordering people about'. There is only one objection to this, and the objection is not in any sense political, it is simply that the method is exceedingly stupid. If there is difficulty or delay in obedience, or eccentricity or 'slackness', the supervisor is expected to yell or bawl or swear, or what is worse, to indulge in lengthy admonition. So he 'talks' and does not 'listen'; and he never learns what is really wrong. The workers are often terrified, they harbour a grievance and at last, if they express it, they tend to overstate or distort.... At once the overstatement is seized for attack, and the possibility of understanding is lost. (Mayo 1930: 331)

7. Personal Equilibrium and Productivity

The individual worker could now be theorized as having sentiments which were not exclusively a product of the work situation, but of the 'personal equilibrium' of the worker concerned, an equilibrium affected by past history and present home circumstances. The Hawthorne studies produced the first intellectual account of the worker as an individual who is different from others, not simply because of differences in output and the measurable characteristics which supposedly accounted for these (as in the psychometric model). Instead it is an account of conditions which affect the worker's output through his or her 'personal equilibrium'. As we shall see from the following example, output is still the central concern. In cases where the researchers had access to output records (that is, in test rooms which were running alongside the interview programme), they specifically investigated the relation of these to events in the individual's life: 'Whenever any pessimistic preoccupation emerged for any reason whatsoever, there was an observable adverse effect on output' (Roethlisberger and Dickson 1970: 315).

To illustrate the point, Roethlisberger and Dickson take the example of W7 (1970: 317ff.), a man from the Bank Wiring Observation Room. W7 was disgruntled because he was getting less money than W9 and also because he had not been regraded when he thought he deserved it. But these grievances were not new. What happened to precipitate an interruption in his acceptance of this (as measured by a drop in output) was that his girl had been placed on shorter hours and was faced with the possibility of unemployment which would mean either that she would have to return to her parents in North Dakota or he would have to marry her, in which case he was not earning enough to support them both:

> His output curve started downward at about the time he was first confronted with this situation . . . The downward trend in W7's output continued all during the period of indecision. Finally on January 7th, after sitting around most of the day and being unable to work, he announced his intention of getting married. He did so two days later. During that week his output curve started upward and in the second week thereafter it reached its highest point up to that time. (1970: 318–19)

W7 made electrical connections by the piece. On 7 January his hourly rate was down to about 525. At the peak later the rate was about 725. 'It was through such cases as those of W7 that the interviewers began to understand better the relation between personal preoccupation and output' (1970: 319).

The changed research method is a necessary condition for the production of this new image of the worker who has a life outside the factory which causes problems:

> It is clear . . . that had there not existed in the test rooms an arrangement for the observation of factors other than those in the immediate work situation, many of the changes in output . . . might have been attributed to 'learning', 'fatigue' or 'monotony'. Therefore, it seemed plausible to assume that wherever obsessive preoccupations were divulged in the interview, a set of factors similar to those revealed in the test rooms were operating. (1970: 319)

The conception of what intervenes between the worker's actions and output had now been radically transformed. Not only was it no longer physiological (for example fatigue), it was not limited to the work situation. Where output was still affected by the work situation, it was usually no longer seen as physical conditions, but conditions pertaining to sentiment – notably relations with supervisors and co-workers. In the authors' discussion of factors affecting output, fatigue is relegated to a much less common phenomenon by restricting its meaning to a state caused by organic unbalance (Roethlisberger and Dickson 1970: 320–1). For mental imbalance (and its partner, personal equilibrium), they had evolved a whole new perspective.

Through this new conception of mental imbalance, Roethlisberger and Dickson were able to draw some conclusions on the effect of repetitive work, which led them back into the importance of group relations. They argued that repetitive work was implicated, not as a cause of mental imbalance, but in creating conditions for 'pessimistic reverie' (a phrase coined by Mayo). When workers were able to have social intercourse with their co-workers on the job, the opportunity for pessimistic reverie was excluded and their troubles did not take on the dimension of morbid preoccupation which led to a fall in output.

This argument is demonstrated by the example of operator 2 in the Relay Assembly Test Room who 'had been considered a "problem case" by her supervisors before her entrance to the test room' (1970: 324). Her domestic responsibilities (dead mother, sole support for three younger brothers) led to frequent displays of 'temper and irritability' but 'when she found an appropriate niche in the social structure so that she could intimately identify herself and her work with a social function, she became an enthusiastic and cooperative worker' (1970: 324). Now that information was sought about the often appallingly difficult lives of the employees, a punitive approach was less tenable. In this case the new discourse led to an understanding of her behaviour as 'opportunity for human comradeship and social conversation [that] played an important part in helping her to meet her personal difficulties' (1970: 324–5).

8. Method and the Production of a New Subject Worker

The clinical interviewing method which permitted such insights produced material of a qualitatively different kind for the supervisory training programme. These case studies were discussed with the supervisors at the Hawthorne Works and the implications for good practice were that it was necessary to know the background to any individual worker's conduct if the correct measures were to be taken. In this way, information concerning the worker as a whole person became recognized as a valuable aspect of management practice. Since all interviewers were Western Electric employees, mostly from supervisory rank, their experience itself constituted training which they disseminated enthusiastically back into the organization (Roethlisberger and Dickson 1970: 284).

Information about workers' outside lives was available in the factory before human relations. The detailed case studies that the authors give (1970: 293–310) indicate that workers with domestic problems would give an account of these to their supervisors when a problem arose. For example:

> I told [my supervisor] that if it was at all possible I would appreciate it if he would let me have my evenings to myself, although I needed the money, because I had a wife in hospital and a fifteen-year old girl at home doing the work around the house, and I wanted to get home to help her. He always told me to stick on the job. I finally took the matter up with the general foreman, and after he listened to my story and later on he talked to my

group chief, why there seemed to be a change in him. (Roethlisberger and Dickson 1970: 296)

Once the theorization of the sentimental worker was available, this kind of information could become legitimate as a part of management practice through supervisory training, rather than being an informal, spontaneous and uncertain part of relations in the plant. A more far-reaching difference was that the nature of the information produced was changed by the occasion and method of its production. For example, one of the interviewees started off by saying 'There's no damn use of you and I going anywhere because I refuse to talk. I talked out of turn once before and got myself in such a mess of trouble that I refuse to talk to you or anyone else' (1970: 301). It is an indication of how powerful the method is that this man ended up by revealing much and even venturing his opinions on supervisors and company politics.

There is a qualitative difference between what an employee might tell his or her supervisor and what can be said in the clinical interview. There is also a difference in the response the interviewee received. The authors acknowledge that this type of interview could not be conducted by a person's supervisor because they are in a 'necessarily authoritarian relation with the interviewee' (1970: 285–6n.). The interviewer succeeded in eliciting information which was at a new level and did not only have implications for the researcher: as a result of the interviewer's techniques 'the interviewee finds himself not only saying things which he never said to anyone else but in many instances saying things which he has not been able to express explicitly to himself' (1970: 285).

From the Western perspective in a post-human relations epoch where self-expression has become an index of mental health, the assumed norm of family life, friendship and even work relations, it is difficult to countenance a time and a set of social relations where that kind of information was essentially absent. When Roethlisberger and Dickson make the claim that their interviewees said things that they'd never expressed to themselves, it means that new knowledge was produced about themselves, creating a different idea of themselves, because of the different method by which it was elicited.

The rules for interviewing are relevant to my argument that, in an important sense, the method produces the subject. They contain many of the principles of interpretation derived in psychoanalytic practice and imply a theory of repression and of the unconscious. When an interviewer senses absences or avoidances and asks questions or adopts postures which are specifically aimed to elicit things a person 'does not want to say' they are instrumental in producing material which never before has been a feature of the interviewee's self-understanding. For example, after energetic talk about the difficulties of her family situation and her dislike of the stepfather who mistreats her mother, one interviewee herself concludes: 'and you know I think the reason I can't stand Mr Jones [her supervisor] is because every time I look at him, he reminds me of my stepfather' (Roethlisberger and Dickson 1970: 310). Mayo comments 'small wonder that the same supervisor had warned the interviewer that she was "difficult to handle"' (Mayo 1949: 69) and goes on to point out the practical benefits of her connection between supervisor and stepfather in 'easing the situation' (we never learn what, if anything, in the supervisor's behaviour precipitated the connection, and if it deserved to be modified). It was because this form of clinical interviewing was seen to have practical benefits by achieving 'emotional release' ('catharsis' in psychoanalytic terminology) as well as in its contribution to supervisory training, that the programme was extended and came to be known as 'employee counselling'. Roethlisberger and Dickson cite one employee as saying 'I tell you, it does a fellow good to get rid of that stuff' (1970: 298). As Mayo has the insight to point out:

> The experience itself was unusual; there are few people in this world who have had the experience of finding someone intelligent, attentive and eager to listen without interruption to all that he or she has to say. . . . To find an intelligent person who was not only eager to listen but also anxious to help to expression idea and feelings but dimly understood – this, for many thousand persons, was an experience without precedent in the modern world. (Mayo 1949: 65, 66)

The account of an employee given in the counselling interview was thus produced in a unique relation, with a skilled interviewer in a position of benign authority, and this situation had effects on employees' self-knowledge. It was indeed 'an experience without precedent' and, as such, it was a significant step in producing the new subject worker of human relations.

Notes

1. Smith (1987) argues that the Hawthorne research was the beginning of industrial sociology. For a good critique of human relations from the perspective of an organizational sociologist, see Perrow (1979 ch. 3). In both the US and UK, industrial psychologists were still preoccupied with scientific measurement, and human relations claimed neither to be scientific nor to measure (see chapter 6 section 3). Although social psychology gradually found a place in industrial psychology, it too was split between 'scientific', laboratory-based versions and the human relations kind.

2. According to John Smith, who has had access to the Hawthorne archives and Mayo's personal correspondence, a psychologist called Imogen Rousseau had conducted a study of output restriction by women before the Bank Wiring Room experiment. This is not referred to in *Management and the Worker*.

3. None the less, the discourse would have been impossible – and would certainly have been different – without the influence of Freudian theory which had pervaded Western thinking. Roethlisberger and Dickson contains many references to a clinical framework derived from psychoanalysis (see section 5 for further detail). They drew on energetic new traditions not only in psychoanalysis but also anthropology and theories of language; see, for example, their footnote on p.272 (1970).

4. See Baritz (1965: 33–4) or Beynon (1984: 34–7) on Henry Ford's moral supervision of his employees' home lives.

5. Myers uses a similar perspective, deploying the psychoanalytic concept of projection to account for workers' unreasonableness in matters of industrial relations (Myers 1920: 166).

6. Roethlisberger was in therapy for a time, with Mayo as his therapist (John Smith, personal communication).

7. By the 1950s the idea of non-directive counselling or therapy had begun to suggest that the therapist played no guiding role, but only the passive one of eliciting what was there. Roethlisberger and Dickson do not suggest this.

8. Large-scale employee counselling never became very common, not least because of the enormous investment required in time and training. Attitude surveys (see chapter 6 section 2) partly met the same need. Counselling methods became a basic part of supervisory and management training, both in general interpersonal skills training and specific training in, for example, appraisal. The principles of non-directive counselling have been widely credited to Carl Rogers in the 1950s, while the Hawthorne research is most famous for the Hawthorne effect and discovery of restriction of output.

6
Motivating Employees: Human Relations Training and Job Satisfaction

An improvement of response on the part of an individual . . . involves a modification or change in himself as well as a change in his relation to his environment. (Roethlisberger 1954: 16)

1. Introduction

The chief importance of human relations to management is that they are manageable. (Gellerman 1966: 1)

This claim, born with human relations practices, offered hope to organizations faced daily with the effects on production of resistant workers and managers who were exacerbating the problem. Human relations approaches were characterized by the belief that workers would control their own relation to the job (though not control their own job) as management desired if they were treated in a way which was consistent with an understanding of the root causes of their behaviour:

He [the manager] must try to understand *why* the employee acts or believes as he does so that the underlying causes can be dealt with. Instead of reacting to superficial symptoms with equally superficial cures, the modern manager tries to get at the roots of behaviour and to introduce any desired changes at that level. (Gellerman 1966: 2)

Here we have a good example of the central tenet of the Hawthorne research taken over and claimed as modern truth by the management thinking of the mid-sixties. It illustrates how human relations affected management values generally. But there would not have been such an effect at the level of management values, or at best it would be a fragile effect, had it not been part of a web of management practices. In this chapter I consider two areas of practice which were a product of human relations: interpersonal skills training and job redesign.

Interpersonal skills training and job redesign developed as rather separate practices because they targeted different groups of employees; the former managers and the latter workers. Yet both emerged from the same starting point: how to induce consent and commitment. Interpersonal skills training developed directly out of the supervisory skills training programme at Hawthorne (Roethlisberger was influential in its development). It was aimed at practitioners – all those 'who were involved in securing the understanding of others in many different kinds of organized human activities' (Roethlisberger 1954: 22). This definition is rather like the wide definition of management which operates today. Like today, it did not include workers as potential trainees. They were the object of its training once removed: managers were to apply their new 'understanding of others' to those employees over whom they had authority, and increasingly to relations with peers too. To increase their range of effect, they trained 'second-level practitioners' (trainers, educators and researchers) who could act as 'multipliers of competence' (Roethlisberger 1954: 23). Aided by the growth of service organizations, this branch of human relations practice was no longer limited to the industrial sphere.

Job design was not a new focus of industrial psychology, but one of its early strengths which had waned once mechanized production was firmly established in manufacturing. However, human relations inserted a new intervening variable between the design of a job and its performance: motivation (or, as conceptualized initially, job attitudes). Enlarging or enriching jobs (job redesign) was advocated as a means of enhancing workers' motivation and thus their performance. The search for a psychological solution to 'poor' performance led back, according to this way of thinking, to technology. But whether the solution was interpersonal competence, leadership style or job redesign, the premiss was that individuals could be motivated to work.

In section 2 I briefly chart the place of attitude surveys in management practice, a slightly different area which was none the less linked to the emergence of human relations. It is usually considered as the terrain of social psychology because of its methods. It uses quantitative methods for measuring opinions or attitudes based on standardized questions administered – usually by written questionnaire – to large numbers of people, in this case employees. In sections 3 and 4 I examine the underlying principles of American human relations training in the 1950s (Roethlisberger 1954) and early 1960s (Argyris 1962) in order to trace post-Hawthorne development in ideas and practices concerning how individuals could be changed in line with the interpersonal conduct which was required of them at work. In section 5 I change the focus away from management training to the continuing problems of regulation in machine-paced jobs. I take up the story of attempts to improve the jobs themselves, which was left behind in chapter 3, in order to trace the history of job design after human relations. I trace a change in two decades (from Walker 1950 to Herzberg 1968), in preoccupation from improving jobs through enlargement of the scope of activities to motivation, a shift which virtually obliterated consideration of the content of the job itself in favour of focusing on the internalized commitment of the individual worker. First, in section 5, I outline the context in which the new debates about job satisfaction emerged. In section 6 I summarize different approaches to job satisfaction. In section 7 I examine an article by Walker, 'The Problem of the Repetitive Job', which represented a new link between industrial engineering and psychology. In section 8 I critically examine Herzberg's two-factor theory, and ask why it was influential in human relations psychology and management thought. In section 9, I summarize my arguments about the legacy of motivation theory (a theme which is taken up again in the following chapter).

2. Attitude Surveys

Mass counselling schemes of the Hawthorne kind were eventually discontinued, but not because the need for information became less acute. Rather, less time-consuming methods were required which could handle mass data. For example, in 1933 the views of 4,500 Proctor and Gamble employees were sought. Whereas the information from a counselling programme was difficult to analyse, attitude surveys produced quantifiable information. They remain the most used method of applied social psychology.[1]

The first major attitude survey was commissioned by Kimberley-Clarke Corporation in 1930 at one of their mills in Wisconsin and was carried out by Kornhauser and Sharpe from Chicago University. Their conclusion sums up what became the commonplace view of the usefulness of attitude surveys: 'an immense part of our industrial discontent is unnecessary. . . . If management knows what its employees are really thinking and feeling, the sources of trouble can usually be greatly reduced in seriousness. . . . Too often the workers' attitudes are guessed at – or ignored – or damned' (quoted in Baritz 1965: 126).

The early connection between attitude surveys and 'intelligence' (in the CIA sense) is illustrated in the case of General Motors. Whilst both Kimberley-Clarke and Proctor and Gamble employed psychologists, General Motors, having initially used a public firm to find out about attitudes, resorted to the use of the Pinkerton Detective Agency to elicit information about workers' activities when they were outside the factory. General Motors' labour relations director finally admitted that 'we are interested to know if there was any particular labor organization going on in town and if so why. . . . What was there about plant operation that would give any need for an outside [labour] organization' (quoted in Baritz 1965: 127).

During the Second World War, the attitude survey became a widely used method to evaluate the state of public morale (Cartwright 1947–8). It was as a result of this application that 'morale' became such a widely used concept in human relations, particularly in industry. Residual management objections to the use of attitude surveys revolved round the fear that high dissatisfaction amongst the workforce would be revealed and would provide unions with a factual basis for their criticisms of management. In fact surveys tended to report high morale and managements came to realize that they could be used to produce a self-fulfilling prophecy effect. For example, Thompson Products introduced an attitude survey despite strong objections from the unions. The initial response rate was so low that pressure was put on supervisors and foremen to get workers to complete their forms. A little later Thompson's produced a booklet telling their workers that only 4 per cent of their colleagues were dissatisfied with their jobs (Baritz 1965: 153). According to Baritz, other companies explicitly copied this approach.

In Britain in 1970 attitude surveys were enjoying renewed popularity. Kay and Warr commented that 'over the last five years or so industrial sponsorship of attitude surveys in this country has increased greatly' (1970: 298). They went on to point out that there was little cross-fertilization between academic and applied psychologists in this area.

3. Interpersonal Skills Training

By the 1950s human relations was firmly on the map in the US. In 1951 the Ford Foundation gave funds to the Harvard Business School whose purpose was 'to design and implement a program which would prepare people to do human relations training and research in a variety of formal organizations such as, for example business, educational and governmental' (Roethlisberger 1954: 3). This Program for Advanced Training and Research in Human Relations extended the central principles of human relations training, both in range and in depth. Roethlisberger's book, *Training for Human Relations*, reports on the progress of the first three years of the programme. The first chapter raises some of the main issues that I shall discuss in what follows: the authenticity of the trainee's subsequent performance; the morality of changing people's values; a learning theory consistent with human relations training and human relations' differences from behavioural science. Argyris tackles the same issues. In 1962, Argyris (also a Harvard professor, but in the School of Education, not the Business School) published a book entitled *Interpersonal Competence and Organizational Effectiveness*, which set out his ideas about achieving changes in managers through the use of experiential learning. He too is concerned with how to change the values of managers so that their interpersonal behaviour is authentic and therefore has the desired effects on the organization. In a chapter entitled 'Interpersonal Authenticity and the T-group', he discusses in detail his reasons for using the T-group,[2] and how he works as an 'educator' to help executives to question their own values and the organizational effects these have:

> The group members need to be placed into a situation where they can see, experience, and evaluate first-hand the impact that their present values (about effective human relations) have upon each other and the group. In our case, this means the T-group experience should first help the executives to experience for themselves the relatively high degree to which they (1) give evaluative, defensive-producing feedback (2) do not own, indeed, are not aware of, their feelings (3) do not help others to own their feelings, (4) are not, or permit others to be open, [sic] and (5) to experiment and take risks. (Argyris 1962: 154–5)

There is a close similarity of approach between Argyris and Roethlisberger, in values and practices, and the differences between their positions provide a fairly sensitive indication of the development of knowledge and practice over approximately a decade.

The initial supervisory training at Hawthorne incorporated the idea of the sentimental worker to the extent that it suggested that workers should be treated by supervisors with due respect for their sentiments and circumstances. However, the model of learning which was directed at the supervisors was still basically behaviourist, that is it was targeted at changing supervisors' interpersonal behaviour, rather than their sentiments. Changed behaviour remained the objective, but the new model was obliged to penetrate deeper into the individual to find an effective locus of change. For example, Argyris maintained that the practice of new behaviour and skills was a vital component in changing a personal philosophy (1962: 165–6). In order to define this object of change, human relations trainers posited entities like attitudes and values. Argyris' model of effective learning intended that there 'may be aroused within them an emotional as well as intellectual awareness of the (unintended) consequences of their present behavior upon each other and upon the organization' (1962: 155). By the 1960s, even the executive had sentiments.

Roethlisberger signalled just how far human relations had moved from earlier psychology when he claimed that the human relations approach questioned traditional assumptions of scientific method, learning and the relation of knowledge to practice (1954: 28). It was from this position that both Roethlisberger and Argyris were critical of behaviourist learning theory, which involved no model of processes internal to the individual. He and Argyris suggested that behavioural scientists were adhering fruitlessly to traditional models of scientific investigation in which it was assumed that correct applications follow from knowledge (Roethlisberger 1954: 4; Argyris 1962: 157).

Roethlisberger regarded these models as without value in the task of changing management's attitudes. The position of Roethlisberger's programme was that 'better practice is more likely to follow from better firsthand observations . . . and that better firsthand observations and hypotheses are likely to follow from the conscious practice of a skill' (1954: 5). 'First-hand observation and skill' later became known as experiential learning and, although neither Roethlisberger nor Argyris use the label yet, they are exploring the principles of experiential learning of interpersonal competence.

Argyris (1962: 153) insists on the inclusion of the 'emotional' as well as the 'intellective' dimension in learning. The old rationalist assumption on which educational practice was based was that correct knowledge would produce correct action. Human relations practitioners had already found out that 'the distinction between making recommendations and getting them put into effect is only too real' (Roethlisberger 1954: 10).

4. Imposing the Choice of Change

The main reason for the decline in emphasis on behavioural training in interpersonal skills techniques and the rise in emphasis on changing the whole person was the problem of authenticity. A method had to be found to solve the problem posed by the recognition that workers saw through inauthentic 'humanistic' posturing by their superiors:

> Too often a foreman, in trying to exercise these discrete skills (more appropriately called 'techniques') of responding to a particular worker, feels silly. He feels that he is not being true to himself and his own immediate experience. This very feeling vitiates the effectiveness of his response. And it is this feeling of his to which his workers often respond. The total effect, far from suggesting skill, is instead tragic or comic depending on one's point of view. (Roethlisberger 1954: 18)

This is a very important comment. It summarizes the reason why human relations had to move on; had to penetrate deeper into the person in order effectively to change managers' behaviour. Managers had to be transformed so that they could live out the democratic and humanistic relations with their subordinates with sufficient conviction. Roethlisberger redefines human relations skill, moving the locus of skill to something intrinsic in order to accommodate this goal:

> By [an] improvement in response on the part of an individual we shall mean an internal way of learning rather than an external technique to be learned. It involves a modification or change in himself as well as a change in his

relation to his environment. It depends upon his capacity to see in a situation something different from what he customarily expects and to respond to this new and altered perception. . . . Skill is not something external to the user, something which he uses only for ulterior purposes. It is intrinsic to him and modifies his behaviour as well as the object or situation upon which it is practised. (Roethlisberger 1954: 16)

Argyris too makes a distinction between methods to 'influence people in order to keep them happy' (1962: 154) and changing values. His terminology puts a further distance between the early skills training and his methods. While Roethlisberger redefined skill in a way which moved the concept away from a behavioural model of technique towards change of the whole person, Argyris brings in the concept of values to indicate 'the emotionally rooted, intellectually expressed "personal directives" that individuals hold that serve to compel their behaviour in a particular direction' (1962: 154). He emphasizes their deep-seatedness and inaccessibility to traditional pedagogic models: 'they cannot be "taught", "issued", "sold" or "plugged into" people' (1962: 154). The manager now had become the target of intensive subjectification. In the terms of the human relations approach, it was necessary to change 'the whole person'.

Human relations training had to steer clear of inauthentic techniques. Instead 'the modification of values is the major objective of the T-group' (Argyris 1962: 154). But this could also make it vulnerable to charges about the manipulativeness of human relations techniques. The dilemma appears throughout the introduction to Roethlisberger's book, and his position is most clearly summarized by what he rejects; he is trying to change neither 'ideals' nor 'techniques' (1954: 20). The former seemed morally intrusive – an imposition of values on those they were training. The latter appeared directly manipulative, but more importantly failed to work. Argyris' dilemma is similar to Roethlisberger's: '[the educator] cannot push very far because if he is not careful, he could create a situation that results in the members feeling that they are being coerced to change in spite of their decision not to do so' (1962: 156).

How do you successfully influence resistant people and yet model democratic values which were such an important part of American identity since the Second World War?

The perceived contradiction between democratic free choice and the need for change illuminates my theme that the human relations movement was involved in subjectification: transforming compliance into cooperation, consent into commitment, discipline into self-discipline, the goals of the organization into the goals of the employee. The critique was made at the time. Chapple and Sayles refer to 'the Pandora's box of ethical questions regarding the use of psychological techniques to persuade, convert, or dissuade employees' (1961: 16). Peter Drucker (1959) argued that human relations often manipulates and adjusts people to management requirements.

How do you ensure change without imposing it? You convince the individual who is the object of the change that they are choosing it. This is what I mean by subjectification. Argyris calls it growth. Growth involves ' "proving" to one's self that it *is* one's self who is responsible for some of the problems that one is facing' (Argyris 1962: 156). I do not want to imply that this makes it inevitably undesirable. From my own experience of experiential groups, I believe that it can involve real and positive change. This is only a contradiction in terms if I maintain the terms of the human relations model, where the individual is the agent of change, facilitated by an outside agent, who therefore has to deny his or her power in the process. In my terms there is no contradiction between subjectification and personal growth, because the production of the subject is a social and historical process. Many diverse forces impinge on any given person's subjectivity, but none of them are free from the relations between power, knowledge and practice which I have been illustrating in the work domain. Individuals differ in their responses because of the diversity of forces, past and present, which act upon them. Many executives in the sixties and seventies went through experiential groups as part of their management training. Some found it liberating, some oppressive; some became better managers, some didn't change, some handed in their notice (Back 1973).

Neither the power of the educator nor the interest of the organization is admitted into this model. Change is assumed to be natural and desirable (Hollway 1989: 94ff.). In Argyris' discussion one can detect the influence of psychoanalytic models as they were being modified in the United States by the early sixties. 'Defenses' and 'projection' are joined by 'openness and risk', 'owning feelings' and 'emotional awareness'. North American psychoanalysis had moved away from the darker and more pessimistic emphases of Freudian theory and placed greater emphasis on the strength of the ego (for example Fromm, Fairbairn and Hartmann). Human relations American-style (and in this it differs from the Tavistock Institute; see chapter 7) was based on the belief that if, by means of a climate of trust leading to openness and the expression of feelings, one peeled off the layers of defence and hurt, the individual would be revealed as basically good and loving. Attempts to change individuals in this direction were thus automatically justified. This was reinforced by, and helped to reproduce, a widespread belief in the value of change in the personal sphere.

5. The High Cost of the Monotonous Job

The idea that jobs could be designed consistently with the principles of job satisfaction held out the hope of curing the problems of productivity associated with monotonous jobs. The repetitive job was a product of Fordism. Meyer (1981, cited in Littler 1985) describes Fordism (the model of production worked out by Ford between 1908 and 1913) as having four basic elements:

(a) standardized product design;
(b) the extensive use of new machine tool technology;
(c) flow-line production; and
(d) the implementation of Taylorism in relation to work processes.
    (Littler 1985: 14)

Industrial engineers were not challenging the established use of technology which was the basis of Fordism as a model of production. It was only with regard to the last of these that there was assumed to be any room for manoeuvre, and only when Taylorist principles of specialization were not tied to flow-line production. Davis identified the relevant engineering principles, as follows:

> The concepts of job design held by [engineers and industrial managers] have exerted an exceedingly strong influence. These concepts are centred around specialization of labor, minimizing skills and minimizing immediate production time. They are based on limited criteria of minimizing immediate costs or maximizing immediate productivity. Thus job design is based upon the principles of specialization, repetitiveness, low skill content and minimum impact of the worker on the production process. (Davis and Canter 1956: 276)

By going over to mass production, Ford gained a massive advantage, which competitors were obliged to copy. Littler[3] points out that there was, however, a recognition of the high cost in terms of turnover, absenteeism and supervision:

> Having developed a new industrial technology based on the flow-line principle and extreme job fragmentation, Ford found that control of the production process was not equal to the control of the workforce. Worker rejection of the new work processes was expressed in high rates of turnover, absenteeism and insufficient effort. For example, the head of Ford's employment department in 1913 cited a figure of $38 to train up a new worker; a small amount, but with an annual turnover of more than 50,000 workers (i.e. 400 per cent) the total cost was two million dollars. (Littler 1985: 15)

By the fifties these costs came to be of paramount importance because of full employment and nearly 100 per cent utilization of plant and facilities.[4]

Scientific management did not solve these problems of absenteeism, turnover, supervision and quality. Tayloristic assumptions were now acknowledged as problematic by social philosophers, industrialists and industrial engineers, as well as by social scientists. Davis points out that the idea of job enlargement 'has been received with great enthusiasm by the public press and business community', and cites articles in *Time* and the *Wall Street Journal* (Davis and Canter 1956: 275). For example:

> The principle of specialization is productive and efficient. But it is very dubious [*sic*] indeed, whether we yet know how to apply it except to machinery. There is the first question of whether 'specialization' as it is understood and practised today is a socially and individually satisfying way of using human energy and production – a major question of the social order in industrial society. (Drucker, quoted in Davis and Canter 1956: 276)

6. Approaches to Job Satisfaction

In 1944, research began in the parts manufacturing department at the Endicott plant of International Business Machines which claimed to demonstrate the success of job enlargement with regard to both productivity and morale.[5] Walker was engaged in this research. His article, 'The Problem of the Repetitive Job' (1950), is the classic early example of the focus on the relation between job design and satisfaction, a topic which was to flood the American management literature and provide a new focus for American industrial psychology. Job satisfaction as an idea had its ancestry in the earlier industrial psychology work on fatigue and monotony (Walker 1950: 54), but by this time it had a human relations face.

Job Design with a Human Relations Face
Human relations provided the possibility of construing workers not as hands but as individuals with emotional and social needs. Being paid for a job did not meet these needs. Thus a human relations approach is a precondition of the idea of job satisfaction. It was consistent with human relations premises to posit that the satisfaction of the whole person was involved in work performance. Morale was a popular early way to refer to the problem. For a while job attitude and job satisfaction tended to be used interchangeably until the latter idea came to dominate. As Vroom (1964: 4) notes in his overview of the field, industrial psychologists tended to use lay terms with little rigour and little reference to any available theory. By the 1960s motivation had become the central concept through which to understand job satisfaction. This was not because available psychological theories of motivation were used (Vroom 1964) but, I suggest, because the

question of motivation offered an object of sufficient depth within the person. I expand this argument below.

The job design approach challenged scientific management's assumption that motivational aspects of work performance could be taken care of by piece-rate incentives. This is the starting point for the classic articles on job design of the early fifties. For example Walker starts by quoting the proposition that: 'jobs have created themselves out of the demands of mechanics alone and have only accidentally become such that men or women, being what they are, could take any interest or satisfaction in them' (1950: 54). The theory of job design came to rest:

> largely on the premise that effective performance and genuine satisfaction in work follow mainly from the intrinsic content of the job. The practice of job design is concerned largely with designing the content of jobs in order to enhance intrinsic rewards such as feelings of achievement and worthwhile accomplishment. (Cooper 1974: 12)

Approaches to job design followed different paths in North America and in Britain (the latter being taken up in Europe and Canada). In the latter tradition, Louis Davis, an American, worked closely with the British Tavistock Institute of Human Relations and is often regarded as the founder of the 'Quality of Working Life' movement. This has been governed by the principle of joint optimization of the social and technical systems (see chapter 7) and has focused on the work group and its relation to the design of work (not the design of jobs). The United States tradition maintained its preference for focusing on the individual and the single job, as is manifest in the dominance of Herzberg's two-factor theory of motivation.[6]

Two Factors in Motivating Workers

The notion of 'intrinsic reward' captured an important practical distinction and led to the emphasis on motivation and needs as opposed to rewards. Based on Maslow's theory, Herzberg asserted that 'two different needs of man are involved' in understanding job behaviour. One set of needs stems from 'animal nature', the other set of needs: 'relates to that unique human characteristic, the ability to achieve and, through achievement to experience psychological growth. The stimuli for the growth needs are tasks that induce growth, in the industrial setting, they are the *job content*' (Herzberg 1968: 56-7).

In this way Herzberg's two-factor theory advanced a distinction between 'hygiene' factors, the absence of which could make a worker unhappy, and 'motivating' factors. As far as Herzberg is concerned 'the only way to motivate the employee is to give him challenging work in which he can assume responsibility' (1968: 53). The practical distinction offered by Herzberg's two-factor theory was that between factors in the work environment, which were being improved on the general assumption that they would lead to higher morale (notably supervisory relations) and the concern with the job itself, the alienating effects of which were now feared to be so strong as to be not susceptible to influence by improvement of external conditions. It is on the basis of formalizing and popularizing this distinction that Herzberg achieved fame.

Job design had to find a new premiss on which to be based. To do so industrial engineering and psychology formed another alliance (the early one being over fatigue), claiming that attention to motivational principles in job design was necessary for productivity, but would also be beneficial to the individual worker. Davis, an industrial engineer, poses the question from both sides:

> From the point of view of increasing motivation, can any human relations program, or any other program undertaken to increase motivation and so productivity, hope to succeed which does not begin with soundly conceived job designs based upon efficient criteria? From the point of view of minimizing total costs of producing can the designer of jobs achieve this goal without integrating the motivational and technical requirements of the job? (Davis et al. 1955: 22)

7. The Problem of the Repetitive Job

Walker's article was written before the field of motivation and job design became inundated with studies aimed at testing different theories of motivation and its relation to job satisfaction. Walker mentions the various attempts that had been made since the First World War to solve the problems caused by repetitive jobs: 'Within industry a variety of devices have been tried for the relief of monotony in highly simplified, repetitive operations, such as the frequent transfer between jobs, introduction of rest pauses, music in the workshop, the grouping of workers into competitive teams, and so forth' (Walker 1950: 54).

Now, he claims, there is a 'head-on attack on the problem through actually enlarging and enriching the basic content of the jobs' (1950: 54). This was happening notwithstanding the obstacle which he identifies as the 'sacrosanct character of certain engineering assumptions'.

Walker's purpose was to use the example of the IBM Endicott plant to demonstrate that managers must be aware of the human and social implications of extreme specialization:

> The story can be briefly described as an experiment in the human possibilities of machine operators. The exercise of greater skills by several hundred factory workmen under a deliberate plan of 'job enlargement'

resulted in a marked rise in over-all efficiency and an increase in personal satisfaction for each of the participants. (Walker 1950: 54)

It had the makings of another panacea.

The president of the company had initiated the research, arguing that job enlargement would improve morale and extend existing company policy of 'teaching workers the significance of particular operations in the total production process' (1950: 55).[7] In particular continued education was promoted in order to hold workers in the company by giving more skills and responsibility, and thus avoid the cost of retraining new employees. In the initial phase, skills and responsibilities were added to the jobs of the single-operator worker. For example, he sharpened his own tools, set up the machine for each new order from blueprints, and made a complete check and inspection of the finished part (1950: 56). Later the job of set-up men was abolished and the personnel relocated. Walker maintained that product quality improved, that there was a considerable saving in costs and that workers were more satisfied (they received higher wages as well as being better satisfied with their work).

Walker is a little disingenuous about the reasons for the IBM programme. It is not surprising that the change was presented, according to the human relations discourse of the day, as being initially concerned with 'the social and human implications' (1950: 54) of altering factory practice. It is only later as an aside that he points out that the war conditions put the cost of 'indirect supervision at an all-time high' (1950: 55). With increasing wartime demand they could not find enough experienced machine setters and inspectors. The extension of responsibility of the machine operators was a practical solution to the problem, particularly given conditions of batch production, albeit one which was consistent with the culture of the company (1950: 55).

Walker's IBM case study puts more emphasis on the organizational and market context than came to be the case when the psychological emphasis of Herzberg was at the height of fashion. It prefigures all the major issues in what came to be called job redesign: the relationships that existed between

— the technology, the content of the job, the organizational structure;
— productivity, quality, cost;
— satisfaction, responsibility, morale and motivation.

Job enlargement was the suggested solution and the idea that linked these issues.

The Conditions of Implementation

Although operators at the Endicott plant had been taught how to perform several related jobs (Walker 1950: 55), the fact that, prior to the job enlargement programme, they did not do them, demonstrates how deeply entrenched the industrial engineering principle of job specialization had become. British trade unions have institutionalized this rigidity as a basis of their bargaining power, as in job demarcation disputes. Kelly points out in this context that 'changes in the organization of work were often introduced as part of a productivity agreement in which employers sought to obtain greater flexibility of workers between jobs in return for higher levels of pay' (Kelly 1985: 43). In the Endicott case there was a similar arrangement, except that wartime conditions obviated much of the resistance that, according to Walker, workers and specialists would have otherwise mounted (1950: 57).

Once an organization is structured on the basis of a strict hierarchy which produces a separation of the interests of different grades of workers (see chapter 3, section 2), it is not surprising that the conditions for obtaining cooperation in job redesign are difficult to achieve. Walker's emphasis on their importance got almost entirely lost with the subsequent psychologization of the topic. His comments about the plant's good relations with foremen are also relevant to contemporary industrial relations efforts where, on green-field sites, companies often take advantage of the lack of entrenched working practices, for example by giving all workers staff conditions of service. Foremen at Endicott were called managers and represented management in all matters of company policy (Walker 1950: 58). This must have had a significant effect on their identifications and willingness to take responsibility.

The responsibility gap between management and workers was institutionalized by Taylorism. In a way which was qualitatively different from the old feudal relationship, it produced division between manual and mental work, between labour power and control. The attempt at Endicott to enrich operators' jobs was seen by Walker, among many, in the context of the dangers of the new division in industrial society between managers and managed. Were the scientific management principles, as they had been applied to industrial design, inevitable or just 'a passing phase of industrialism' (1950: 58)? Walker does not attempt to answer his question. None the less it became widely recognized at the time that these divisions contradicted Taylor's claims concerning the benefits of specialization and managerial control for profit, efficiency, pay and industrial relations.

Job redesign never achieved anything like the depth and breadth of application which was achieved by scientific management. It was certainly never aimed at reversing it. Rather it tried to meet a need to make some adjustments, a need which arose from the contradictions inherent within scientific management and Fordism. As we shall see in its subsequent developments, particularly its Herzbergian manifestation, job enrichment was most easily applicable to work which had never been subjected to Taylorist principles and their incorporation in the technologies of the assembly line. Job enrichment (that is building up the responsibility and control of a job) has been primarily practised in quasi-managerial and professional jobs.

8. Herzberg and Human Relations

Herzberg's original research, on which the two-factor theory of work motivation was based, was originally published in 1959 in a book by Herzberg, Mausner and Snyderman called *The Motivation to Work* (hereafter referred to as H,M&S). This book sets out the position for which Herzberg became renowned. In it Herzberg is still somewhat cautious about the generalizability of his conclusions. By 1968 Herzberg's tone had changed from scientist psychologist to management guru. True, the conclusions were based on a sample of 1,685 interviews (Herzberg 1968: 57) as opposed to 200 and the breadth had been improved (but see section 9). But Herzberg's claims to the sole theory of job motivation were fuelled more by his wish to appeal to a management audience which was still seeking a simple solution to the problem of job satisfaction. Addressing himself to managers, as he was in the 1968 *Harvard Business Review* article, Herzberg was brash and populist, dismissing all approaches save his own, misrepresenting many, and sacrificing to the imperatives of managerial application the complexities of what must be one of the most difficult questions in psychology – the nature of motivation.

Herzberg's two-factor theory of motivation was based on Maslow's hierarchy of needs (Maslow 1954). Instead of conducting a critique of this and other theories of motivation, he recast Maslow's theory entirely on the grounds that it could meet management's need for 'general laws of job attitudes' (H,M&S 1959: 110):

> [Maslow's hierarchy of needs] has led many people to feel that the worker can never be satisfied with his job. How are you going to solve the dilemma of trying to motivate workers who have a continuously revolving set of needs? . . . Is the answer to the question 'what do people want from their jobs' always to be, 'It depends'? We certainly need a less pessimistic approach if the rewards from better motivation for both industry and individuals are to be gained. (H,M&S 1959: 110–11)

Herzberg's two-factor theory of motivation is probably still the most widely used piece of behavioural science theory in management training, despite increasing criticism over the years which amounts to a rejection of the theory.[8] Herzberg's presentation and tone begin to explain his outstanding success (commercially if not academically) but the deeper reasons must be sought in the climate of North American organizations and the prevailing approaches to their problems.

Looking for the Key to Job Attitudes

Herzberg, Mausner and Snyderman begin their book by supplying a plausible explanation of the prevailing climate:

> During the period when the study . . . was conducted the answer [to the question why study job attitudes] seemed obvious. There was full employment, with nearly 100% utilization of plant and facilities. It was questionable whether the utilization of manpower was complete. Thus industry seemed to face a situation in which one of the crucial ways to expand productivity was to increase the efficiency of the individual at the job. On the other side of the same coin, there was the continuing dread of the mechanization of people as well of jobs. . . . It seemed overwhelmingly necessary to tackle the problem of job attitudes. Let us be precise. To industry, the payoff for a study of job attitudes would be increased productivity, decreased turnover, decreased absenteeism, and smoother working relations. (1959: ix)

The authors go on to mention the benefits to the community and the individual and quote the evidence of their previous survey (Herzberg et al. 1957) that 'the rosy prospect' of an answer to the problem of job attitudes was 'viewed very seriously by a great many people'.

How you Install a Generator in an Employee

Herzberg wants to show that workers should be internally motivated to increase productivity. He is against incentive schemes because, even if they succeed in improving productivity, the 'Kick In The Arse' (KITA) has to be repeated, unlike when a generator is installed in an employee (1968: 54ff.). This distinction is at the heart of the two-factor theory.

Herzberg discusses evidence about incentive plans in relation to hygiene factors (HM&S 1959: 118–19). He interprets workers' 'liking' of a company which offers good incentive schemes as 'little more than the absence of dislike' and their satisfaction 'little more than the absence of dissatisfaction'. He wants total commitment. Herzberg raises the issue of ethical justification only to pronounce that it was 'settled to our own satisfaction' because of the work's 'potential social usefulness'. Herzberg offers to tap workers' true production potential by manipulating motivators in job content rather than hygiene factors. His theory reflects this attempt to secure workers' total commitment by construing work motivation as something self-driven. It constitutes a further attempt (in parallel with human relations training) at subjectification. To the extent that it succeeded, it bound people to their job. Extra effort, even if productive, was not enough.

Herzberg (1968) has a section entitled 'Myths about Motivation' in which he caricatures both behaviourist[9] and human relations approaches to employee motivation, subsuming them both under the 'KITA' umbrella (despite their opposite theoretical positions). His attachment to the idea of internal motivation enables him to attack the reduction of the working week, increases in wages, fringe benefits and welfare provision (Herzberg 1968: 55). Standard human relations approaches are subject to the same criticism, namely that improvements in interpersonal relations (like other hygiene factors) only make for escalation in expectations and require constant increases in whatever benefit is involved in order to maintain motivation. In this way he dismisses human relations and sensitivity training, communicating with employees, job participation and employee counselling. Nonetheless, Herzberg's two-factor theory, with its value emphasis on motivators as the solution to job satisfaction, harnesses the 'whole person' of human relations to productivity:

> We would define first level factors of achievement – responsibility – work itself – advancement as a complex of factors leading to this sense of personal growth and self actualization . . . we postulate a basic need for these goals as a central phenomenon in understanding job attitudes. (HM&S 1959: 70)

Herzberg's Individualism

A part of the answer to the question of Herzberg's popularity rests in the state of the dominant human relations approaches, both in formulating the problem and in attempting to solve it. The starting point for his disagreement with most human relations approaches is what he characterizes their 'group' approach: 'the idea has grown that a supervisor is successful to the degree to which he focusses on the needs of his subordinates as individuals rather than on the goals of production' (HM&S 1959: 10). He mentions Argyris' work with approval as concentrating on the individual rather than the group. What Herzberg means by the group is interpersonal relations between supervisor and supervisees. He likewise criticizes the approach of the Michigan School (the work associated with Likert; see chapter 7) which claims the success of democratic over autocratic leadership style. These approaches might lead to improved morale, but there was no evidence, according to Herzberg, that improved morale led to higher productivity (HM&S 1959: 131). Ironically Herzberg's work is itself criticized for concentrating on job satisfaction outcomes at the expense of behavioural ones (Cooper 1974: 13). This is consistent with his reliance on Maslow's theory in which satisfaction is the major motivational outcome.

Herzberg's theory of motivation, following Maslow, is emphatically individualist. In this sense it takes the human relations approaches to their ultimate extreme. They began as an attempt to go beyond the individualist and mechanistic approaches of scientific management and working conditions. They discovered the informal group and sentiment. They proceeded to a focus on interpersonal relations, personal growth and leadership style, and with Herzberg they are back to a problematic of the relation between individual and the single job, but with a focus on motivation as the solution to job satisfaction.

9. The Legacy of Motivation Theory

Herzberg's outlook is entirely dependent upon making generalizations – across types of job, across classes, across nations and national culture and across the sexes. For example in relation to technology he pours scorn on the idea of 'job enlargement' without discussing the different exigencies of job redesign in mass production jobs. His cavalier approach to generalizability reflects the legacy of orthodox psychological theories of motivation. Motivation was based in instinct and assumed to stem from a series of needs, the number and content of which differed according to the theorist (for example McDougall 1923 added 'gregariousness'). Maslow parted with this tradition only to the extent of positing that the potency of needs (that is their ability to motivate behaviour) could be conceptualized as a hierarchy. He did not question the location of needs within an essentially asocial individual nor shift the focus of motivation theory from a description of needs to questions concerning their cause (if they were biologically based, that question was irrelevant). The effect of this legacy on work motivation theory was that it has no way of conceptualizing the limits of its generalizability: if it is biological, it can be true of all humanity. Herzberg claimed that 'the findings of our study have some implications for an understanding of primitive man' (HM&S 1959: 121). In this model the need for self-actualization is as natural as the need for food. In the same tradition McGregor (1967: 10) regards humans as 'by nature motivated'.

At about the same time McClelland (1961) was popularizing the idea of 'achievement motivation' (labelled nAch when quantified) and applying it to training for entrepreneurialism in Third World countries. Although he started off with the specifically historical work of Weber who analysed the growth of the Protestant Ethic within Western capitalism, he still tried to socialize nAch into Indian farmers without attention to context or culture. Maslow's and Herzberg's assumptions about motivation are universalistic despite the fact that they are expressions of American human relations values and assumptions concerning personal commitment to work. Respondents who might have attached different significance to the experience of having control over their work still had their responses coded according to categories derived from what Herzberg himself called 'middle-management men' (HM&S 1959: 112), that is North American white, male, middle-class (by education if not birth) professionals. Turner and Lawrence (1965), building on Herzberg's work, found evidence of what they believed were rural–urban differences in work culture. Later Hackman and Oldham were to turn these into individual differences (of 'growth need strength'), a move which is commonplace amongst psychologists, particularly those involved with psychometrics (see chapter 4).

Herzberg initially included production and clerical workers in his study and his account of why he dropped them has no theoretical legitimacy:

> In our first pilot study we talked with clerical and production workers as well as professional and managerial people. We discovered that the professional and managerial groups were more verbal, showed a quicker grasp of the technique, and gave more and better delineated sequences of events than the clerical and production groups . . . it was vital that we mine where the metal was richest. (HM&S 1959: 32)

This is tantamount to saying that, since workers didn't produce the accounts he was seeking, he didn't sample them. He suppressed the question whether these workers held the same values in relation to their jobs, or experienced the sort of ego involvement that the management and professional groups did. (There is some evidence that the two-factor theory is not applicable to blue-collar or working-class workers; Blood and Hulin 1967; Whitsett and Winslow 1967; Nichols 1975.)

Herzberg made his choice of interviewees based on his interest in employees who were – or were potentially – internally committed to their work, and thus to the organization. With the so-called scientific results which he produced, he then claimed universality for a theory of internal work commitment. In my view this is the single most important aspect of Herzberg's theory and the fundamental reason for its enduring popularity.

Notes

1. The tardy acceptance of the attitude survey in industrial psychology is exemplified by the addition of a chapter on 'The Measurement of Attitude and Morale' in the 1961 edition of Tiffin and McCormick's classic textbook in industrial psychology. Sills (1973) provides an example of its take-up in the personnel management literature in Britain.

2. There is a full account of the first 'T-group' – in 1947 – in Bradford et al. (1964). It originated in a training event for adult educators.

3. See Knights et al. 1985 for an excellent collection of articles on job redesign.

4. More recently the connection between job satisfaction and high quality has become paramount with the rise of Japanese competition. In Japan, due to its late and rapid industrialization, Taylorist principles of job specialization had never become entrenched: 'Instead Japanese factories depended on a tradition of work teams incorporating managerial functions and maintenance functions, associated with few staff specialists. . . . Job boundaries were relatively few, allowing considerable job flexibility' (Littler 1985: 13).

A study by Garvin (1983), also cited in Littler (1985: 20), compared assembly-line production of air conditioners in the USA and Japan. The average production defects of the American conditioners were 63.5 defects per 10 units compared to 0.95 in the Japanese machines. The failure rate of products from the highest-quality Japanese producers were between 500 and 1,000 less than those of the lowest-quality producers in the US. That this problem of quality already existed is indicated by the fact that, even in the fifties, Walker introduces the problem in these terms: 'no matter how accurate the machines, operators who are bored do not turn out a high-quality product' (1950: 54).

5. Job enlargement and job enrichment are, strictly speaking, methods of job redesign, in the sense that they are trying to modify existing jobs in accordance with the above criteria. Later the distinction was made between enlargement meaning horizontal loading (more tasks without more control) and job enrichment. Herzberg argued that horizontal job loading 'merely enlarges the meaningless of the job' (1968: 59). In the Walker article the same distinction is not made, since he uses job enlargement to incorporate 'enriching the job in variety, interest and significance' (1950: 55) and 'responsibility' (1950: 56).

6. Hackman and Oldham's (1980) Job Characteristics Model illustrates the dominance of the perspective on the single job in the United States. By the early 1970s they, among many other psychologists, were critical of the reductionism of Herzberg's theory, and particularly of its exclusion of the work group and of a notion of work defined more widely than the tasks making up an individual job. None the less, they argued that work group variables would make any model so difficult to operationalize that they would limit their own work to the single job. They produced an exhaustive list of job variables, operationally defined and measurable, which formed the basis of their Job Diagnostic Survey. The lack of widespread managerial popularity for their model might be partly to do with the fact that it did not tap the managerial ideology of the day. It talked almost exclusively about job characteristics and not individuals' motivation. By the time that their survey was well validated, popular managerial (and to some extent therefore psychological) interest in motivation and job satisfaction had waned, along with the boom years.

7. This policy is similar in the last two aspects to Cadbury's, discussed in chapter 2.

8. Several studies have conducted a critique of the theory within its own terms, for example Blood and Hulin (1967), House and Wigdor (1967), King (1970), Lawler (1969), Oldham et al. (1976), Whitsett and Winslow (1967). However, in my view it is traditions that have developed independently of the theory which show up its limitations most powerfully, for example Blauner (1964), Goldthorpe et al. (1968), Hackman and Oldham (1980), Knights et al. (1985) and the Quality of Working Life movement.

9. The basis of Skinner's account of learning was that behaviour was learned as a result of either negative or positive reinforcement (negative and positive KITA, in Herzberg's terms). Skinner was dogmatic in the view that a simple S-R model was sufficient to explain learning (from stimulus to response with no intervening theory of the organism, animal or human). Significantly the Skinnerian model would have the opposite implications to the subjectification involved in human relations approaches.

7
Organizational Change and Development

> The attitude of the hourly-paid employees had been formed over the years by the way in which they had been managed. In seeking to change shop-floor attitudes, therefore, it was essential first to secure changes in attitude among supervisors and managers. (Hill 1971: 43)

> There are many circumstances when the exercise of authority fails to achieve the desired results. Under such circumstances, the solution does not lie in exerting more authority or less authority: it lies in using other means of influence. (McGregor 1960: 31)

1. Introduction

The story of human relations has taken us as far as the 1970s. Human relations moved the understanding of people at work from a psychology interested in measurement and performance to one in which the whole person of the employee, including sentiments and interpersonal relations, had to be addressed in the interests of changes at work. Within this human relations paradigm, organizational change was seen in terms of interpersonal skills and attitude change on the part of individuals. Managers were no longer only being trained in order to have the skills to induce the cooperation of workers. The survival of the organization in a turbulent environment was seen to depend on the ability of middle and senior management to embrace changes. Thus a far-reaching elision was made between personal change ('personal growth') and organizational change. The emphasis on organizational change coincided with booming economies in the West in general (and the US in particular). The large organization had become paramount as the structure within which the majority of people spent their working lives. The term 'organization' began to dominate the labels, if not the conceptual perspectives, of academics and practitioners whose interest was planned change at work. Organizational change comes to be seen as the key to success in the market-place and human relations experts became 'change agents'.[1]

While many kinds of change can occur in organizations, the term organizational change normally refers to planned changes; specifically intervention or action research which is conducted primarily by social or behavioural science consultants, internal or external to the organization, on behalf of senior management. Since the 1970s the object of planned change typically has been managers, since they have been seen as the people through whom the key practices of the organization can be changed. New knowledge and new forms of intervention targeted their leadership of teams or groups, their interpersonal skills and their decision-making. The T-group and other experiential training methods brought managers or executives together in groups and interpersonal relations within these groups became the focus for change.

In sections 2 and 3 I discuss two terms, organizational behaviour (OB) and organization development (OD) which inform organizational change. These describe respectively the disciplinary background to understanding organizational change and the dominant techniques. In section 4 I discuss the dominant role of private sector industry in organizational change and contrast this briefly with other cases in public sector service organizations. This chapter revolves round a detailed analysis of two case studies of organizational change in the 1960s in the British oil industry; one at Esso and the other at Shell. These are the subjects of section 5 and 6 respectively. They have been chosen because they illustrate some of the dominant approaches to organizational change, and in doing so highlight the tensions and problems of these strategies within the highly politicized world of organizations. Lisl Klein wrote *A Social Scientist in Industry* (1976) using her experience at Esso to analyse the role of social science in industry. She documents a period in the late 1960s when she was an internal social scientist at Esso UK, working in the Tavistock tradition. At the same time the company brought in an American team from the Michigan Institute of Social Research. The contrast is illuminating. Paul Hill, the coordinator of the Shell intervention from his base in the Employee Relations Planning Unit, wrote *Towards a New Philosophy of Management* (1971). It deals with the ambitious, company-wide intervention by the Tavistock Institute of Human Relations which began in 1965. Together the cases provide an opportunity to look at three kinds of intervention research, Klein's and Michigan's at Esso and the Tavistock's at Shell, in companies manufacturing similar products, in the same market and labour conditions. The two institutes are fairly representative of British and American approaches at the time (although there was considerable similarity between practices in the two countries as well).

2. Organizational Behaviour

Human relations premises underpinned much of the theory of organizational behaviour, through their influence on the development of social psychology. They also informed the intervention techniques which by the 1970s had come to be known as organization development, or OD. Yet despite this homogeneity, there were tensions between the academic and business ends of the spectrum. Organizational behaviour is usually defined as an interdisciplinary subject within applied social science, largely composed of psychology and sociology. One definition, by a British academic, emphasizes the sociological aspects of organizational behaviour: 'Organizational behaviour is the study of the structure and functioning of organizations and the behaviour of groups and individual within them' (Pugh 1969: 345). In the US, OB has been the academic wing of human relations practices as they have been applied in organizations (Perrow uses the terms synonymously; for example 1970: 3). It is helpful to be aware of two distinctions in this connection. One is between managerial and academic approaches, a distinction which appeared to be problematic twenty years ago: 'organizational theory has often been stifled because it has worked on problems that managers thought were problems and it has studied them using managerial concepts rather than psychological ones' (Weick 1969, quoted in Buchanan and Huczynski 1985: 433).

The other distinction is between psychological and sociological contributions to OB. The dominant concepts of organizational behaviour have been largely at a psychological level, as opposed to a sociological one, in the sense that they focus on the individual in the organization, rather than on structures and technologies. This tendency has been more extreme in the US than in the UK. Nonetheless, of a typical British textbook on organizational behaviour, approximately three-quarters is about the individual or group and only a quarter about structure and technology (see, for example, Buchanan and Huczynski 1985). Categories such as perception, learning, personality and motivation refer to the level of the individual, but only rarely do these concepts derive from experimental or 'pure' psychology. I have already pointed out that the concept of motivation developed a completely new meaning in the human relations tradition than it had had in the physiological psychology tradition (see chapter 4). The concept of technology was influential in a strand of British work starting with Joan Woodward in the fifties. From the data derived from a survey of one hundred manufacturing companies, Woodward (1958) concluded that differences in technology were likely to influence organizational structure. Influential work in a similarly organizational mode was published by Burns and Stalker (1961) and the Aston Group (see Pugh and Hickson, 1976) as well as a considerable amount of work in which the Tavistock was involved. In the US, Lawrence and Lorsch (1967) focused on the environments of organizations.

Social psychology was assumed to play an adequate integrating role between the individual and the organization. Social psychological categories such as formal and informal groups, roles, leadership, conformity, norms and attitudes are the mainstay of organizational behaviour (particularly in the American tradition). Although those who identified as social psychologists were more likely to be strict in their use of the experimental method and therefore maintained a partially independent, experimental approach, the emergence of social psychological concepts was profoundly influenced by the human relations tradition in the United States and the subsequent rapid expansion of social psychology during and after the Second World War (Cartwright 1947–8). Early research on leadership was overwhelmingly funded by the US military and its assumptions were extended from military hierarchy to hierarchy in other work organizations.[2]

3. Organization Development

In the 1970s, in the US, work on organizational change from a human relations perspective continued in the same vein as the previous decade, but with another name: organization development (OD). Douglas McGregor, in the context of his work with Union Carbide in 1957, has been identified as 'one of the first behavioral scientists to talk systematically about, and to implement, an organization-development program' (French 1978: 540). Its connections with human relations and social psychology and the concern with planned change can be seen in the following definition (quoted by Rowlandson 1984: 90): 'OD is an intervention strategy that uses group processes to focus on the whole culture of the organization in order to bring about planned change'. French and Bell define OD as:

> a long-range effort to improve an organization's problem solving and renewal process, particularly through a more effective and collaborative management of organization culture – with special emphasis on the culture of formal work teams – with the assistance of a change agent or catalyst and the use of the theory and technology of applied behavioural science, including action research. (French and Bell 1973: 15)

We shall see in chapter 8 that the tradition has been carried into the 1980s under the banner of organizational culture, a term which in the above definition is closely linked to the human relations idea of what makes an effective work group. According to French and Bell, OD has taken the 'ongoing work team, including supervisor and subordinates' as its key unit and 'puts a primary emphasis on human and social relationships' (1973: 15, 20), thus again demonstrating its continuation in the human relations tradition. The stock in trade of the OD consultant was a series of experiential group exercises which developed within human relations management training: sensitivity, T-groups, encounter groups and laboratory training. According to Bass and

Barrett (1971) (quoted by Rowlandson 1984: 91), 'this sensitivity training, making heavy use of T-groups or encounter groups, now often called team-building, is the single practice that most consultants or change agents are likely to agree is "definitely doing OD"'. This emphasis on experiential group processes is evident in the influence of American institutions such as the National Training Laboratories Institute for Applied Behavioural Science, who in the seventies coordinated the publication of the OD network, *The OD Practitioner*.

Because OD has been so fashionable and dominant, criticism has not been salient in the literature. But there have been criticisms and these tend to centre on two charges. The first is that experiential groups did not achieve organizational goals (though they were charged with achieving nervous breakdown, resignations and inappropriate – from the organization's point of view – managerial behaviour).[3] More broadly, the criticism became that OD's claims for change were too ambitious and they had not succeeded because they relied on personal changes in trust and openness, rather than taking on board the politics of the organization (for example Friedlander and Brown 1974). That OD listened, to some extent agreed, yet was not able to take the criticism on board, is a testimony both to the limitations of the conceptual framework available, which was focused on a human relations psychology of the individual, and to the politics of OD consultancy, whose interventions were kept at arm's length from top management and business decisions.

A rather different charge is that OD, along with its human relations predecessors, is ideologically biased against strong management (what in Britain in the eighties would be called 'the manager's right to manage'). From a management point of view, Lee (1982, 1985) has been a consistent and vocal detractor of OD. He cites research evidence to suggest that OD consultants' values mean that they promote things like democratic participation in decision-making over growth and development of the corporation (Lee 1985: 12). He also argues that organizational training has 'abandoned the foreman' (1985: 17) and that 'the glamour of "management development" has, over the last twenty five years, pushed the once excellent first-line supervisory training and development work into the background' (1985: 17). According to Lee: '(I)n 1950, 13% of personnel and training journal articles were devoted to supervisory training. By 1970 this had dropped to less than 1%, where it remained. Management development and related topics, as we might expect, grew from 4% of the articles to 15% during this period' (1985: 17).

In Britain, OD became a popular topic of discussion in management and personnel publications. Its definitions tended to be wider than in the US, influenced by the more sociological tradition of organizational behaviour in the UK. For example, an article on OD in *Personnel Management* by the head of organizational effectiveness at Shell was summarized as covering 'the whole gamut of techniques – from quality circles to improving the quality of working life' (Pritchard 1984: 30). She includes the open systems and socio-technical approaches (see the section on the Tavistock below), strategic planning and industrial democracy. It would seem that, by 1984, the term OD in Britain was beginning to refer to any techniques of planned organizational change and to acquire some distance from the sensitivity approach. Pritchard and others point out that OD practitioners can have many different titles while performing a similar job: 'adviser, consultant, facilitator, change agent, occupational psychologist, third party, behavioural scientist' (Pritchard 1984: 30).

In Britain, occupational psychology and OD had a rather ambivalent relationship. In 1979, the British Psychological Society working party on the future of occupational psychology conducted a survey of occupational psychologists, of whom they managed to locate 745. The survey found that the most common activity of occupational psychologists was organizational consultancy (followed by training and development consultancy). The report comments 'At the moment it seems that very little attention is given in degree courses for occupational psychologists to the theory and practice of consultancy' (Rowan 1979: 1). Occupational psychology training was still keeping human relations at arm's length. Yet the respondents' estimates of what they would be doing in five years had a distinctly human relations flavour:

Interpersonal skills (38 per cent)
Occupational health and stress (38 per cent)
Organization development (37 per cent)
Quality of working life (36 per cent)
Participation (34 per cent)
Interpersonal behaviour (34 per cent)

A factor analysis of respondents' specialities revealed three clusters, which were named organizational consultancy, ergonomics and personnel.[4] Organizational consultancy was by far the largest, while the other two represent the traditional areas of industrial and occupational psychology (Rowan 1979: 3).

4. Private and Public Sector Interventions

An emphasis on manufacturing industry, as in the two case studies of this chapter, is consistent with the whole history of industrial psychology. From scientific management, through human factors to human relations, manufacturing industry has provided the terrain on which industrial psychology has been founded. The most fundamental of these problems has been the relation of factory workers to deskilled, machine-paced, externally controlled jobs. Moreover this problem has almost always been in the context of private sector companies who are dictated by the market to prioritize profits or profitability.[5] However in the sixties, more than in any previous epoch, service organizations in both public and private sector were growing rapidly and organizational psychology was expanding its scope to address their requirements (for example, Roethlisberger in chapter 6 section 1). In the 1979 survey of British occupational psychologists, 76 per cent worked in the public sector. Of these, 29 per cent worked in academic teaching units, 7 per cent in academic research units, 29 per cent in government departments or agencies, 5 per cent in nationalized boards or corporations and 6 per cent in other public sector organizations (Rowan 1979). One of the reasons why human relations training expanded so rapidly in the fifties and sixties was that it could be applied, with no modifications, to bureaucracies whose main purpose was information handling or service provision (for example government agencies). A service perspective and a 'people' perspective were easy to merge.

Once outside the grip of the private sector, action research did not have to become fixated on variants of the problem of productivity. The Tavistock, for example, has a long tradition of action research in the National Health Service, where the governing premiss has been (until the 1980s) the need to improve patient care. For example, Menzies (1960) used Jaques' (1947–8, 1955) psychoanalytic concept of social defences against anxiety to provide an innovative analysis of why so many trainee nurses were leaving the profession (see section 5). In this context it is easy to see that, since nursing is usually chosen as a vocation, 'motivation' as a starting point for analysing the problem would have been unhelpful. Miller and Gwynne (1972) have reported at length on problems within residential institutions for the physically handicapped and the chronically sick, using similar psychoanalytic concepts, and also the open systems model (Miller and Rice 1967). Small organizations such as social work agencies have a tradition of using consultants, initially often to help at the level of the small group (for example Bayes and Newton 1978). Their traditions have been fairly separate (again not starting with the problematic of motivation) and have drawn on the psychotherapeutic model in social work. Contrasting these little-known studies with the famous ones, it becomes clearer just how much the dominant concepts of industrial and human relations psychology have been produced by the problems that were facing management in private manufacturing industry. Work psychology is the product of such history.

5. Esso Petroleum and Organizational Change

In the late 1960s, the Esso Petroleum Company (UK) had two kinds of social science intervention being conducted simultaneously; two kinds which provide interesting contrasts in theory, method, style and culture. From 1967 to 1969 Esso Petroleum Company UK brought in an American team to carry out some research and intervention. From 1965 to 1970 Lisl Klein was an inhouse social scientist employed in the Employee Relations Department at the London office of Esso. Her training was in the Tavistock tradition, and her book gives some insight into the clash of perspectives between the Michigan Institute of Social Research (deriving from the work of Rensis Likert, 1961 and 1967) and Tavistock-based action research, and also between internal and external consultant roles. In what follows, I shall outline the Michigan and Tavistock approaches to organizational change and then discuss what happened at Esso, drawing on Klein's account.

The Michigan Institute of Social Research

Rensis Likert's model of the organization is a good example of the inseparability of a managerial human relations perspective, the social psychology of groups and leadership style and the theorization of organization at a reductively psychological level. His work, which has been immensely popular in management training and practice, represents a long historical link which goes back to Hawthorne and extends forward from 1961 into organizational behaviour and OD. The Michigan University Institute for Social Research was formed in 1947 when the MIT Center for Group Dynamics (established by Kurt Lewin) joined with Michigan's Survey Research Center. In addition to Likert, there are many famous names associated with the Michigan Center: Festinger, Lippitt, McGregor, French, Cartwright and Deutsch – a collection which illustrates the inseparability of social psychology and human relations management.

In *New Patterns of Management* (1961), Likert developed a model of effective organizational structure which consisted of democratic/participative work groups, each linked to the organization as a whole through overlapping memberships. He reiterated the by now conventional wisdom of the Hawthorne research in his emphasis that work groups were an important source of individuals' need satisfaction and that, if managers created work groups which fulfilled this need by developing 'supportive relationships', the work groups would also be more productive (Likert 1961: 97–118). Likert is most famous for what have come to be known as 'systems 1, 2, 3 and 4', clusters of style characteristics which he found to be consistent up and down an organizational hierarchy, and which he therefore used to theorize

organizations. The numbers refer respectively to exploitive authoritative, benevolent authoritative, participative consultative and participative group management systems. The last of these – 'system 4' – is
regarded as being most successful. It claims to tap and use the
motivation of the employee; develop positive attitudes towards other
members and commitment to the organization; involve group participation in setting goals, improving methods and appraising progress;
establish a climate of trust and confidence and a sense of responsibility
for the organization's goals. Michigan's usual form of intervention in
an organization is described by Klein as follows:

> Projects in organizations generally take the form of first diagnosing
> whereabouts on this [the four system] schema an organization is located, by
> means of a questionnaire survey. Members of the organization are asked to
> complete a long and detailed questionnaire giving their views on the way in
> which motivation is tapped, the nature of communication, interaction,
> decision-making, goal-setting and control processes, as well as their
> opinions about the organization's performance. They are also asked how
> they would like the situation to be in respect of these variables. There is then
> some form of intervention, by means of a variety of strategies, designed to
> shift the behaviour of people in the organization further . . . towards 'System
> 4' or a 'participative group' style. The survey is repeated, either at stages
> along the way or at the end, so that shifts in perceived management style can
> be measured. At the same time actual performance is measured through
> whatever form of productivity measurement is in use or can be installed, to
> test the hypothesis that morale will improve and that productivity will
> improve with it. (Klein 1976: 141, 144)

Participation and Democracy

Participation occupies a central position in Likert's work, and in the
human relations literature on organizational change. For example in
his introductory chapter to the Shell intervention, Paul Hill uses the
heading 'participation' to refer to 'the most promising approach to
deal with the problem of motivation' by social scientists (Hill 1971: 10).
The probable reason for the centrality of the idea is that it provided a
compromise between the job redesign school and the management
style school of human relations in that it purported to involve workers
in decisions, giving them some feeling of control or responsibility,
without having to make dramatic changes in the technology or the
structure of control (though preferably cutting out one level in the
supervisory hierarchy). The contemporary fashion for quality circles is
an instance of the same strategy. To understand the place of
participation in the discourse, it is necessary to review the idea of
democratic leadership style.

The distinction between democratic and authoritarian leadership
styles, and particularly the scientific evidence that the former was more
successful in engendering cooperation, can be traced back to Lewin,

Lippitt and White's (1939) experiment with different leadership styles in a boys' club. Belief in the superiority of democratic leadership in organizations became the credo of American human relations, influenced generally by the post-war political ideology of the United States. More particularly, American managerial culture was affected by the knowledge and fear of the negative effects of the early coercive and absolutist management which was now associated with authoritarian leadership style (for example the comment by Mayo, chapter 5 section 6).

In the sixties, the language of democratic leadership style and participation had swept through management thinking in the US and to a lesser extent in the UK (see section 6). But voices were beginning to be heard which questioned just what was meant by 'democracy' and 'participation' in this human relations context. The strongest critique of human relations eventually came to be that it was manipulative. Despite the fact that most of those involved in the human relations approach seemed genuinely to believe that it had emerged because of 'deliberate efforts to improve the condition of the working man' (Gellerman 1966: 16), when talking to management, social scientists were quite clear that this change was not primarily for welfare reasons (see, for example, the quotation from McGregor at the head of this chapter).

In the culture of the time (which after all was partly a product of human relations ideas in management practice), more authoritarian methods were resented and tended to lead to opposition by subordinates, which made it more difficult for management to exercise control. This was the fundamental reason for the dominant emphasis on democratic style. Child points out the inconsistencies this necessitated:

> The irony in having to make known to employees what was supposed to be a shared purpose, and of having in effect to create a co-operation which was supposed to be spontaneous and eagerly desired, indicated the manipulative features in what was put forward as a democratic and participative system of industrial control. (1969: 119)

A few writers (for example J.A.C. Brown, cited in Child 1969: 127) acknowledged that for human relations thinkers 'participative' and 'democratic' referred only to techniques of communication and motivation. Shell is a good case in point. The Employee Relations Planning Unit, having advocated a 'participative management style' in order to encourage subordinates 'to commit themselves and their energies wholeheartedly to the objectives of the company in the tasks they undertake', goes on to comment that 'this style by no means equates with "soft management". The boss . . . still takes the decisions' (Hill 1971: 45).

Leadership Style

Likert (1961, 1967), Argyris (1957, 1962) and McGregor (1960) all share the central assumption that work motivation and job attitudes can be changed by changing the interpersonal behaviour of managers towards more democratic leadership style ('leadership' can be taken to mean managerial in this context). However, there are some differences between the theorists.

On the basis of management policy, practice and literature, McGregor (1960) identified two contrasting sets of management assumptions which guided managers' behaviour; theory x and theory y. They are based on a historical shift in management values, but such a recognition is not incorporated into the account. Theory x assumptions reflect scientific management beliefs and practices, for example the irresponsibility of the worker who thus requires external control. Theory y assumptions incorporate human relations values and are based on Maslow's beliefs about people being naturally motivated and it only requiring trust by managers and a certain amount of autonomy in their work for this to become realized in their behaviour. In this theory, the problematic of work motivation is reduced again to the relation with managers, but this time the emphasis on skill or style has shifted slightly to an emphasis on the beliefs or 'theories' of managers; the focus is deeper within the individual manager, as in Argyris (see chapter 6). By this time, I hardly need to point out that the way that McGregor propounded his description, and the way that it has been taken up (nearly as popular in management training as Herzberg) is suffused with the universalistic value that theory x managers are bad and theory y managers good and effective. Only rarely is it said that this depends on organizational culture, structure or technology.

Because of their sociotechnical perspective, Tavistock consultants were able to recognize the effects of different technologies on strategies of management control. For example in their Statement of Philosophy for Shell (see section 6) they say:

> the most important human task in running process operations is identified as information handling. As this is a skill which cannot be controlled by external supervision, employees must be internally motivated to carry it out efficiently. It follows that the key human characteristics required are responsibility and commitment. (Hill 1971: 58)

Likert's description of systems 1 to 4, in which leadership styles are the causal factor for changing motivation and commitment, is very similar to McGregor's in underlying values and paradigm. In Likert's system, the polarity described by theory x and theory y has become a continuum, and incorporates the belief that enhancing group processes will tap motivation.

In discussing the industrial relations climate at Shell UK (below), it will become clear how closely these human relations ideas coincided with the dilemmas facing management. Hill's concise summary of the problem at Shell was that:

> the historical authoritarian system of management by control through rewards and punishments is no longer appropriate or effective today since the 'punishments' available to management no longer carry any weight. Effective management in modern industry can only be practised by the consent of those managed. (Hill 1971: 43)

I shall return later to the Shell case to show how the concepts of motivation, participation, attitude and job redesign shaped the diagnosis of the problem at Shell and the Tavistock intervention.

The Tavistock Institute of Human Relations

The Tavistock Institute of Human Relations (TIHR) was, like the NIIP, a product of wartime – not the First, but the Second World War. As Jaques put it:

> the group of psychiatrists and psychologists who formed the original nucleus of the Institute had been brought together in the British Army during the war. . . . The psychiatrists joined with their fellow technicians in psychology and the other social sciences to initiate and develop a number of new techniques, including procedures for the selection of both officers and men, a new approach to battle conditioning, battle training and tactics, new methods in psychological warfare (both in military intelligence and in broadcasting) and techniques for solving problems of repatriation and resettlement. In addition they made practical contributions to the assessment and maintenance of morale and discipline. (Jaques 1947a: 4)[6]

The most striking change in the conditions for an Institute in Britain since the First World War was the intervening growth in social science, and the emergence of a social psychology. Also by this time 'organizations' had become a much more common object of theory and intervention than 'industry'. Jaques stresses interdisciplinary collaboration in the social sciences (Jaques 1947b: 59). These trends are reflected in the TIHR's definition of its object of intervention: not industry, not only organizations, but also 'the richness and variety of the problems of community life must be reflected in the work of the Institute' (Jaques 1947a: 7). Despite the danger of spreading its energies too widely 'a full range of activities must be developed . . . to break down the barriers to the application of social science in a wide variety of social regions'. The regions cited are 'the individual, the family, the school, industry and the living community' and the range of industrial activities are rather predictable: 'selection, training and morale' (1947a: 7). The aims of the TIHR are an example of the expansionist aims of social science, which was now defining an ever more extensive range of objects. The general goal of such interventions was 'the changing of human behaviour' (Jaques 1947a: 60). Jaques exemplifies the Tavistock approach when it was first established: 'it is our belief that the study of how social scientists work with the community is one of the central problems of social science today'.

The model used by the TIHR problematized the role of interventionist and theorized the relation between applied social science research and the client. The emphasis is a clinical one, using the principles of the psychotherapeutic method of psychoanalysis to inform the sociotherapeutic method of action research. The model contrasts strongly with the scientific model of research and intervention in industrial psychology, which assumes objectivity on the part of the researcher or consultant.[7] The psychoanalytic model does not see the consultancy relationship as a problem to be got round in order to achieve scientific objectivity. Rather it is the central tool for influence towards change. Jaques identifies the process, which is the basis of psychoanalytic therapy, whereby the patient's ambivalence towards treatment is directed to the therapist as transference (Jaques 1947b: 64). The application of this model to social therapy is the central feature of the early TIHR approach. It constitutes not only a way of understanding the client/interventionist relation, but the central tenet of the method of intervention, since 'social change can be accomplished only as rapidly as resistances are overcome and removed' (Jaques 1947b: 65). In this way the model for organizational change is based on that for individual change. The sorts of defence mechanism operating between individuals to produce individual pathology are generalizable to the relations and processes to be found within any organization. Jaques' work with Glacier Metal – a relationship he maintained for sixteen years – is a classic example of these principles in action (Jaques 1951). In his introduction to the Glacier Metal work, Jaques sums up his approach as follows:

> The specific study here reported shows how unconscious forces in group behaviour and the unwitting collusion between groups for purposes of which they are only dimly aware, are important factors in the process of social adaptation. It also shows – and this is perhaps more important – how such forces, and such unrecognised collusion, may be a main source of difficulty in implementing agreed plans for social development and social change. (Jaques 1951: xvii)

Isobel Menzies (1960) developed the psychoanalytic idea of defence against anxiety to analyse social defences against anxiety amongst nurses in a large London teaching hospital. The hospital was losing student nurses at a serious rate and requested Menzies' help to prevent what senior staff felt was an impending breakdown in the system of allocation of student nurses to meet staffing needs. Using her analytic experience she took this as the 'presenting problem', that is a problem which is acceptable and can be consciously articulated. Her diagnosis was achieved through intensive interviews, discussions and observations. Her interpretation of the hospital organization proposed that the defences of the nursing staff produced and maintained rigidities in the organization's structures, social relations, rules and procedures.

Notwithstanding the Tavistock's psychoanalytic tradition, it is best known for its approach to organizations as sociotechnical systems. This emphasizes the interdependence of two subsystems in an organization; the technical, based on plant and machinery, and the social, consisting of social relations and the way work is organized. The principle of joint optimization of the social and technical systems emerged from the work of Trist and Bamforth (1951) in the Durham coalfield at a time when a mechanized system of coal getting was being introduced and the old group system of work had therefore been discontinued. They concluded that the groups should be reintroduced. The belief that the autonomous work group was a good way to optimize the joint working of the social and technical systems has been central to the Quality of Working Life (QOWL) movement and related job redesign innovations, notably at the Scandinavian Volvo Kalmar plant in 1974. The stress on the interdependence of the social and technical systems meant that the Tavistock consultants did not regard intervention in group processes as a sufficient strategy. Instead an intervention had to be based on a particular technical system and this was likely to involve work design or redesign.

Differences within Social Science in Esso Petroleum
Klein's work at Esso was based on the principle of joint optimization of the sociotechnical system. For example, her work to improve the refuelling service at London's Heathrow airport involved a system redesign using ergonomic as well as social psychological principles (Klein 1976: ch. 8; Shackel and Klein 1976). Marie Jahoda, in the preface to Klein's book, points out that: 'The point that Miss Klein makes so convincingly is that it is the structure of the work itself, rather than personal virtues and failings of individuals which requires a social science input' (Klein 1976: xii).

Relating to the Michigan team's activity presented Klein with 'a big dilemma' since the theory:

> took no account of structural variables, the nature and content of tasks . . . or of any aspects of technical or economic structure as causal variables, either in explaining why differences in behaviour arise in the first place, or in assessing whether behaviour is appropriate to a situation, or as a means of modifying behaviour. (Klein 1976: 144)

The Tavistock meaning of 'action research' entails conducting a unique piece of research based on a unique problem and shaping generalized concepts and methods to the solution of that particular problem. Klein's projects at Purfleet (a distribution centre) and West London (airport refuelling) were examples of this approach. Klein's approach involved case studies of problems identified by managers in the organization (possibly with her help), an approach which is particularly suitable to the role of internal researcher/consultant.

In the Michigan model a standardized intervention is conducted (in this case it attempted to move managers towards system 4 styles) on the basis of standardized questionnaire data. The questionnaire is a psychometric instrument. It is devised to be used across whole populations and, through quantification, to arrive at its information in a way which renders results comparable. In the Michigan research the measured characteristic is leadership style and the unit to be measured is the organization (or sub-unit such as the marketing department).

Likert claimed his systems to be empirically proven, based as they were on statistical analysis of quantitative data. This is their strong selling point as a basis for organizational change: if system 4 styles could be empirically correlated with positive attitudes, then an intervention geared to moving leadership styles closer to the system 4 end of the continuum will produce those desired outcomes. Within this paradigm, no thought need be given to structural conditions in the organization that are major factors in producing both worker and management behaviour. Indeed Likert explicitly excluded them (Likert 1967: 139).

Performance, before and after the change event, is measured against system 4 practice (Klein 1976: 141–2). Through Likert's work the human relations norm of participative management was claimed as the scientifically established norm of successful management style for organizations.[8] Such instruments were popular in applied social psychology because they could deal with information *en masse* (in this case 5,000 respondents at Esso). Moreover, they had the respectability of science and could claim statistical reliability and validity.

However, there are contradictions in this case between the goals of social science and of solving organizational problems. First, whereas Klein was interested in parts of the organization with the most severe problems, the Michigan team, according to Klein, was interested in the success of their model and therefore 'wanted a degree of shelter from problems' for their research (Klein 1976: 153). Similarly, one Michigan consultant said he liked the 'Hawthorne effect' (Klein 1976: 156) because it enhanced the changes in management behaviour which they wanted to establish. (The Hawthorne effect refers to the favourable changes in behaviour of those being studied which are not the result of changes in working conditions, but of being the object of intervention.) Secondly, the research team was interested in replicating its findings by getting data from as many different sources as possible using the same instrument. So when it came to making changes in the American version it was not possible for several reasons. Codification had become highly mechanized because the method depended on treatment which is generalizable to all populations. This has been a very common occurrence in applied psychology and social psychology using psychometric-type methods.[9]

The fact that this kind of research is popular with organizations as well as researchers needs to be explained. First, although the focus on management styles and behaviour is not particularly credible with operational managers, it coincides with their dominant belief that the technology is sacrosanct. Secondly, it is seen as scientific and therefore legitimate. Klein comments that for the employee relations manager (who was trained as an engineer), 'one of the chief attractions [of the Michigan project] had been the emphasis on experimental control and measurement' (Klein 1976: 168). However, these reasons are compounded by considerations which revolve round interests and power.

Power and Access
In my view the main reason for the popularity of questionnaire and training-based research is that the scope and direction of the research is limited and known in advance, and so the repercussions to the department or organization appear to be more controllable. Usually employees are taken out, 'trained', and put back in: the organization is not subjected to scrutiny. When Klein confronted someone from the Michigan team with questions on how changes would be accomplished, the answer was quite vague: that once the motivation was released in those involved in the change programme, 'structural' changes would follow (Klein 1976: 157). It is now a standard criticism that attitudinal changes on their own rarely survive re-entry into the workplace if structures and practices remain unchanged.

A further reason for the method's acceptability is that the object of the research is employees who are lower in the hierarchy than the person who allows access. One example of this was the subsequent research proposed by the Michigan team. After the reorganization of the Marketing Department at Esso and the failure of the initial Michigan project, the Michigan team came back with an entirely new proposal which was formulated in terms much more reminiscent of the sociotechnical approach and which did not concentrate on leadership style but rather on decision-making processes (Klein 1976: 168). Klein was enthusiastic about it but the employee relations manager recorded his 'extreme disappointment'. In the event 'the Marketing Director emphatically rejected the proposal, saying that his decision-making processes did not need looking at, thank you very much' (Klein 1976: 169).

The case study approach does not limit in advance what will be relevant information. If it is informed by adequate organizational theory it is more likely to succeed in grasping the complexities of power and influence that surround the problem, and will affect its solution. Yet this was one of the reasons why several of Klein's projects never got off the ground (Klein 1976: 160). Another is that social scientists do not tend to have high status within large organizations. The fact that Klein was not consulted by the employee relations manager about the Michigan project is one example. Another is that the managing director did not know of her existence.

Such power dynamics invariably affect inhouse and external consultants differently. Inhouse consultants are permanently a part of the usual power plays that are being conducted in different quarters. External consultants who have been invited in to conduct big projects will have the backing of top management. The problem then is support from lower down, amongst those managers who will be required to participate (as discussed earlier). In Klein's strategy, managers' participation was guaranteed by their initiation of research into the problem and by the use of departmental budgets rather than central finance.

Is it the case that the more on target and insightful social science research becomes, the more threatening it is and the least likely to be accepted? In what circumstances might this be the case? Can it retain its integrity, be effective and be accepted? It is worth holding these questions in mind for the discussion of the Shell case.

6. Shell and the Tavistock Intervention

Hill's account of the industrial relations and market situation of Shell in the mid-sixties and the initial study of the Employee Relations Planning Unit gives a clear illustration of the conditions for planned organizational change, and social science participation, in large private sector companies. The theme of my analysis, which runs through my subsequent comments, is to suggest that it is inevitable that social-science-based intervention will come to be shaped by the priorities and constraints of the company. The same analysis suggests that organizational psychology is already, for historical reasons, in a position which facilitates such a collaboration. It has become so through just the same processes as I analyse here. Finally I do not argue that social science interventions are therefore not effective: on the contrary, I shall try to show that the Tavistock intervention in Shell served the needs of that company at the time excellently,[10] although there was a discrepancy between these needs and the formal objectives of the intervention.

The Background to Shell's Intervention

The oil business had entered troubled times. From the late fifties on, Middle East nations became stronger in their control of crude oil prices, from Suez through to the formation of OPEC. Moreover, within Shell UK there was the fear that Shell's competitors were gaining an advantage: Esso, the closest rival, had struck the much celebrated productivity bargains in 1963. Shell's productivity deals in 1960 and 1963 had had only restricted impact, as Hill shows in his account of the 1965 industrial relations problems. The changing market climate and 'the web of restrictive practices which at Shell Haven were stifling productivity and threatening the possibility of future expansion there' (Hill 1971: 26) were the reasons for the company's determination to engage in planned organizational change. The aims of the change programme were 'to improve the motivation of employees at all levels and to remove unnecessary conflict from the work situation' (Hill 1971: 16). The Employee Relations Planning Unit (ERP) was set up to diagnose the problem, partly because managers and the personnel department were too busy with day-to-day trouble-shooting to do any long-term planning. The power of unions to engage in restrictive practices over a fairly long period had led to a feeling of fatalism amongst managers and a serious morale problem amongst supervisors (Hill 1971: 23).

'Productivity deals' is the shorthand term for the outcome of negotiations between management and unions whereby unions agree to drop certain restrictive practices or increase production in return for improved pay or conditions. It was taken for granted amongst management that far-reaching deals were necessary. The problem, in the light of Shell's recent history,[11] was how to achieve this. The ERP's report had to go further and it did so in the following terms:

> We consider that there are definite limitations to the amount of progress we can hope to make in the future in achieving greater productivity by more effective use of manpower through conventional bargaining tactics, given the present climate of relationships at Shell Haven and Stanlow. . . . Fundamentally the men are not committed to the company's objective and the most we can hope for is that they will honour the bargains they have entered into. (Hill 1971: 42)

Motivation, Participation and Attitude Change

What kind of solution was there to this state of affairs?

> We should . . . make it our long-term policy to secure a fundamental change

in attitude on the part of employees to the point where, in a climate of
mutual trust and confidence between men and management, it becomes
possible for them to commit themselves fully. (Hill 1971: 43)

No informed manager could be unaware of the pervasive human
relations literature which addressed just that problem: how to induce
employees' commitment. Hill spent his initial time in the ERP
reviewing the literature to help diagnose the problem and come up with
a new solution, so it is not surprising that his picture of the Shell
situation is permeated with the perspective of 'motivation'. His title
'History of Motivation Problem in the Company' (Hill 1971: 19) heads
a section on industrial relations problems. He describes structural and
power features of management–union relations: the difficulty of
national and local agreements for operator and craft unions and the
piggy-backing effect of their respective settlements; demarcation
disputes preventing flexibility and producing overmanning; the use of
overtime. These are assumed to be symptoms of a problem of
motivation (which by definition is a problem at the level of the
individual). What this tends towards is an attempt to change
individuals, bypassing the industrial relations structures where conflict
is institutionalized. It supports my earlier point that psychological
concepts have been taken up by management because they provide
solutions that focus on the individual (which, as we shall see, were
effective in the Shell case) and bypass organized labour.

In a separate chapter Hill reviews the literature on motivation and
concludes, not surprisingly, that Herzberg and McGregor appeared to
be most relevant to Shell's problem. The ERP report also explicitly
argues that attitudes should be changed at managerial and supervisory
levels (see the quotation from Hill at the head of this chapter). This sets
the stage for Hill's discussion of a solution in terms of managers
adopting participative styles: 'it was suggested that a more participative
management style would need to be adopted if people down the line
were to become more effectively motivated' (1971: 43).[12]

The ERP concluded that an attitude change programme was needed.
Hill's account of the ERP's reasoning is an almost perfect example of
how, why and in what circumstances management takes up the
discourse of human relations. Much of the rest of the story will be
concerned to answer the question 'with what effects?' First, though,
there is an important rider to ERP's recommendation: attitude change
was the first problem area identified, but productivity bargaining was
tacked on as the second (it didn't take much identifying, as I have
already pointed out). The ERP suggested that 'the company should be
aiming for such changes as: staff status for all hourly paid employees;
annual salaries in place of hourly rates; abolition of overtime

payments; increased flexibility and a reduction in demarcation restrictions' (Hill 1971: 46). Hill saw the two action proposals as interlinked:

> It was thought that the attitude change programme would have a favourable effect on the general climate of the workplace and on people's attitudes. This should enhance the chances of successful joint development of productivity bargains. Satisfactory bargains with the unions, by eliminating, for example, overtime payments, would in turn make it simpler to introduce further changes on the shop floor, such as different working methods or different job structures, which, it was hoped, would flow from the adoption of a more participative management philosophy. (1971: 46–7)

This argument makes quite clear that the attitude change programme is intended to smooth the path for better productivity deals. The flexibility of manning that this would permit would be a precondition for job redesign, which could then further reduce manning. It again illustrates the use of job redesign, presented as an exercise in enhancing job satisfaction, as a way to achieve more flexible working practices (see also chapter 6, section 7).

The Role of the Tavistock at Shell

All of the thinking outlined so far was done by the ERP prior to contacting the Tavistock. Certainly the Tavistock would have had to recognize the importance of the productivity deals in Shell's plans. What they did in the event was to build their interventions around the attitude change plan, and leave the productivity bargaining outside the scope of their direct intervention. This was to have significant consequences.

The ERP had already decided to write a statement of policy based on the belief that 'management should adopt a more participative style' (Hill 1971· 45) if attitudes were to be changed. They had attempted to draft one, but recognized that they needed more than 'a plea for participative management' (Hill 1971: 50). If it were to succeed in influencing members of the company, it had to be improved. This was the first thing that the Tavistock team did, and in the process made the statement of philosophy represent a more subtle and complex blend of social and economic purposes (see Hill 1971: 59–65 for the full text of the statement). Their other two roles were to design and facilitate the conferences which were convened to discuss the statement and to act as consultants to work design and job redesign experiments, including the design of a new plant on a green-field site at Teesport.

The Statement of Philosophy

The statement of philosophy written by Trist and Emery, the senior consultants from the Tavistock, in conjunction with the ERP, began by identifying not only the objective of long-term profitability but what Hill calls the company's social objective. In this the company has 'stewardship' of both human and environmental resources; that is it should protect and develop the resources, and meet the needs, of the community. The inclusion of the social objective was meant to enshrine an ethic which was consistent with good treatment of employees. Without this, what grounds would managers have for believing that the company really required them to change their practices? It is a long-standing debate whether social and economic goals are compatible in the way that is necessary for these two statements to coexist.[13] Blackler and Brown in their critical evaluation of the Shell intervention argue that 'efficient business management and humanitarian social ideals were made to appear both compatible and even complementary' (1980: 159). The principle of joint optimization of the social and technical systems was advanced as a way of assisting the company to pursue both. The sociotechnical approach was put in the position of resolving a conflict of ethical objectives in such a way as to make it appear that Esso was not going to prioritize profitability over its social objective.

Blackler and Brown discuss at some length the beliefs of Trist and Emery. They point out Trist and Emery's emphasis on a systems model where the environment could be turbulent and throw an organization out of balance (Emery and Trist 1965). This linked to their belief that society at the time was increasingly turbulent and they were committed to developing social science which enhanced control of these forces. They identified the emergence of new social values as coping mechanisms that could help to deal with such uncertainty and claimed that to do research into these issues was 'a compelling task for social scientists' (Emery and Trist 1965: 31, quoted in Blackler and Brown 1980: 13). In this context, a piece of social science action research based on introducing a new system of social science values in a large organization threatened by a turbulent environment must have seemed a wonderful opportunity. Their purpose, like Mayo's, was to maximize cooperation and diminish conflict. The strategy was to use a series of conferences (cascading down the hierarchy) to promote attitude change. The idea was that conferences would provide a forum for managers to participate in discussing the philosophy, and that, if they then accepted it, it would enhance their commitment to putting its principles into practice.

According to Blackler and Brown, the conferences were a failure. They were 'safely insulated from the forces, issues and decision-making frameworks which, in practice, determined company actions and strategic policies' (1980: 149). They accuse the Tavistock team of 'pseudo-innocence' in denying or ignoring the internal political and economic forces in organizations which, in their view, made it predictable that managers would not adopt the social objectives, but only the profitability objectives in the statement. My interpretation of this inconsistency is that the Tavistock's naivety was necessary if the intervention were to be acceptable to the company's overall goal of profitability through the pursuit of wide-ranging productivity bargains.

'Joint optimization' as a principle was lost in the way the socio-technical approach was used in the statement to provide a sophisticated analysis of the requirements of the technical system in terms of workers' commitment. Technology was treated as determining work organization. In the statement of philosophy the key characteristics of the technical system are set out in such a way as to improve the analysis originally made by Hill, which was in reductive human relations terms (Hill 1971: 61–5). It then goes on to analyse the implications for the social system and workers' attitudes. For example, the analysis emphasizes that the technology requires flexibility and that improved performance will inevitably be based on the efficiency of plant utilization (Hill 1971: 61).

Kelly, in a critical analysis of the sociotechnical approach, argues, on the basis of other case studies, that the concept of joint optimization has little connection with the reality of sociotechnical practice and that it should be replaced with the notion of intensification of labour (Kelly 1978: 1069). The Teesport case (reported in detail in Hill's book) supports this thesis: there the design cut out one level of the hierarchy and used many fewer operatives since jobs were designed, and operators trained, to be flexible between as many as eight different jobs (Hill 1971: 139).

The statement's analysis of the implications of technology for the social system (note that the relation is treated only this way round) is based on the characteristics of information-processing jobs. In effect it is argued that old forms of control are not adequate for these jobs, and that change in management practice and/or job design is required in order to achieve self-control in these jobs: 'The only promising way of avoiding these faults [in information handling work] is for the individual to be internally motivated to exercise responsibility and initiative. Any external control can only act after error has occurred or had its effect' (Hill 1971: 63).

In continuous process technology, the stoppages caused by such faults are very expensive. The distinction made by the Tavistock team between these information handlers and manual workers illustrates an important historical process affecting social science interventions: with increasing automation changing the nature of jobs, and with the spread and sophistication of computer technology controlling industrial processes, the need to change management practice from reliance on external modes of control became of paramount importance.

Outcomes

According to Blackler and Brown, the intervention had left little trace on the climate of the Shell UK organization by the time they conducted research there in 1977:

> Each of the main channels which 'emerged' through which the philosophy was to be implemented led to disappointments. Too much was promised from job redesign, inadequate organization theory led to unrealistic expectations for managers to be change agents, the experience with the productivity deals contradicted the spirit of the philosophy they allegedly demonstrated, and what developments at Teesport really owed to the philosophy remains uncertain. In terms of effectively lasting changes the philosophy did, indeed, amount to little more than a drop in the ocean. (Blackler and Brown 1980: 156)

But in the short term, the effects of the intervention were not inconsiderable. Involvement of union officials in discussions did generate at least a temporary culture of cooperation.

> The Joint Working Parties [JWPs] were to be a completely new departure. They were to bring together representatives of management and shop stewards, not in the usual bargaining frame of reference, but in a new, collaborative problem-solving frame of reference. . . . Their terms of reference would be to consider how to remove impediments to efficiency; and to work out what in their view would be the most appropriate set of terms and conditions of work for the existing hourly-paid employees. This was to be done without any regard to price whatsoever. . . . (Hill 1971: 151)

Only the shop steward members of the craft Joint Working Parties at Shell Haven refused to change their frame of reference and this JWP was wound up. In others, the shop steward members cooperated fully, even running the risk of losing the trust of union members (Hill 1971: 153).

There were many successes in terms of the ERP goals on overtime, flexibility, overmanning and annual salary (Hill 1971: 154ff.). One example of changed attitudes will serve to illustrate:

> In previous years, these TGWU shop stewards had been known for their determined opposition to any reduction in the number of operators manning a unit, even where technical advances had clearly reduced the work load. . . . These same shop stewards had now enthusiastically accepted the company's philosophy statement and had entered the JWP discussions in a truly collaborative frame of reference. (Hill 1971: 156–7)

Hill goes on to detail their suggestions for obtaining job flexibility and time flexibility on one site, with the operators themselves devising shifts which reduced the amount of overtime available to them (1971:

156–7). This change of attitude must have been based on the conviction that the company was serious in espousing its social objectives, and indeed at the time it may have been (to the extent that it is possible to impute unitary intentions to the multiplicity of forces which make up an organization). However, if Blackler and Brown's verdict is accepted, only the sceptical craft union stewards at Shell Haven were correct about the company's behaviour in the long term.

With regard to the productivity deal with the TGWU, Hill concludes that although it was costly in the time and resources invested in it:

> Considering . . . the unfavourable climate of pre-philosophy days, the outcome must rank as a very great success, and a tribute to the determination of both management and union representatives to make it so. It must also be seen as a striking example of the impact which the company philosophy programme had on some people's attitudes and motivation. (Hill 1971: 166)

Hill concludes the chapter by saying that it was the opinion of the managements concerned that productivity deals could not have been achieved without the philosophy dissemination programme (1971: 167).

The Implications of the Shell Case

It is clear to me, from the evidence in Hill's account, that the philosophy of management was a crucial plank in the attempt to win the cooperation of workers, particularly union representatives, in radical reformulation of terms and conditions to produce greater efficiency. Central to greater efficiency was the need for flexibility of working, which had been prohibited by the old demarcations and other conventions of unionized labour. Here job redesign exercises, advanced on the same platform as the company's social objective, played a part.

In general, the emphasis was on a new management style characterized by participation, to change individual workers' attitudes. This strategy was a success. Wide-ranging productivity deals were struck in which unions conceded most of the restrictive practices and other conventions which had formed the basis of their bargaining power. It is not at all surprising that once the deals had been struck, the philosophy fizzled out, so that a few years later it was remembered as an insignificant and short-lived fad.

To say this is not to accuse the social scientists involved of a conscious conspiracy to manipulate the workforce into cooperation with managerial objectives. The relatively peripheral position of social scientists and the ERP in the activities of managers and the over-whelming (but unmentioned) forces compelling managers to continue practising as they had done before (including a capitalist international environment), meant that the social objectives of the intervention never stood a chance of making anything but a short-term impact. This was exacerbated by lack of a theory of organizational change which could take into account the power relations of the organization and their effects on planned change. It is an indictment of organizational theory (of which, after all, the Tavistock approach is a sophisticated variant) that social scientists could believe that such an intervention could achieve anything else.

Applied social scientists are in a double-bind which will be all the stronger in the future as we are increasingly required to make ourselves self-financing through research and consultancy. If the Tavistock team had been clearer about the discrepancy between the stated objectives of Shell, which they helped to formulate in the statement (and which apparently reflected their own values), and the more pragmatic objectives which can be seen in the outcomes, they might have decided not to participate. But the Tavistock is a self-financing institution. If it had challenged Shell's prioritization of productivity bargaining over long-term change in philosophy, it might not have been given the contract. Alternatively it might have been led to believe that the company was serious. In a sense – and probably quite unintentionally – this is what happened. Hill in the ERP and the senior managers at the first high-level conference where the statement was discussed, did believe in the new philosophy. The discourse was very convincing. Their authenticity was a condition of its success in changing attitudes lower down.[14]

In such a situation, what should social scientists do? It may be that the values of Emery and Trist were consistent with the profitability objective of Shell, which dictated their approach to attitude change and productivity deals. In that case was there an ethical problem? Yes, in so far as there was a discrepancy between the explicit values of the statement of philosophy and its effects. One could argue that they tried, but their eventual failure was only apparent after the contract finished. The trouble with this approach is that applied social science does not incorporate into its understanding the conditions of its successes and failures, so that social scientists do not stand a better chance in future of working out in advance the likely effects of their interventions. It may be argued that the discrepancy between the statement and the eventual outcomes is the responsibility of the company. Maybe. But who in the company is in a position to overrule the imperatives of international competition?

Despite their weak position and probably their good intentions, social scientists as individuals become implicated in the effects of planned organizational change. More important, social science knowledge is implicated in the process and this has the effect of blinding subsequent social science practice to the power relations involved in organizational change and therefore to their likely effects.

Notes

1. Schein and Bennis (1965: 206) identify the first time the term 'change agent' was used in a lay context: in 1963 the *New York Times* ran a large classified advertisement announcing a search for change agents.

2. The organization of work since the industrial revolution owes a lot to the models of social relations already functioning in military organization.

3. See Back (1973) for an early, balanced critique of the American use of sensitivity training, particularly chapter 1. *Management Today* (November 1984) exemplifies the popular criticisms.

4. The factor labelled organizational consultancy included group decision-making, intergroup processes, group problem-solving, role problems, group dynamics, participation, conflict resolution, leadership styles, communication, interpersonal behaviour, organization development and so on (Rowan 1979: 3).

In 1986, the Training Committee of the BPS Division of Occupational Psychology came up with similar factors (BPS 1986).

5. The prominent exception is ergonomic research for the armed forces, where psychology focused on the problem of monotony in jobs, for example monitoring radar screens.

6. In 1947, very soon after the TIHR was founded, the American *Journal of Social Issues* (*JSI*), itself recently founded as the mouthpiece of the Society for the Psychological Study of Social Issues (and of which most of the subsequent big names in social psychology were members; see *JSI* 1 [1945]) invited the members of the TIHR to produce a whole issue. Since it was so soon after the TIHR was founded, and since through the journal it was to present itself for the first time to like-minded American social scientists, the material contained in it is of enormous interest. In both countries, the writings of concerned social scientists during this period give the impression of freshness, a concern with values, the preparedness to pioneer new methods, and to transcend discipline boundaries in the process.

7. It is because of this assumption that the NIIP journal never contained any discussion of method.

8. This is parallel to my argument in chapter 3 in which the norm of the normal curve conflates the statistical and the social norms.

9. Although he used interviewing as the basis for codifying responses, Herzberg (see chapter 6) demonstrated the same phenomenon: he was interested in claiming the universal validity of the two-factor theory and therefore had to 'prove' it by using a standard method over a large number, and wide variety, of cases.

10. The group employed by Shell was called the Tavistock Centre for Human Resources, and was headed by Eric Trist. Another group existed at the TIHR, the Centre for Applied Research, headed by Kenneth Rice. The two had split in the early sixties as a result of a serious power struggle. Throughout this chapter I shall refer to the Shell group generically as the Tavistock.

11. In 1964 Shell UK had undertaken an 18 per cent reduction in the number of hourly paid employees at its refineries. At Shell Haven, which was a focus for the Tavistock intervention, the reduction was 26 per cent. Union opposition was strong and the effects of this exercise on a simultaneous attempt to negotiate greater flexibility and reduce demarcation restrictions was that the latter were abandoned. According to Hill,

resentment and distrust from this exercise spread over to the plans put forward in the change exercise (Hill 1971: 25–6). Hill summarizes the effects as follows: 'The demolition of the old "Joe Shell" image had its greatest effect on the longer-service employees. Along with it tended to be demolished also the tradition of loyalty to the company, which had provided a form of motivation, a sense of obligation to do a fair day's work'.

12. These two statements together neatly summarize the history of human relations thought from Hawthorne to the 1970s.

13. My own belief is that they are not, given the dominance of competitive international capital. The case which is on my mind as I redraft this chapter (in January 1990) is that of the international nuclear industry, the subject of a recent television documentary, *Food Irradiation*. Its evidence convinced me that the governments of Britain, the US and Canada, among others, have been targeted by a marketing campaign by the International Atomic Energy Authority (IAEA) in a long-term attempt to find profitable uses for nuclear waste. The so-called benefits of food irradiation are implausible, given the advanced state of refrigeration technology, and the dangers of genetic distortions, cancers and increased malnutrition as the result of food irradiation are real. Evidence of these dangers in scientific studies has been suppressed by the IAEA, in what amounts to a clear prioritization of profits over the health of population worldwide.

14. The case exemplifies the relevance of Argyris' stress on authenticity (chapter 6, section 4).

8
Organizational Culture

Employer attitudes of 'collectivism' are giving way to 'individualism'. . . .
This individualism is linked to the search for commitment and the winning
of the 'hearts and minds' of employees at all levels. (Molander 1989: 7)

AT&T people had taken to their hearts the precise new pro-competitive
values senior management believed should be emphasized. No commentary
on a felicitous cultural shift could be more dramatic than the acceptance of
these new values over others long embedded in and thoroughly characteristic
of the corporate value system. (Tunstall 1985: 60)

1. Introduction

When I began to hear the term 'organizational culture' creep into
writings and discussions to do with my work, I was impressed and my
scepticism was momentarily silenced. Culture to me connotes a more
complex, less reductive analysis of social phenomena. Has OB really
taken culture on board, I marvelled, has it progressed from seeing
things in terms of the individual and small group? Is it really
recognizing cultural differences within organizations? (I should have
already noticed that 'culture' is used in the singular, which is a bad
sign.) Then my scepticism started taking over as I heard the term used
in the context of the same old human relations imperatives: participative management, democratic leadership, team building, consensus,
planned change, conflict resolution and employee opinion surveys. My
scepticism turned to dismay when I read phrases like 'more culture',
'strong and weak cultures' and finally 'culture is manifest in . . . human
nature' (Kilmann ct al. 1985: 5).[1]

How then is organizational culture defined by the academics who
have made a name for themselves in this field?[2] Schein points out the
confusion surrounding the use of the term 'culture' and instances six
quite different usages (Schein 1985b: 6). He comments that they all
'*reflect* the organization's culture, but none of them *is* the essence of
culture', and argues that 'the term culture should be reserved for the
deeper level of *basic assumptions* and *beliefs* that are shared by
members of an organization' (1985b: 6; original emphasis). Kilmann,
Saxton and Serpa use a similar definition:

> operationally, culture is defined as shared philosophies, ideologies, values,
> beliefs, assumptions and norms that knit a community together . . . all of

these interrelated psychological qualities reveal a group's agreement, implicit or explicit, on how to approach decisions and problems: 'the way things are done around here'. (1985: 5)

They are correct to specify 'operationally'. One of the defining features of organizational culture seems to be the lack of theory informing its approaches.[3] As I have already argued in several contexts, this is not surprising, since it is a product of an area which is defined by managerial problems. To the extent that theory is discernible, it is social psychological. Sapienza defines organizational culture as 'a shared appreciative system' (1985: 66) and then commonly uses the term 'shared beliefs'. This seems to be the most common usage and it refers back to a commonly used definition of a group in social psychology as a collection of invidivuals who have shared beliefs.

Business Week captured the central problem around which the organizational culture bandwagon has formed, in its title 'Corporate Culture: The Hard-to-change Values that Spell Success or Failure' (*Business Week* 1980: 148). Culture was a (not so) new word for an old problem: that 'invisible force' (Kilmann et al. 1985: ix) which has to be controlled if planned change is to be successful. Alternatively culture is what gives a competitive edge to one company over another whose market conditions are the same: 'Cultural uniqueness is a primary and cherished feature of organizations, a critical asset that is nurtured in the internal value system' (Tunstall 1985: 144). These definitions refer to an organizational problem, as seen from the perspective of top management.

So what purpose does it serve to include the term culture? It refers to the norms, values and so on which – so the term implies – must be shaped and shared to make for more effective working. This means improved productivity, but productivity achieved through the human relations principles of work group satisfaction, high morale, loyalty and consensus. Maybe the new ingredient is that employees are not just expected to do their job well, but to give management the information which will enable it to be done even better. The Japanese have quality circles. American industry began to see that, as Chairman Brown of the new AT&T put it: 'we have to open up channels of communication so that new opportunities . . . don't die on the organizational ladder' (quoted in Tunstall 1985: 47).

Despite the fact that considerable doubt has been cast on the idea of consensus as a valid basis for understanding organizations (see chapter 8), it remains a basic principle. So, for example, Kilmann, Saxton and Serpa continue their introductory discussion of culture (cited above) by saying 'The best way to make a company successful is to have a culture that influences all members to adopt by tacit agreement, the most effective approach, attitude and behaviour on the job' (Kilmann et al. 1985: 5). That is why, in the words of Edgar Schein 'the hunt is on for "right" and "strong" cultures' (Schein 1985a: 18).[4] The reason for this lies in the managerial purposes in the context of which this new knowledge, like the old human relations knowledge, has been produced. In other words, what purports to be a neutral body of knowledge and practice has been produced principally at the behest of management.[5]

2. Child of Human Relations

As is evidenced by the foregoing definitions, the study of organizational culture remains within human relations and social psychology, a position from which successive approaches to organizational change have not departed since the 1930s. OD used the term culture as follows: 'a more effective and collaborative management of organizational culture, with special emphasis on the culture of formal work teams' (French and Bell 1973). The term culture could be dropped in both places in this quotation without affecting the sense of the statement. In fact my experience of reading Kilmann, Saxton and Serpa is that often no distinction is made between the organization, as it is treated by behavioural science, and its culture. This is particularly evident in discussions of change, where all the old mechanisms of 'organizational change' can be applied to 'organizational culture' (see for example Schein 1985a, 1985b). At one level this shows up the continuity of writers, such as Schein, who were involved in OD and are continuing in the same business.[6] At another level it suggests that there have been no significant advances in understanding.

Edgar Schein is significant in the field of organizational culture both because he personally exemplifies the continuity within the field from the late 1940s (he got his PhD in social psychology from the Harvard Department of Social Relations in 1952) to the present prominence of organizational culture, and also because he is one of the few writers in the field who have engaged in critical analysis of the term and attempts to theorize organizational culture. He criticizes 'the simplistic and cavalier statements about culture' (Schein 1985b: 5) and the tendency 'to link culture with virtually everything' (1985b: 4). The primary purpose of his book, *Organizational Culture and Leadership* is 'to clarify the concept of "organizational culture"' (1985b: ix).

Schein's enthusiasm for an analysis of organizations in terms of culture derives from his own experience of failure with earlier premises on which he based his practice as an organizational consultant. He gives an example where he attempted to intervene at the level of interpersonal process to improve the functioning of a group of managers:

> I made many suggestions about better listening, less interrupting, more orderly processing of the agenda, the potential negative effects of high emotionality and conflict, and the need to reduce frustration level. . . . However, the basic pattern did not change. I could not understand why my efforts to improve the group's problem-solving process were not more successful. (Schein 1985b: 2)

Schein goes on to argue that he needed to understand the cultural assumptions of the group, and challenge his own, different ones, before he could be effective: 'Once I shifted my focus to improving the *decision* process instead of the *group* process, my interventions were more quickly acted upon' (1985b: 11).

This illustrates how one practitioner experienced the inadequacy of OD based on interpersonal skills interventions, which were themselves dependent on an ideology of what constituted good human relations. Despite twenty years of effort, this principle was not uncritically shared amongst the managers in Schein's example. OD was looking for theory which permitted it to escape from this interpersonal tunnel vision.

Managers needed less reductive tools in order to understand and improve their performance:

> When managers observe communication or problem-solving failures, when they cannot get people to work together effectively, they need to go beyond individual explanations. The problem may not be their own lack of managerial skill or limitations in the personalities of the people involved. Often the problem is that those people started with different assumptions, different language, different world views – in short different cultures. (Schein 1985b: 315–16)

To the extent that 'culture' as a concept provided Schein with a way of identifying the basic assumptions of the clients with whom he was consulting, and helped to make visible content as well as process, it was a useful tool (see Schein's chapter 5 on method).

Culture has not provided a paradigm for OD which raises its interventions above the level of the individual and the skills of influencing others. Yet it has achieved a shift of emphasis, from feelings to meanings, in how people can be influenced (see section 6). The continuity of theme is unsurprising, as the arguments in part 2 of this book predict. OD is a technology which is practised on behalf of senior management, and its preoccupation remains the problem of producing adapatable consensus in line with senior management's changing objectives for the organization as the market environment of the organization changes. Change remains the watchword.

Schein identifies various weaknesses in the analysis of organizational culture (see Schein 1985b: 44) which his own analysis does not, in my view, overcome. This is largely because the weaknesses of a human relations, social psychological perspective, with its managerial premisses, are not transcended. Although there are many inconsistencies in the way that the term culture is used by Schein, his formal definition is as follows:

> a pattern of basic assumptions – invented, discovered, or developed by a given group as it learns to cope with its problems of external adaptation and internal integration – that has worked well enough to be considered valid and, therefore, to be taught to new members as the correct way to perceive, think, and feel in relation to those problems. (Schein 1985b: 9)

For Schein, organizations exist near the bottom of a size hierarchy of social units that have 'cultures', with occupations or professions above it and groups below, at the lowest level where cultures operate. According to Schein, it is at the group level that culture forms: 'culture is a learned product of group experience' (1985b: 8).

Schein's definition falls into different traps. First, he relies almost entirely on the group level of analysis and, because of the traditions of American social psychology, that means assumptions about small groups. Given that the word 'organization' features in his book's title, the omission of analysis at the organizational level is very striking. While he mentions markets and technology in the context of his case studies, he does not analyse culture in the perspective of hierarchy, structure or formal authority in the organization. Conceptually, Schein does distinguish culture at the organizational and group levels by his correct insistence that organizations can have more than one culture, because culture is produced at the group level and the organization is made up of many groups (whether they do have more than one is 'an empirical question'; 1985b: 7). However, in practice there is a constant slippage from group to organizational level, so that he ends up referring to organizational culture in the singular. For example: 'culture should be reserved for the deeper level basic assumptions and beliefs that are shared by members of an organization, that operate unconsciously, and that define in a basic 'taken-for-granted' fashion an organization's view of itself and its environment' (1985b: 6).

The group in Schein's analysis is not quite like the group of Argyris' managerial training group (see chapter 6). It seems to have a group mind, at least at the basic assumption level, and to this extent the theoretical focus has shifted from the group as a collection of individuals with feelings which characterized human relations training. Here Schein is harking back to the earliest traditions of the American group relations movement, before the small group was reduced, analytically speaking, to the constituent members as individuals. He also explicitly uses Tavistock group psychoanalytic theory (see chapter 7) in which the unconscious works at the group, rather than the individual, level. Yet Schein does not integrate group analytic notions of the irrationality of the group, or its use of defence mechanisms, into his analysis of culture. This can be seen in the above definition, where the group evaluates whether its actions work well enough, considers them valid (or not, presumably) and proceeds to teach these basic assumptions to new members. This comes across as rational and purposive and is a travesty of Bion's (1959) theorization of basic assumptions in a psychoanalytic tradition. It depends more on socialization and learning theory. Moreover, it implies a model of power or influence which is entirely one-way, as if 'the group' confers the culture on new members, but they do not modify it (do they bring no culture with them?). No wonder that, as we shall see, established leaders are seen as the only motors of change in organizational culture. Schein's model apparently cannot envisage a group culture which is dysfunctional, yet his consultancy experience has primarily been to improve the functioning (in senior management's terms) of small groups. Indeed Schein explicitly regards culture as functional for the group; functional in coping with external adaptation and internal integration. The potential clash between these two could lead Schein into a theorization of culture as multiple and non-unitary, but it does not.

3. Leadership and Culture

Although Schein's formal definition of culture does not refer to leadership, the direction of his analysis cannot be understood without this *deus ex machina*. This brings me to a further weakness of Schein's analysis of organizational culture, which is central because it is where he specifically analyses organizational, rather than group, culture. Leadership functions as a *deus ex machina* in the sense that the concept is introduced, without any critical analysis and only prescriptive definition, as a solution to problems of organizational culture. He defines leadership as 'the ability to see a need for change and the ability to make it happen' (Schein 1985b: xi). He uses the term without theoretical consistency and usually refers to founders of organizations in his examples. It turns out that what interests him is not whether or how culture is produced at the level of groups (though that is where all his theory is located) but the importance of leaders: 'leadership is the fundamental process by which organizational cultures are formed and changed' (1985b: ix); 'I realized that culture was the result of entrepreneurial activities by company founders, leaders of movements, institution builders and social architects' (1985b: xi); 'organizational cultures are created by leaders . . . there is a possibility that *the only*

thing of real importance that leaders do is to create and manage culture'
(1985b: 2; original emphasis). At the end of the book, the 'possibility'
has gone and in its place is the bald statement that 'the unique and
essential function of leadership is the manipulation of culture' (1985b:
317). Here Schein has moved into the realm of the prescriptive and
clarified his basic managerialism.[7] The leader is invoked as the
mechanism which ensures that the group and organization don't just
evolve their own culture, but that their culture is under the control of
someone at the top who has responsibility for the successful
performance of the organization. For example:

> We need to understand . . . how the individual intentions of the founder,
> leaders or convenors of a new group or organization, their own definitions
> of the situation, their assumptions and values, come to be a *shared,
> consensually validated* set of definitions that are passed on to new members.
> (Schein 1985b: 50; original emphasis)[8]

Thompson and McHugh point out the links between the principles
of the 'corporate culture merchants' and heightening anti-union
stances as part of human resource management policy:

> Collective bargaining and unions are bad words in the new world of
> unmediated relations between the organisation and the individual. An
> example of the new practices is that of direct communication with the
> workforce. Winning companies have a culture that enables 'a passion for
> disclosure of information' (Goldsmith and Clutterbuck 1985: 73), hence the
> rash of briefings, videos, house magazines, open days and consultative
> forums. Trade unions are not given much of a part in strong culture
> companies. (1990: 229–30)

Old-fashioned personnel management has associations with an epoch
in which management dealings with the workforce were mediated
through the trade unions. The new Human Resources Management
(HRM) has been recast and does not intend to remain confined to a
narrow specialist department:

> Instead the emphasis is on the integration of 'personnel' issues within the
> overall business strategy, with employees becoming a 'resource' equivalent
> to something like finance. Strategic is a term continually invoked to refer to
> the management of employees at all levels directed towards the creating and
> sustaining of competitive advantage. . . . The intent to move away from an
> industrial relations approach is clear. (Thompson and McHugh 1990: 229)

The invocation of the leader who creates, manages and manipulates
culture has all the weaknesses of the old managers-as-leaders paradigm
which, after many attempts at a revival, was, I thought until recently,
finally and deservedly laid to rest. Sociological analysis of managerial
effectiveness has constantly tried to emphasize the conditions within
which a manager must exercise both formal and informal authority

and challenged psychological views of leaders which reduce, ultimately, to ideas of strong personality or charisma. Perrow, for example, comments that 'the history of research in this area is one of progressive disenchantment with the above theses' (1979: 98). With organizational culture, it seems the ghost of managerial leadership has come back to haunt the field, but with one adjustment: managers are not needed in organizations, only leaders. This rejection is occasioned by orthodox management continuing to ignore the 'human element' (for example Bennis and Nanus 1985: 221).

The theme of leadership is also central to the work of Tom Peters, whose three books (Peters and Waterman 1982; Peters and Austin 1985; Peters 1988) have been at the centre of a management cult of epic proportions. Peters starts his latest book with a quotation from the *Financial Times* saying that the American economy is struggling against competition from the Far East. Peters asserts that no firm is safe (not even IBM).[9] It is from this premiss that he goes on to propose changes which reject the gentle and familiar rhetoric of change in favour of words like 'chaos', 'management revolution' and 'a world turned upside down'. A quantum leap of change is demanded by the world market, an idea which functions as an external and objective determinant of Peters' forty-five prescriptions which: 'specify what managers at every level must do – and do fast – if their organizations are to survive, let alone be superlative in today's and tomorrow's chaotic environments' (jacket of *Thriving on Chaos*, 1988).

The role of visionary and inspiring (that is, charismatic) leader is a fundamental requirement in Peters' prescriptions. For him, leaders are not just founders (though his earlier book *In Search of Excellence* is sprinkled with admiring anecdotes of successful American entrepreneurs). Peters claims that anyone can be a visionary leader (well nearly) (1985: 292); anyone, that is, who learns to live for the organization. A leader must Love Change; Involve Everyone in Everything; Listen, Celebrate and Recognize; Develop an Inspiring Vision; Manage by Example; Bash Bureaucracy and Create a Sense of Urgency. These are some of the forty-five prescriptions. Anyone? He makes no reference to some of the structural and normative limitations on the actions of managers (let alone, for example, secretaries). He seems to be obeying a well established but well hidden principle of human relations in organizations: if a feature of organizational life doesn't support your prescriptions, ignore it, and if managers ignore it as well, maybe it will disappear. It is precisely this voluntarism which has caused the widespread scepticism about human relations interventions in organizations. Peters appears to push the earlier fashion for 'democratic' leadership to extremes in advocating the sort of manager who will inspire such total identification with the organization in all employees that external regulation and control will be rendered obsolete.

Whereas managers were meant to achieve this through interpersonal skills, now they achieve it through manipulating culture:

> Leaders articulate and define what has previously remained implicit or unsaid; then they invent images, metaphors and models that provide a focus for new attention. By so doing they consolidate or challenge prevailing wisdom. In short, an *essential* factor in leadership is the capacity to influence and *organize meaning* for the members of the organization. (Bennis and Nanus 1985: 39; original emphasis)

With evident enthusiasm, Peters quotes a leader as saying of his team 'the brainwashed members of an extremist political sect are no more conformist in their central beliefs' (Peters and Waterman 1982: 16). Interpersonal skills were greeted with scepticism, 'authenticity' failed to convince. The organization of meaning is now hailed as the vehicle which will do the trick of producing self-regulation of the individual at work. Despite the historical record, Peters believes that invoking good human relations can achieve this goal. Management must recognize 'the importance of making the average Joe a hero and a consistent winner' (1982: 29). He insists 'how strongly workers can identify with their work . . . if we give them a little say so'.

Given that these ideas are more than fifty years old, and the problem of self-regulation at work has not been solved to senior management's satisfaction, you might be forgiven for concluding that it was time to pension off human relations principles with a gold medal for long service. How come Peters has revived them as if they were the latest new product from R&D? If we go back to the 1982 book, it is clear that he was pitting these solutions, not against human relations management principles – he rather disingenuously admits to tapping an old stream in the work of Mayo (Peters and Waterman 1982: 5) – but against Taylor and Weber, against 'the numerative, rationalist approach to management which dominates the business schools' (Peters and Waterman 1982: 29). It is a timely reminder that human relations management ideas, which look so dominant from within the human resource management field, have never dominated management training. So, over half a century later, Peters still sees the mission as 'to remind the world of professional managers that "soft is hard"' (1982: 11),[10] and to convince them that the intractable, intuitive side of the organization 'can be managed' (see the epigraph to chapter 6 for an almost identical claim). How can employees be managed? Having 'gone back to the drawing board on organizational effectiveness' (1982: 3), Peters and his colleagues 'found the obvious, that the individual human being still counts' (1982: 8).[11]

The well-known hostility between people management principles and other branches of management seems to have taken another turn. People management, rather than responding by attempting to integrate into its perspectives an understanding of the non-psychological conditions of organizational life, digs itself deeper into a defensive position: people can achieve anything. While this proposition may be attractive enough to create a cult following, management practice as a whole will not embrace it; it is far too exclusive and unrealistic. But human relations does not learn from history.

4. An Overview

In summary, the term culture, like its human relations predecessors, is a product of the power of top management to define a practical problem, and employees' relation to its solution, with the help of consultants, academics and inhouse specialists whose services they buy. So what, you may think. This practical concern is appropriate for applied behavioural science. My criticisms illustrate two of the basic arguments which are demonstrated by the case studies in this book. First, knowledge is not produced in a neutral environment and then applied: it is produced as part of management–employee relations, with the complex of interests and influences which characterize them. Second, this has an effect on what knowledge can be produced. Certain insights are 'unthinkable' today in organizational psychology because of the specific power relations governing its production and reproduction. Paradoxically, so far this has not necessarily been helpful in solving top management's problems. After all, there is a significant body of opinion which says that human relations training and OD have not worked. To the extent that organizational psychology is incapable of escaping from its human relations groove, so-called new approaches turn out to have the same weaknesses as the old ones.

I have argued that in terms of broad assumptions and values, organizational culture is the direct descendant of human relations and organization development. It is certainly produced in the same constellation of interests, which is why it has been so hard to learn any theoretical lessons. Its conceptual shifts are only accomplished on the condition that they do not challenge the legitimacy of management authority, the primacy of productivity over other concerns and, if and when other concerns appear to conflict, the values of organizational consensus.

Within these boundaries, 'organizational culture' does seem to have achieved a shift which is largely a product of changes in wider business strategy, like the worldwide move to privatization and the consequent emphasis on entrepreneurialism. The individual employee lower down the hierarchy is being encouraged to take more responsibility and initiative. Decisions taken correctly at these levels would mean a quicker response to the market, more flexibility and thus a more competitive organization. In this view, the individual is still the target. Although the idea of culture suggests a theoretical shift of target to a domain outside the individual, as I have argued, 'culture' has been quickly reduced to concepts such as attitudes and values which themselves are contained within a social psychological set of assumptions. Not just the individual, but the 'sentimental individual', is still the target for the production of loyalty and consensus. When individuals lower down the hierarchy are required to take initiatives, it is all the more necessary that they have embraced company values wholeheartedly; that is with hearts as well as minds. After all: 'Self-generated quality control is so much more effective than inspector generated control' (Peters and Waterman: 1982: 29). However I argue below (section 6) that the *methods* for changing employee attitudes have shifted towards an emphasis on leader-produced meanings.

The eighties quickly became recognized in the West as the decade of free market economics, the rolling back of the state and the triumph of commercialism, not least because they coincided with the Thatcher and Reagan years. It has also seen a sustained, and relatively successful, attack on trade unionism. It is precisely in this environment that 'organizational culture' has come to mean what it does. The 'strength' of culture has become a central, if ambivalent, concept in organizational change, where changed market conditions or company status require changed priorities in top management and equivalent adjustments throughout the company.

A paradox has been recognized, which is illustrated in the following quotation:

> To many executives, two lessons seem especially clear: First, in a relatively stable business environment, the elements of a well-entrenched and adhesive corporate culture are supportive of the company's mission and success and this should be nurtured and encouraged. Second, and conversely, in the face of significant change, these very same elements may threaten adaptation – and thus corporate fortunes – if they are not modified to fit new business realities. (Tunstall 1985: 45)

The case of change in corporate culture at American Telephone and Telegraph Company (AT&T) has become famous as an example of the successful resolution of this dilemma. In what follows I shall look at it in detail.

5. 'Ma Bell Doesn't Live Here Any More'

> For the better part of a century, the Bell System possessed a corporate culture that, as much as any other factor, created the energy to drive the entire enterprise. It was a culture uncommon not only in its singleness of purpose and its creation of a sense of family, but also in its demonstrable contributions to corporate success. Then, in the mid 1970s, the inexorable march towards deregulation of the telecommunications industry began to unfold and with it came a recognition that internal changes were needed at AT&T. Among them, of course, were attendant 'cultural' changes in value systems, behaviour patterns and corporate symbols. In the midst of these gradual changes came the Justice Department Consent Decree, which required the breakup of the Bell System by horizontal divestiture of its local exchange companies. That divestiture decree served as a potent catalyst to the normally slow chemistry of cultural change. (Tunstall 1985: 46)

Thus Tunstall, Corporate Vice-president for organization and management systems at AT&T, sets the scene for his discussion of change in the corporate culture at AT&T.

According to Tunstall, the 'corporate mission' and 'corporate culture' had been ideally matched. They shared a 'superordinate goal of universal service' (1985: 49). What was to happen to this goal? This is where top management was faced with a dilemma: it had to get employees (including managers) to change their priorities without allowing them to think that dedication to customer service at affordable prices was no longer a company principle: 'with divestiture, certain bedrock values – so indispensable in the regulated past – had to be discarded, or at least reshaped and redirected' (1985: 49) and Tunstall adds:

> Of course, any tampering with the value system had to be executed with great care. If employees began to question whether the corporation had their best interests at heart – or, indeed, whether the corporation's commitment to customer service was diminishing – the company would be challenged by a severe setback that could not be easily repaired. (1985: 49–50)

As the incoming President put it: 'The challenge will be to change our culture without changing the character of our business' (1985: 60).

The problem of cultural change was perceived to be different at two levels. At lower levels of the hierarchy it was essential to preserve the sort of employee loyalty and commitment to the organization and its goals which had helped the corporation so much in the past. The most important strategy here was for top management to be informed of how employees were taking the changes. This could then be the basis of a public relations exercise. At management level, the problem was more difficult: managers had to embrace a new competitive climate in order to make appropriate decisions. A new management culture was deemed to be crucial: 'the corporate value system had to recognize and reward a more entrepreneurial type of manager' (1985: 50). The old managers 'were thought to share certain beliefs that to some extent predisposed them to "internal service standards and corporate traits that were appropriate to a regulated environment"' (*Wall Street Journal* 1984: 32, quoted in Sapienza 1985: 68).

One solution to this was to buy in managers from other companies, particularly on the marketing side (13,000 employees were retired early, but this figure is not broken down into categories of job). The new managers were predisposed to 'competitive zeal . . . and risk-taking'. The resultant conflict (which in OD terms would have been called intergroup conflict, but now would be called conflict between cultures) was 'cited as the single element more critical to AT&T's success than either strategy or structure' (*Wall Street Journal* 1984: 32). 'The cultural wheat must be separated from the chaff', said Tunstall (1983: 18). 'Decisions must be made about which elements support future goals and strategies, and thus must be retained' (1983: 18). We are left in some doubt whether the 'elements' are the managers themselves or just their beliefs.

6. The Methods of Culture Change

A study was commissioned by the retiring president: to provide senior management with the means not only to understand the dislocations and strains caused by divestiture but also to determine what new initiatives might be required to adapt current cultural values to the new environment. (Tunstall 1985: 53)

Tunstall devised an approach with three elements. The first involved the President asking twenty key executives in the company 'for their detailed assessments of the impact of divestiture on AT&T's culture, and for their recommendations' (1985: 54). Second, 'leading management consultants familiar with Bell's history, the trauma of its disaggregation, and its current condition' were interviewed. Third a survey questionnaire was sent to a sample of 6,000 employees 'the "soul" of the organization'. Twelve questions dealt with their perceptions about the company, its future and their own after divestiture. There was a better response rate (50 per cent) than ever before 'in the corporation's abundant history of employee opinion sampling' (1985: 56). A thirteenth free-form question was included:

What were your feelings as the new year and the new AT&T era dawned on January 1st 1984? Feel free to share your thoughts, about the passing of the old Bell System, the birth of the new AT&T and its impact on you as you begin work this year. (1985: 56)

An impressive 57 per cent of respondents replied in detail. The responses to this question were not quantified, as the others were. Its purpose appeared to be twofold. First it 'brought to life and reconfirmed the conclusions that issued forth from the quantified statistical data' (1985: 58), thus enabling management to be more confident about the significance of the quantified responses. Second the responses were cathartic in a similar way to the Hawthorne counselling programme: 'It was as if they had been waiting for an opportunity to tell someone in authority of their sadness, anger and outrage at divestiture, of their stubborn pride in their heritage and of their mingled hopes and concerns about the future' (1985: 56).

The employee opinion survey provided the basis for an information campaign – in essence, a public relations exercise – to reassure employees and provide a new positive image with which they could identify. The survey provided information about which values they needed to incorporate into the new rhetoric – if not the actual practices – of the new AT&T. It also provided reassurance that:

> AT&T people had taken to their hearts the precise new pro-competitive values senior management believed should be emphasized. No commentary on a felicitous cultural shift could be more dramatic than the acceptance of these new values over others long embedded in and thoroughly characteristic of the corporate value system. (1985: 60)

From the small number of examples quoted by Tunstall, and from his commentary, it would appear that most employees felt angry and bitter, but that they knew that the forces imposing the changes of AT&T were too powerful to resist. They had to accept divestiture and they realized that AT&T had to accept it too. The company was not responsible: they were on the same side. For example, one employee who implies by his metaphor that he was 'wedded' to the company, said 'I felt I had gone through a divorce that neither my wife nor my children wanted. It was forced upon us by some very powerful outside forces and I could not control the outcome' (1985: 56-7). The metaphor is testimony to the success of previous policies of securing the commitment and loyalty of employees.

While employees had little choice in whether to accept the changes, they could, of course, have become sceptical and uncommitted employees, which was what top management feared. In the AT&T case, the problem of ensuring employee commitment was superseded at this point by the problem of maintaining commitment under changed conditions. Change raises the question of what employees have been committed to. These were asked to commit themselves to new, in many ways diametrically opposed, values.

The methods used by Mr Brown, the new chairman, after the

analysis of the employee opinion survey, were not out of the human relations stable, but drew heavily on public relations techniques. Brown's talk, entitled 'A New Vision for AT&T', which among other things discussed how management style had to change, was widely distributed. A videotape, transmitted company-wide, featured the chairman and a panel of top corporate officers answering questions from employees. A series of inhouse publications featured articles on the new AT&T. Officers gave talks to employees on new desired behaviour such as 'the new bias toward action, risk-taking, individual initiative' (1985: 61). This was backed up by recognition for special achievements such as the 'Eagle Awards for marketing ideas or super sales' and the 'Golden Boy [*sic*] awards for exemplary customer service' (1985: 62). These awards are an example of Peters' category of 'well-constructed recognition settings' which 'provide the single most important opportunity to parade and reinforce the special kinds of new behaviors one hopes others will emulate' (Peters 1988: 307). The 800 top executives attended week-long corporate forums. A two-volume document detailed the new organization structure, relations, principles and values. Finally AT&T sponsored an advertising programme directed at their external constituencies which 'proved equally useful in aiding the change process inside the corporation' (Tunstall 1985: 62).

During this period the new corporation did indeed introduce an impressive array of new ventures. While these could not have happened without dramatic changes at the decision-making level, it is important to remember that such changes were underpinned by a transformed legal and financial status which must have continued to act as a spur to changing behaviour. Material conditions change behaviour and conditions at AT&T changed dramatically. So myopic is the preoccupation with process that this dynamic in cultural change is not discussed in the prolific literature on cultural change at AT&T. Any scholarly treatment of cultural change would necessarily theorize the relations between culture on the one hand and material conditions, structures and rules on the other.

I have argued that human relations likes to leave material and structural conditions untouched. The preference for treating culture in isolation is a further example of how 'organization culture' has not broken out of that mould. Meanwhile, top executives such as Mr Brown make the required structural and policy changes and the employee relations people continue with their damage limitation work.

The case is a suitable exemplar of the 1980s, expressing conditions which may well extend to the 1990s, for example in Eastern Europe and the Third World under the structural adjustment policies of the World

Bank and IMF. From the protection of state ownership, organizations are being exposed to market conditions. Customer service ceases to be a priority unless it enhances competitiveness. The company can use the most advanced PR and advertising techniques to give employees the answer ready-made, even, in the case of AT&T, beaming it into their own homes via television.

While the target is still self-regulation by individual employees, there has been a shift towards influencing them through the didactic production of meanings. In the Hawthorne counselling programme and later managerial human relations training, the interests of the company were not in the foreground, and employees were encouraged to discover their own feelings (now it might be referred to as organizing their own meanings). At AT&T in the 1980s, meanings were produced by a paternalistic leadership and employees were expected to identify wholeheartedly with the goals of the organization so produced.

Notes

1. Two pages further on, this assertion is reversed to read 'culture is the collective manifestation of human nature', a position which is at least arguable. This is not just a mistake. It illustrates the lack of conceptual clarity which pervades this field, the reasons for which I discuss in more detail below.

2. The majority of these appear to be American professors in business administration and management.

3. Thompson and McHugh point out that the organizational culture approach has also been weak on the use of evidence, relying heavily on anecdotal accounts from 'leaders' (1990: 231): 'the lack of rigour in research methodology has been a persistent theme of critics' (1990: 233).

4. The use of 'strong' with reference to culture assumes that culture is unidimensional and a question of amount or quantity. Such an assumption masks the question of the content of culture, which would be best approached through understanding differences within organizations. The 'process' emphasis of human relations concepts like consensus and democratic style makes it all the easier to take for granted the question what and whose are the values on which cultural consensus is to be based? For example, a discussion of resistant employee cultures of the kind that was documented in the Bank Wiring Room at Hawthorne is absent from the literature.

5. I am in danger here of conducting my analysis as if 'management' were a single entity. I am using the term to refer to those management problems which bear upon the domain of the regulation and maximization of workers. To the extent that this is seen as affecting economic success in the market-place, it concerns management as a whole, although there could be – and invariably are – different primary interests within managements, varying across time and space, type of organization and also within an organization. An example of the last of these is the usual dislike by financial and economic management of human resource expenditure and ideas.

6. Examine the similarities and differences between, for example, Schein and Bennis (1965) and Schein (1985b).

7. In the following quotation, 'we' involves an identification with management goals: 'if we respect what culture is and what functions it serves, we will find that it is a

potentially friendly animal that can be tamed and made to work for us' (Schein 1985a: 42). If 'us' means the organization, then this term as usual is concealing differences of interest, which are none the less central to this passage: the thing which needs to be tamed – the workforce?

8. Elsewhere Schein is more cautious and stipulates that 'although the final form of an organization's culture [as if there were such a thing as a final form, particularly in what is meant to be a dynamic perspective!] reflects the complex interaction between the thrust provided by the founder, the reactions of the groupmembers, and their shared historical experiences, there is little doubt that the initial shaping force is the personality and belief system of that founder' (Schein 1985b: 319–20).

9. Peters uses a different angle in *In Search of Excellence*. There he had 'an upbeat message. There is good news from America. Good management practice today is not resident only in Japan' (Peters and Waterman 1982: xxv). Popular – and chauvinistic – packaging has been one factor in the successful marketing of these old ideas in the 1980s.

10. The significance of gender in this metaphor is not irrelevant. Arguably the whole human relations management movement has had to be invented to curb the dysfunctional masculinity of modern organizations, but it is partly because human relations principles and skills are regarded as 'feminine' that they have made so little impact on managers, who (apart from personnel managers) are still predominantly men.

11 Peters emphasizes the obviousness of his prescriptions. In the preface to *A Passion for Excellence*, he claims that 'practice common sense' turned out to be the biggest selling point of his first book. If human relations ideas are by now 'common sense' (which is questionable), his use of this term makes it all the more impossible for him and other management thinkers to examine the weaknesses of their 'common sense'. In this case, Peters is blind to why these prescriptions may have failed in the past. The label 'common sense' encourages one to ignore history – the history of production of ideas.

9
The Future of Work Psychology and Organizational Behaviour

If behavioral science has ever won out over an amalgam of engineering and economics, the case has not come to my attention. (Hackman 1978: 3)

The days of the large employment organization are over. (Handy 1984: 86)

1. Introduction

What conditions have produced work and organizational psychology in their eighty-year history and with what effects? The perspective I have used to frame and answer this question has been that of the regulation of work and of the workforce. The history of work psychology (I use the abbreviated term to refer to the whole) is the history of some of the tools produced to help in this endeavour; specifically the tools whose object is the individual at work. The first object of the endeavour, in the early twentieth century, was the shop-floor worker; the worker in manufacturing industry who was attached to a production process according to a formal division of labour. The collection of this kind of labour in large factories posed a problem of regulation which, while not entirely new, was qualitatively different from anything in the previous history of production.

The problem of regulation was not entirely new. According to Foucault, the eighteenth century saw the emergence and growth of a new mode of domination in the Western world; a shift from the traditional mode to the disciplinary mode. Disciplinary modes of regulative organization grew up, for example in barracks, schools, lunatic asylums and prisons. Factories did have a model on which to build, but the mode of domination was characterized by coercion and in the factory it treated workers as labour – as hands to perform jobs. This proved problematic, not least because self-organization by labour proved to be a very effective means of countervailing power: prisoners, schoolchildren, lunatics and even army conscripts had never been in a position to stage such strong resistance.

In the early days of scientific management, regulatory strategies began, uncertainly, to target individuals and this has been particularly relevant in work organizations ever since because it has offered the potential for undermining organized groups. Industrial psychology emerged soon after this period as part of an attempt by the new management to introduce technologies of regulation which were not dependent on overt, coercive and impersonal control and therefore might be more effective for workforces which had been rendered suspicious and sceptical by their treatment. Very soon it changed radically with the emergence of a new psychology of individual differences which promised to resolve a contradiction: it regulated groups and large numbers, *en masse*, but it targeted individuals. Not long after, human relations emerged as a strategy which targeted the individual not in terms of performance or ability, but in terms of sentiment. It was a time of burgeoning new discourses in psychology, catalysed by two world wars which disrupted established organizational forms on a massive scale. Since the 1950s the flurry of activity has been maintained, but largely as a result of the staggering growth in the Western economies. Western economies and the practice of management in Western organizations have been based on the principle of profitability engineered through permanent growth in consumption. There is now evidence, notably ecological evidence, that this principle is not viable in the longer term. At the same time, however, we are witnessing the expansion of that principle into Eastern Europe and its consolidation, through structural adjustment, in the Third World.[1]

I have argued that there has been a movement within the disciplinary mode of domination whereby the object of regulation – the individual – has become differentiated. The human relations discourse has produced a 'deep' target within the individual. The central question it posed is the product of the alliance between human relations and management: how to create internal commitment in individuals at all levels of the organization, in order to solve problems of regulation and resistance which were seemingly insoluble by the old disciplinary strategies. For Herzberg, it was the internal generator which was to replace the 'Kick in the Arse'. For McDougall it was 'other means of influence' where 'the exercise of authority fails to achieve the desired results' (chapter 6). For Bennis and Nanus, it is 'to influence and organize meaning for the members of the organization' (1985: 39).

I am not saying that self-discipline is successfully replacing discipline. It may be that no single mode of domination will be sufficiently successful over time to replace other modes. I hope so. From the history charted so far, it looks more like a story of several strategies of work regulation which coexist and compete. Each strategy uses a different model of the individual: scientific management, human factors, vocational selection, interpersonal skills training, work design and leadership. They vary in the advantages that accrue to employees from their use. Amongst these there is little theoretical coherence, and even within each broad strategy there are differences. This is because they are not primarily the products of theorizing, but of changing regulative problems in a variety of workplaces. They do share one common feature, however, and this testifies to the power of work psychology: they all target the individual.[2]

It follows that, in the future, different categories of employee will continue to be the objects of different psychological strategies of regulation, depending on their position of power within the labour market and, more broadly, the society. A necessary component of predicting the future of work psychology is therefore to look for changes in the structure of the labour force and differences in status and treatment within it. The differentiation of core and peripheral workers will probably be the basis for different regulatory practices, based in the first case on self-regulation and in the second on a contractual relation in which the quality of output will be the focus of regulation. I discuss this in more detail later in the chapter. Strategies of regulation are modified in the context of different traditions of domination and resistance, and so they are constantly in flux and in need of revision. There will therefore continue to be a role for something – a class of agents and a cluster of discourses – to do the job that work psychology has done for eighty years. Whether it will be done by work psychology is much less sure.

This theoretical analysis informs my speculations about work and work psychology in the future. Many of the trends are international, or at least shared by Western societies. But where they are specific, I take the example of Britain, with which I am most familiar. The analytical principles can be applied to other specific locations by those who know their situations well.

In chapter 8 I discussed the modern form of human relations in 'organizational culture'. In section 2 I bring up to date my picture of work psychology in one country, Britain. I go on to look at the way the future of occupational psychology has been characterized by the BPS Working Party on the Future of the Psychological Sciences (BPS 1988). I then discuss the question of the boundary around work psychology in view of the recent professionalization of British psychology through the establishment of a register of chartered psychologists.

In section 3 I look at predictions about changing conditions at work, on the basis that these will affect regulation, which will in turn affect the issues that work psychology will address. Many predictions have emphasized the effect of computer technology, for example on the location of work. Some have taken a wider look at the structure of work organizations and changes in the relation between them and their workforce. I extrapolate from trends in a different area of applied psychology to predict the differences of technique that work psychology is likely to apply to different statuses of worker.

In section 4 I discuss the role of state intervention in directing work psychology to different issues from those defined by the employer. I discuss two historical examples, health and safety at work and equal opportunities, and also introduce a contemporary issue, sick building syndrome, which might engage work psychology in the future.

In section 5 I move from a British to a world perspective, concentrating on the relationship between Western forms of organization and management and the Third World and how these are mediated by work psychology and behavioural science management training more generally. In section 6 I consider the possibilities for alternative management practices and knowledge. Finally I discuss work psychology and organizational behaviour's part in the production of worker subjectivity; that is the extent to which they impinge, not just on management practices, not even just on workers' performance, but the self-experience of people in relation to their work and its effects on them.

2. UK Work Psychology in 1990

What does work psychology consist of today? What has happened to the various approaches that have emerged in and dominated the eighty years which I have documented? In the UK, over the last decade, many commercial consultancy businesses have been set up who employ occupational psychologists, or who call themselves occupational psychologists:

> The most conspicuous and profound change in the practice of occupational psychology in Britain in recent decades is the unprecedented growth of private, psychological consultancies . . . (I)n the last ten years the boom in management consultancy of all kinds has provided opportunities for occupational psychologists. Client demand for these consultancies is almost entirely from management and not from trade unions, nor from individuals, for whom the provision of specialised services is less than formerly. (Shimmin and Wallis 1989: 17)

What do these commercial consultancies provide? In most of the positions which require a psychologist, rather than say a behavioural scientist or management specialist, the central feature of the job is assessment. Individual assessment by means of tests is the jewel in the crown of work psychology. It occupies this place principally because it is the only area to which work psychology can lay special professional claim. There are some tests which only psychologists are allowed to administer and interpret. In the 1960s the British Psychological Society was involved in setting up standards for test usage (BPS 1960, 1965,

1969). In 1970 'the trend [was] toward a greater professionalism which can protect test constructors, test users and test takers' (Lancashire and Cohen 1970: 224). So individual assessment is the area that provides work psychology with something approaching an area of practice which is exclusive to it and protected by a professional boundary (see section 2). This boundary protects very few assessment practices, however. For example, most if not all of the array of techniques included in an assessment centre (see Hollway 1984a) could be applied by non-psychologists working in personnel departments. Work psychologists are expected to know about assessment centre design and to develop the assessment side of the work. Typically in the case of human resources consultancies, the target of psychological assessment is the selection and subsequent development of management, in particular senior management. Here no expense is spared to find and develop the right people, since a lot is perceived to depend on them. They are the ones who are expected to be totally committed to their job and organization. The most striking and significant difference between the industrial psychology of the twenties and thirties and work psychology in the UK today is not so much the methods (although they are more sophisticated), but the target, which has shifted from industrial workers to managers in all kinds of organization. Managers are the immediate target of regulation by work psychology.

There is a tension between the attempted precision and objectivity of work psychology in the assessment sphere and the prescriptions emanating from the recent popular management literature. Peters, for example, recommends that organizations 'spend time lavishly on recruiting' (one of the forty-five principles of his 1988 book) and emphasizes the primary importance of assessing a person's commitment to the organization, their motivation, love of change and potential to be a good 'team player'. He mentions the likely objection that these characteristics cannot be measured and asserts that if you try hard enough, they can. Work psychology (occupational in Britain, industrial or personnel psychology in the US) will certainly continue to contribute in this sphere, trying to discipline the informality of judgements that is condoned in the popular management literature.

The term 'climate survey' now commonly refers to that tradition which started off with surveys to measure employees' opinions or attitudes (see chapter 6, section 2) and was still going strong in the 1980s when AT&T was deregulated (see chapter 8). As long as large-scale organizations exist in which employees are not democratically represented in decision-making, the need will continue for ways of finding out their opinions.

Sales training has not had a high profile in work psychology, but its connections with interpersonal skills training are not difficult to see. Interpersonal skills training has been about how one person can influence another. With increasing competition and emphasis on marketing in manufacturing companies, the success of the sales force in creating a market, or increasing market share, is paramount. The ethos of international capitalism and consumerism means that sales people cannot be allowed to rely on the old combination of the quality of their product, the customer's perceived need for it, and personal contacts. Work psychologists are helping companies to train their sales people in sophisticated methods of pressure selling.

Performance-related pay became common at management level in Britain only in the 1980s, along with a government-led emphasis on accountability. In the United States it has a longer tradition and American organizational psychology has generated a massive literature on the relation between pay and performance. This work has largely fallen under the heading of motivation (hence my categorizing it under human relations), but the question originates in scientific management. The related area of performance management may be new in its designation, but draws on the long history that work psychology now has in devising strategies of regulating the performance of individuals in a variety of positions and organizations.

Counselling is often cited as one skill which psychologists can deploy in the service of employees, rather than on behalf of management. Its most prominent role in occupational psychology is in its integration into vocational guidance. I have described the emergence of counselling within the human relations tradition and shown how its methods became transformed into interpersonal skills training for supervisors and later managers (chapter 4 and 5). Counselling the mass of shop-floor workers was discontinued essentially because it was time-consuming and expensive, but it continues to feature in management training. Subsequently counselling skills became a part of vocational guidance. With the growth of counselling psychology, largely associated with the influence of Carl Rogers (1957, 1965),

> the client is no longer assigned the role of a subject passively assessed and advised, but that of an active partner learning to take full responsibility for the definition of his situation and for the development of realistic vocational plans. Since the interview is not now expected to serve as a once-for-all assessment, its opportunities for encouraging personal growth and mature decision-making can be freely utilized. (Lancashire and Cohen 1970: 224)

Counselling has, however, remained on the periphery of work psychology in the sense that it has usually taken place outside the workplace, in connection with schools and employment advice agencies. Within the workplace, counselling is a tool which may be used occasionally by personnel managers although their roles permit little time for this, and the old-style 'welfare officer' has not enjoyed the come-back that some predicted (Stewart 1983). In this area too, psychological attention is bestowed upon those senior people whose malfunctioning may cost the organization a lot of money and whose cost of replacement, and security of job tenure, make it appropriate to attempt to improve, rather than replace, the individual incumbent. When this kind of personal attention is required, counselling methods are seen to be highly appropriate, even though their success is uncertain. Stress counselling may be provided and counselling on alcohol dependency could be a massive growth area if the funds were provided within organizations. With the widespread decline of traditional areas of employment such as manufacturing industry, redundancy counselling was forecast to be a necessary new area in the early 1980s. Yet this service was never made widely available, presumably because funds for the benefit of those who were about to become ex-employees were not forthcoming. In espousing redundancy counselling, work psychology was, as usual, taking a structural problem and treating it at the level of the individual.

The main area of counselling that work psychologists undertake is as part of the personal development programmes for managers. 'Staff development' has been accepted for quite a long time as a desirable goal by employers and employees alike and it has been linked to appraisal systems in many organizations. Counselling techniques are often taught in the context of training appraisal interviewers. But it is mainly at middle and senior management level that individuals are provided with the luxury of considering their future careers with the help of an attentive counsellor. The growth of development counselling is fairly new in Britain and is associated with demographic trends which mean that middle and senior managers are going to be in short supply. Employers are not paying for development counselling for altruistic reasons. They want to know what will keep promising managers and senior managers in the company and what kinds of benefits, training and experience will both be compatible with the requirements of the company and will induce him (and occasionally her) to stay. Large companies in Britain are employing help from inhouse and external consultants on this question.[4] Given the history of counselling within human relations, which has had at best an ambivalent status within work psychology, these skills are as likely to come from outside work psychology as from within it.

The Future According to the BPS
The British Psychological Society (BPS), in its 1988 report by the Working Party on the Future of the Psychological Sciences, identifies a 'trilogy of traditional topics of occupational psychology' (1988: 25) as

having future importance: personnel selection, training and leadership. It also identifies several developing topics in occupational psychology: health at work, human–computer interaction, women and ethnic miniorities at work, new cognitive approaches and organizational change. Organizational change is maybe only 'developing' in terms of occupational psychology's interest in climbing late on to the bandwagon. It tends not to look for psychologists but behavioural scientists (which includes the former, but is a wider category). Human–computer interaction is attracting major research funding: 'As more and more offices, factories, hospitals, and small businesses are using micros, word processors and the like, the more important the relationship between the person and machine becomes, in terms of productivity, health, career development, and work roles' (BPS 1988: 26).

Health at work is re-emerging as a topic with 'the growing costs of health care for employees in most companies in terms of sickness absence, premature death, alcoholism, and other problems' (1988: 25). Occupational stress has led to this area of interest and continues to be important when it 'has been designated one of the top ten industrial diseases in the United States' (BPS 1988). I discuss this area further in section 4. Women and ethnic minorities at work are identified as areas needing systematic applied psychological research. In the case of ethnic minorities, the report says:

> There are grounds for concern stemming from the fact that few psychologists seem to have academic interest in such matters, and have tended to leave the research to other social science disciplines. It is important for the future of the psychological sciences that topics like this one become more important focal points of our interests, since they are and will continue to be mainstream occupational and societal problems. (BPS 1988: 26)

From the point of view of my analysis, the lack of interest by occupational psychologists in issues of race discrimination is unsurprising. Management, predictably, has demonstrated no interest either in paying for research, or commissioning consultancy on the subject. I discuss issues of equal opportunity and work psychology further in section 4.

Finally, the Working Party report cites development in cognitive theory, an area of theory which is dominant in psychology at the moment. The report suggests in an approving tone that cognitive theories specific to occupational psychology, for example derived from appraisal situations, are beginning to be produced. Since it is practice-led, theoretical development has been unusual in occupational psychology. Shimmin and Wallis 'are not convinced that any recent theoretical developments, even in applied psychological theory, have had any major impact on occupational psychology in practice' (1989: 19).

In summary, the BPS comes up with nothing new and demonstrates its inability to step outside the theoretical and methodological assumptions of work psychology in order to think itself into the future, let alone to generate anything fresh. The picture is of a core of psychological skills based on the measurement of individual differences, and peripheral skills which overlap with those of other specialists but are deemed to be psychological to the extent that they target the individual employee and have a history within organizational strategies of regulation. The trend is continuing towards the application of individually based strategies to higher-paid, higher-status, higher-qualified job occupants. With regard to these job occupants, the principle of self-regulation becomes the basis of work psychology's strategies.

The Boundary around Work Psychology

Work psychology has never had well-defined professional boundaries in the way that accountancy or medicine has. Its practitioners have been almost interchangeable with a range of others (depending on the area of intervention): management consultants, trainers, personnel specialists, business, or business administration graduates, behavioural scientists, engineers or sociologists. In the training of these, psychology has often provided an input.[5]

> The bulk of occupational psychology teaching now takes place outside mainstream psychology departments. As in the United States, it is in schools and departments of Business and Management in universities and polytechnics that the subject flourishes and 'student demand' for it is greatest. (Shimmin and Wallis 1989: 20)

In clinical or educational psychology, a career structure can be mapped out within a sector, and consequently professional barriers can be erected around specific categories of personnel. Work psychology has never been able to create such a niche for itself. In Britain, the closest it has come to such a position has been within a variety of central government ministries and agencies.[6]

This picture may be affected by recent moves to professionalize the practice of psychology in Britain. Supported by parliamentary legislation and by the majority of its membership, in 1989 the British Psychological Society introduced a register of chartered psychologists, the purpose of which is to be able to monitor and control the activities of those who practise as psychologists. Much of the debate on this decision has been about the protection of the public through this measure and, by distinguishing psychologists from charlatans, the protection of psychologists' reputation with the public. In the case of occupational psychology, the chartering of psychologists also raises the question of what sphere of practice is exclusive to psychologists. This question is usually posed in the context of worry about its survival without boundaries, for example: 'it is evident that occupational psychology has no clear boundaries. It could easily become absorbed or submerged within the amorphous subject of "management" or the emergent field of "organisational behaviour" ' (Shimmin and Wallis 1989: 20).

How might chartering strengthen the claims of psychologists to practise in certain specialist kinds of work? The most likely scenario is that psychologists will continue to claim expertise in the wider sphere of practices which target the individual at work. For example, in a 1986 discussion paper, the BPS Division of Occupational Psychology Training Committee concluded:

> The Policy of the Division and of its Training Committee is that Occupational Psychologists should be broadly trained so that they, rather than other people, decide whether a particular problem is best solved by organisational development, by selection or training or by redesign of a job or piece of equipment. Breadth of training is essential if Occupational Psychology is to remain an autonomous profession. (BPS 1986: 112–13)

Yet this breadth is what makes its boundary so unclear. If we practise in these areas as chartered psychologists, is there any difference between our services and those of non-psychologists? When I taught at Birkbeck College Department of Occupational Psychology, I introduced a discussion on work psychology for the BPS Conference on the Future of the Psychological Sciences with the following observation:

> We turn out students whose M.Scs are either Occupational Psychology or Organizational Behaviour, depending on whether they came to us with a psychology degree or a different degree. In principle there is no difference . . . except that occupational psychologists are allowed to call themselves registered occupational psychologists (with the required experience) and are allowed to train in the use of tests which it is illegal for an organizational behaviour graduate to use. In terms of the students' ability when they leave the course, these are spurious distinctions. (Hollway 1987: 4)

Will being chartered psychologists make us better practitioners than non-psychologists? What in our training might produce this? Underlying the idea of the well-trained chartered psychologist is the belief that training in scientific method and statistical analysis distinguishes the psychologist from the behavioural scientist or management consultant and makes him or her more rigorous and objective. While I sympathize with the wish to avoid the traps of popular management psychology, none the less, as should be clear from the foregoing chapters, this is a belief which I do not share and cannot support.

3. Changes in the Character of Work

The history of work psychology that I have charted in this book is conditioned by the history of technological changes at work, albeit mediated by varying strategies of regulation on the part of management. It is essential therefore, before I took further than the present, to survey changes and prognoses in the technology of work. Changes that affect the relation between management and the workforce transform work psychology, since it is within that relationship that work psychology has been produced. In this category, three interrelated predictions are common:[7]

> Computerized information processing could wipe out the jobs of many middle managers or change them so much as to make them unrecognizable. The distinction between blue-collar and white-collar workers is almost certain to narrow and perhaps disappear altogether. The giant manufacturing plants of today, with thousands of workers on a single site, will become museum-pieces. (Clutterbuck 1979: 17)

What will replace these fundamental forms of work organization?

New Technology and the Regulation of Work

Rosenbrock, a British professor of control engineering, has argued that industrial nations have reached a turning point regarding how interactive computing can be used in the design of work. He draws parallels between this and the point that was reached nearly a century ago when Fordist principles were established. He raises questions about the adverse effects of the division of labour then and asks whether there was a choice between designs that enhanced skills or eliminated them:

> Was there a similar choice of alternatives a hundred years ago in the role of the manual worker? Was an alternative technology possible in which machines would be used not to eliminate the skill of the workman, but to enhance it and make it more effective? We shall never know, because if that choice existed it was closed off by the path actually followed. (1977: 8–9)

According to Rosenbrock (writing in 1977), a similar choice exists since 'Over the next twenty years it seems certain that the whole technology of production will change beyond recognition' (1977: 7). He concludes optimistically: 'Perhaps it is open to us to guide this transformation towards a technology which does not seek to eliminate the skill of the workman: a technology which cooperates with his skill and interacts with it to make it more productive' (1977: 9).

Rosenbrock's emphasis is on the effects of new technology on skill. Historically we have seen the effect of deskilling on the question of regulation, but this would also be affected by the location of work. Supervision was a problem created by gathering workers together in large factories. Large organizations can decentralize many information-based jobs as a result of new technology. How is supervision accomplished in those jobs which are newly decentralized by means of work stations electronically connected to central computers?

In 1978 Hackman, an American professor of administrative science and psychology, was raising questions directly concerned with supervision, using what has been the dominant American approach, that is job satisfaction (see chapter 6). He applied it to the routes that might be taken in the 1980s:

> One route, which derives from the conclusion that many people are underutilized by the work they do, leads to increases in the level of challenge that is built into jobs and in the degree of control jobholders have in managing their own work. In effect, we would attempt to change jobs to make them better fits for the people who do them.
>
> The other route derives from the second conclusion; namely that people gradually adapt and adjust to almost any work situation, even one that initially seems to underutilize their talents greatly. This route leads to greater control of work procedures and closer monitoring of work outcomes by management to increase the productive efficiency of the workforce.
>
> Technological and motivational devices would be used to attempt to change the behavior of people to fit the demands of well-engineered jobs. The expectation is that in a carefully designed work environment employees will adjust to having little personal control of their work, and the efficiencies gained by using sophisticated managerial controls of work and workers will more than compensate for any temporary dissatisfactions the workers may experience. (Hackman 1978: 7–8)

Hackman predicted different outcomes based on these two scenarios. Route one would lead to employees experiencing, 'legitimately, that they are both responsible and accountable for their own work' (1978: 10); that motivation and satisfaction considerations would affect work design; that technologies would vary more, according to more complex variations in organizations. Organizations would have fewer hierarchical levels, fewer managerial and personnel jobs.

Route two would mean that:

> External controls are employed to ensure that individuals do, in fact, behave appropriately on the job. These include close and directive supervision, financial incentive schemes for correct performance, tasks that are engineered to minimize the possibility of human mistakes, and information and control systems that allow management to monitor the performance of the work system as closely and continuously as possible. And throughout, productivity and efficiency tend to dominate quality and service as the primary criteria for assessing organizational performance. (1978: 12)

It sounds like more of what we already have in non-professional, non-managerial and non-technical jobs, except that automated instrumentation and control greatly enhances managerial control of work. Moreover 'the gap between those who do the work and those who control it will grow' (Hackman 1978: 13).

Hackman concludes that the only remaining requirement will be 'devices to ensure that the person actually does what he or she is supposed to do'. He concedes that 'it is doubtful that employee motivation . . . can be created and maintained from intrinsic rewards', that is, he believes that self-regulation would not work under these conditions. The alternative is 'extrinsic rewards' and Hackman predicts that 'behavior modification programs will be among the standard motivational techniques used in work organizations in the 1980s' (1978: 13). He believes that 'we are moving with some vigor down Route Two', and predicts increases in employee 'craziness', including drug abuse, as a result of his scenario about the future of work (see also Handy 1979).

According to Hackman, companies would sponsor aid programmes to help employees adjust, including 'systematic "attitude development" to foster high job satisfaction and organizational commitment' (1978: 13). There seems to be a contradiction here. On the one hand, Hackman does not think that self-regulation will work under route two conditions, and on the other, he predicts attitude development programmes to foster job satisfaction and organizational commitment. It may be that companies will simply fail to learn from the first round of human relations experience and try to reinvent the wheel of self-regulation in alienating jobs. (I suggested in chapter 8 that this is what the fashion for organizational culture is doing, albeit armed with some sophisticated new techniques which owe more to PR and marketing.) Or it may be that Hackman and the companies whose behaviour he is predicting are failing to make that crucial distinction between managerial or professional jobs and the rest. This failure is systematic in work psychology, motivated perhaps by the desire to believe that self-regulation without structural change, and without genuine democracy at work, is possible and would finally solve conflict at work.

Internalized Commitment

I have suggested that, in its treatment of managers, work psychology will assume, and help to produce, internalized commitment or self-regulation. Powering the belief in motivating workers has been the evidence that large numbers of those who work – including all the researchers and consultants who comment on the subject – are self-regulated in their work. Indeed some are what is now popularly referred to as 'workaholic'. Yet as I have pointed out, work psycho-logists like Herzberg and Hackman are prone to generalize about motivation and job satisfaction in all employees because, although their paradigm has acknowledged differences in discretion and autonomy afforded by particular technologies and forms of supervision, it has skated over the fundamental differences between management and those who are managed. The rhetoric of organizational culture – leaders 'everywhere' and the breakdown of hierarchy – tends in the same direction. In the case of AT&T, however, the strategies chosen for employees at different levels in the hierarchy were quite distinct. The human relations rhetoric of no difference between managers and managed is paradoxical. On one hand, it is trying to produce no difference by suppressing those differences in its discourse. On the other, it is structural differences of control, responsibility and reward which are more powerful in determining difference than management psychology. This makes management psychology both inapplicable and at the same time seductive to apply.

None the less, the distinction between blue- and white-collar workers has been an object of organizational change attempts because of the perceived difference in self-regulation in these two groups. If blue-collar workers were treated like white-collar workers, so the argument goes, would they not identify more with the interests of the organization and not support trade unions so strongly? The Japanese experience is brought in to support this argument. Alternatively, one can argue that, although they do not have such long-standing traditions of organized opposition, when white-collar workers are subjected to deskilled jobs and disciplinary modes of regulation, they too are likely to engage in forms of resistance to organizational goals. The balance between blue- and white-collar jobs is changing for technological reasons as robots and other forms of automation take over manufacturing jobs and people monitor information in front of VDU screens. But the distinction between self-regulated and externally regulated workers will not disappear without fundamental changes in the organization and control of work.

Reference to the desirability of a 'classless' management style in Japanese organizations often suggests that a similar reduction in the trappings of hierarchy in British organizations would help to transcend the blue-collar culture which is traditionally opposed to management: 'we may be too concerned with power and authority and not enough with the main objectives of an organization' (Halley 1980: 12). The concern with symbolic authority is not limited to the factory floor. For example, McTierney, speaking on behalf of the British Bankers' Union, BIFU, commented on the inability of office workers to control their own environment because of 'authoritarian managements for whom a removed tie or jacket is tantamount to anarchy' (Nicholson-Lord 1990: 3). In contrast, or maybe in response, Peters routinely advocates that senior people take their jackets off before they wander around, and that they immediately get rid of their reserved parking spot. The reduction of symbols of hierarchy is intended to enhance the dignity of those lower in the hierarchy and to remove the obstacles (obstacles at the symbolic level) to their commitment to the organization. Yet ever since supervisory training began at Hawthorne the majority of managers have been rejecting such pleas, and work psychology does not know why. This position, coupled with the deskilling of office jobs through computer technology, looks set to produce a repetition of the history of individual psychology which was set in train by the technology of the assembly line and the emergence of management as a separate function. The fundamental principles governing management have not been re-examined by work and organizational psychology, however much it plays around with the symbols.

The Employment Organization and the Contractual Organization

I have argued that undifferentiated predictions about the future of work regulation are unlikely to be helpful and a distinction must be made between professional, managerial and technical jobs and the rest when predicting the application and success of self-regulation (or, as Hackman has it, fostering attitudes of high job satisfaction and organizational commitment). But there is an additional distinction in the way that organizations govern the relationship with their workforce which is essential when considering the decentralization of work and the future of regulation: a distinction between the employment organization and the contractual organization. According to Handy, 'the contractual organization in which as much as possible is contracted out to individuals or to autonomous groups is becoming more common' (1979: 25):

> Whether we like it or not (and there are many who don't), the contractual organization is with us, is growing and is likely to grow faster. We would be wise to wake up to that fact because the management of contractual organizations is different from, and in many ways more difficult than, the management of employment organizations. (Handy 1984: 81–2)

In contractual organizations 'the focus of control changes from input and process to the outputs that are contracted to it' (Handy 1979: 25). This represents a dramatic redefinition of the problem of supervision, a redefinition based on the organization bearing little or no responsibility for those working under contract but only for their product.

The rise of contracting organizations would have profound consequences for the regulatory functions of management. Except in times of labour scarcity, contracts increase competitiveness. The criterion of regulation will be what is produced, not how. 'How many' or 'how much' and 'how good' will be governed by the contract (and more widely by the production of consumer needs through advertising and marketing): how much do I need to produce this week to pay my bills?[8] But quantity and quality often conflict and quality is the crucial issue in what is produced. Quality is the question around which self-regulation could revolve and much depends on the type of product. For example in service industries, particularly in face-to-face service situations, quality of service depends upon performance where the social relation involved is not that which centres on supervision but on client service and sales. A work psychology of interpersonal skills is already intervening in this area. Thompson and McHugh make the point that 'emotion management' is a necessary feature of many service jobs (1990: 321–2). They quote Hochschild: 'It is not simply individuals who manage their feelings in order to do a job; whole organisations have entered the game. The emotion management that keeps the smile on Delta Airlines competes with the emotion management that keeps the same smile on United and TWA' (Hochschild 1983: 185–6).

The contractual organization will not entirely replace the employment organization: 'subcontract as they may, organizations will still be left with a core of employed persons – their career staff and labour' (Handy 1984: 25). So the same organization is usually both an employment and a contractual organization, differentiating its workforce into the two categories; the core being employed and the periphery contracted. The latter are 'casualized', deprived of job security and benefits such as insurance, sickness pay, paid maternity leave and pension. This distinction is already commonplace and has threatening implications for those with no special skills to sell in a context where full employment is unlikely to return in their lifetime.

Core and Peripheral Workers

The distinction between core workers and peripheral workers does not coincide with that between managers and professionals in contrast to the rest. Many professionals and managers may opt for 'self-employment' or freelance work, and their services to organizations can be contracted. It is fairly common for professionals to set up their own businesses, often without the blessing of their previous employers. Handy documents a trend whereby, in order to reduce central staff costs and related overheads, large employers are systematically encouraging professional, managerial and technical staff to set up satellite businesses, whose services they then contract (Handy 1984: ch. 4). The increased profitability of this arrangement for the original enterprise more than compensates for the initial financial support provided for the satellites (Handy 1984: 77). These staff are in a different position from the office cleaners, hotel workers, porters, home workers and the like who have little bargaining power or job security. It is largely the latter type of job which is being casualized in increasing numbers. Given these trends, the distinction between core and periphery is an important analytical tool for predicting the future, not only of work, but of work psychology. How will it reflect this distinction?

I came across a striking example of applied psychology's ability to deal separately with socially differentiated groups when I was conducting some research on applied psychology in Zimbabwe two years after independence in 1982. I discuss it here because I believe it offers a suggestive parallel for the situation work psychology is facing in relation to core and peripheral workers. Educational psychological services in Rhodesia, like all services, were segregated along racial lines. The white population was provided with resources which were modelled on those available to wealthy Britons at home. Educational psychological services were individualized to provide help for white children to compete successfully in their educational attainment. This involved individual profiling through the use of tests, individualized remedial help and vocational guidance. Ninety per cent of the education budget went into educational provision for the 5 per cent of the population who were white.

It was only when Rhodesia faced a shortage of skilled labour that Africans were admitted into education. By the 1970s, many African children had access to a rudimentary primary education, but only 15 per cent were selected for secondary school. The selection of these Africans posed a problem which required the use of mass methods on this large and unknown population. Consequently a different psychological service was set up to test Africans. A standard British intelligence test was modified, new norms were produced and the psychologist responsible prided herself on doing an objective, and therefore fair, selection job.

The different theoretical principles which have informed these two approaches in applied psychology have sometimes been called the ideographic and nomothetic approaches; the first based on the specificity of the single individual and the second based on differences within a large population, in which individuals are only of interest to the extent that an administrative problem has to be solved by placing them in one category or another. In the case of an apartheid educational system, the wider political purposes served by these two different applications of psychometric psychology are starkly evident.

Applied to the work psychology parallel, the Rhodesian example suggests that individualized adaptations of psychometric assessment will be applied to valued members of the core workforce, whose present and future performance will affect the organization. According to Handy, senior managers would retain a coordinating function in the new contracting organizations, but their numbers would decrease. Their recruitment, development and retention will involve a similar array of assessment and development as that used already for senior managers: profiling through tests, counselling, interviews, group activities and so on. The non-professional, non-managerial, non-technical periphery will be treated as a mass, since their individuality is not of interest to the contracting organization. If skilled work is required, ability can be measured by the mass application of standardized tests of performance similar to those that industrial psychology has developed since the 1920s. As is already the case, unskilled workers with no job security will merit no psychological intervention at all.

The funding, interest and status would reside in practices whose object was individual managers. The predominant discourses of work psychology would tend even further in this direction than at present. Funding, knowledge and visibility go together to a great extent, and increasingly so in a climate where higher education funding depends on organizational sponsorship.

It is probable that new small businesses of the entrepreneurial type will buy in many specialist services on a consultancy basis which might have been provided inhouse in a large organization. The technical skills associated with the psychometric assessment of a new business colleague in a small firm do not differ in kind from those which have been developed in the context of large employment organizations.

How will the suitability of self-employed professional workers be assessed? The contracting organization will not be interested in investing as previously in their selection, appraisal and development because they are not tied to them as in an employing organization. The mechanism will be much closer to one where freelance individuals or small firms are hired on the basis of their past performance (mediated by their reputation). The contracting organization will develop techniques of quality assessment (likely to be outside the province of work psychology) and the small enterprise whose product is quality tested will have to take responsibility for quality control, including where this impinges on the regulation of the workforce.

Management training will pose work and organizational psychology with a new set of emphases. For psychology management training has centred on the problem of providing managers with the interpersonal skills to inspire loyalty and commitment in their subordinates in the context of large, hierarchical and often impersonal organizations. At the core, with far fewer workers given the status of employees, it is likely that their minority position will appear privileged and engender self-regulated work performance in line with organizational values. The concerns of popular management texts like Peters' increasingly reflect the needs of these organizations, particularly when they are high-tech and do not involve unskilled labour. That part of their operation, for example the assembly of electronic components, is probably farmed out to Singapore or some equivalent location. For those working for a fee, the same issues would largely be taken care of by contractual means. Those managers who remained at the core would be required to control the quality of output, communicate with peers, plan strategy and make decisions. The last twenty years already suggests a shift in this direction in management training, but there is still a long way to go:

> The textbooks of management are all about employment organizations: how to organize, motivate, lead and control the people whose time you have bought. They have little to say about the management of organizations in which you can control *what* people do but not *how* they do it. (Handy 1984: 82)

Engaged as it has been inside the managerial point of view, work psychology has not had the distance or independence to comment critically. Its role has been limited to changing managers' styles, so that some of the unwanted effects of their roles might be mitigated. This history does not put work psychology and organizational behaviour in a strong position to perceive the effects on management's role of a widespread change to a contractual form of work. How will the quality of service be assessed and how will its assessment be part of the contractual relationship? Put another way, how will the contractual relationship perform regulatory functions to parallel those developed by employing organizations?

In summary, I have argued that, from scientific management to human relations management, there was a partial shift from discipline to self-regulation in which work psychology was involved. It was paralleled by a shift in the object of work psychology from shop-floor workers to managers. Self-regulation constitutes what I have called a 'deep target', that is it aims to engage something that comes closer to what I call subjectivity; an identification with the goals of the organization which would render supervision obsolete. The attempt has not been a success with blue-collar workers (for a British case, see Nichols 1975) and it is probable that in some sectors the attempt has been virtually abandoned in favour of the new forms of work I discussed earlier. The application of human relations techniques to managers has not suffered the same problems. Not surprisingly, managers themselves are positioned less ambiguously by management discourses and identify more closely with them. None the less, human relations techniques have had a poor record in changing managers' behaviour.

If the contractual relationship does not point in the direction of 'deep target' work psychology discourses, surely it will still require self-regulation through the contract, in the sense that the contracting organization would still have a considerable interest in that self-regulation and seek to exercise it. There is an apparent contradiction in this statement, but one which seems to suit the 1990s quite well: 'You, the individual, are entirely responsible for yourself; expect nothing either from the state or from those for whom you work. You are free to choose, but only within the constraints of the contract market. Fail to regulate yourself at your peril; in a situation of plentiful and cheap labour, we need not protect you.' This could be applied to unskilled, replaceable, 'casualized' contract labour, but would break down in a situation of skill shortage, where those in possession of valuable skills would have the bargaining power to extract concessions from organizations, without being dependent upon one organization.

For contracted workers, perhaps market forces are going to replace those 'deep target' parts of work psychology's activities, such as development counselling and appraisal, which are to do with subjective ties to a work organization. In such a climate, psychometric techniques could emerge as even more dominant to respond to contracting organizations' attempts to control the quality of the product. If work psychology wants to have a role which goes beyond what it does at present in a contracted sphere, its history suggests that it will hone its activities to the regulative needs of new forms of organization and new principles of relation with its workforce.

4. Back to Worker Protection?

So far I have implied that work psychology's activities will be closely determined by the interests of the work organization, be it as employing or contracting organization. This was particularly the case for the private sector in the 1980s as a result of British government policy of 'rolling back' the state, that is of reducing state intervention in this sector in order to encourage 'market forces'. The same government has, however, actively interfered in the affairs of the public sector. It has forced many public sector employing organizations to become contracting organizations, notably local authority and hospital services, in order to cut costs, thereby transferring large numbers of employees from public to private sector. The resultant (and questionable in many cases) 'improved efficiency' has partly been achieved at the expense of the pay and other benefits which workers received as public sector employees. There are also certain areas which the government has not yet succeeded in devolving on to the private sector, for example employment training.

As more people fall outside the provision hitherto extended by employing organizations, it may be that governments are obliged to change direction and take more responsibility for setting minimum standards which apply to fee as well as wage employment. The principle of the minimum wage and its regulation by the Wages Council has been abandoned and the least organized, least powerful workers are possibly less protected than at any time this century. There are probably half a million home workers in Britain and many are not registered with councils by those who employ them. They are mainly women with family commitments involved in undervalued, traditionally women's skills such as sewing and knitting. Even relatively well-paid workers receive no sick pay or holiday pay. The magazine *Outworkers' Own* documented the case, in 1981, of 'a firm in London paying Leicester outworkers £5 for the seventy-two hours it takes to knit an Arran jumper' (quoted in Handy 1984: 127).

Work psychology has mainly been involved in regulation of workers on behalf of employers. Who, if anyone, regulates employers? In the nineteenth century when extreme exploitation of workers was still rife (see chaper 3, note 5) government was forced to intervene in the affairs of private sector employers. It still occupied that role in the early twentieth century when industrial psychology entered the scene. As I have shown in chapter 3, early human factors work emerged within that tradition of government regulation of industry. In 1990, the government's principle of non-intervention, coupled with high unemployment and a significant collapse of trade union power, has led to the point where there is serious disquiet about pay and conditions at work. Coupled with the movement towards new and less protected forms of work such as contracting and remuneration through fees rather than wages, active resistance and public disquiet might lead to a new wave of government intervention. In this case, work psychology might have the opportunity to broaden its base to include the implementation and supervision of government-initiated regulation of employing and contracting organizations.

Occupational psychologists were involved in health and safety at work issues in the wake of successive legislation, particularly in the 1960s. The prospect of active government intervention meant that employers were moved to initiate the necessary changes, sometimes preceded by work psychologists' research, to protect workers' health and safety. This strand of research continued in the Quality of Working Life movement, but was lost from view in the political climate of the 1980s. It suggests the importance of a close link between legislation, active monitoring and the scope for work psychology.

Equal Opportunities

Such links are demonstrated by the intervention of work psychology into equal opportunities issues following the legislation of 1974 and 1975. At that time, equal opportunities was heralded as a potential new field for occupational psychology (Pearn 1976; Goodman and Novarra 1977; Wallis 1981). Some training and consultancy work in the field was conducted before the interest faded. Now there is little activity within occupational psychology and the area is dominated by a legal perspective (for example see the *Equal Opportunities Review*). Work psychologists were reliant on employers taking the new legislation seriously and this depended in most instances not on whether employers agreed with equal opportunities principles (most denied that there was a problem), but whether the law would oblige them to change their practices.[9] The record of successful cases brought against employers was, and still is, dismal (Snell 1979; Atkins 1986), and most employers soon settled back into the stae of complacency which did not require the services of the (few) occupational psychologists who could give advice about equal opportunities legislation and how to comply with it.

Where occupational psychology has been involved, it has been largely in encouraging the use of psychometric tests for selection, based on the argument that this is an objective method of assessment, not subject to stereotyped judgements based on race or sex.[10] I have already pointed out with regard to occupational psychology's boundaries that its contributions have usually been incorporated into wider personnel or training practice. This has also been the case with equal opportunities in the UK, where the use of psychometric measurement became a small, contested and sometimes negligible, part of equal opportunities practice. In some local authorities, especially Labour-controlled urban authorities, a considerable amount of experience of equal opportunities policy and practice has been gained over the fifteen years since legislation was introduced. Equal opportunities practice centres on the following: devising precise job and person specifications against which applicants can be assessed consistently; training selection interviewers in fair and consistent questioning, for example not to raise questions which concern women's domestic responsibilities, or use such criteria in their judgements; making selectors aware of criteria which would lead to indirect discrimination, such as specifying age limits which would rule out the eligibility of women who have taken time off from work to bring up children; setting out procedures which help to ensure equal access to training and promotion for those from discriminated-against groups; developing policy on sexual and racial harassment and working out ways to implement it successfully and providing awareness training on sexism and racism. Work psychology has been able to contribute its specialism in psychometric assessment and some expertise in interviewing method derived largely from the social psychology of interpersonal skills which, however, has never been race or gender sensitive.

By using the methods of psychometrics, work psychology compares individuals with others (and potentially social groups with each other; see chapter 4, note 3) and is blind to the organizational conditions and wider environment which produce and reproduce discrimination at work. Psychometrics measures the problem individual (the woman, disabled or black person) against the norm (the male, white norm which was also originally built into psychometric tests; see Hollway 1984a). It has a tendency therefore to blame the victim. Equal opportunities more generally has focused on changing management and personnel practice in order to ensure equal opportunities, yet organizational behaviour has made virtually no contribution.

Given its present, dependent position on work organizations themselves, work psychology needs convincing government intervention that will impose responsibilities on work organizations, which work psychologists (and others) can then help to implement. In the US, although government intervention into private organizations is minimal, legislation obliging organizations to follow non-discriminatory recruitment practices was strong. Under Reagan and since, there has been a reaction against equal opportunities legislation and the restrictions on management that it was experienced as imposing. While popular management thought never embraced the goal of equal opportunities, nor the regulation that that required, it seems that the current popular management emphasis is advocating a kind of informality of management which would probably be antithetical to state regulation of equal opportunities. 'Bureaucracy bashing' (one of Peters' (1988) prescriptions) is advocated because bureaucracy is equated with rigidity and slow decision-making. Other characteristics of bureaucratic organization are also reviled, for example the sending of memos. This is to do with the advocacy of direct communication, as in Peters' MBWA (Managing By Wandering Around). Peters appears to advocate in all seriousness that memos should be entirely replaced by phone calls and face-to-face communications. These and other similar strictures amount to his advocating an organization based almost entirely on informal communications. The absence of a formal record means that action cannot be judged by reference to it. Government regulation cannot function in such a climate.

Work psychology needs to provide an analysis of gender and ethnic relations in organizations which can support change. Enlisting the support of women and black people already present in the organization has not been a central strategy in equal opportunities practices and even this formulation retains a managerial perspective. An example is provided by my own experience as a woman employed in the university sector, which in Britain has recently come to attention for its worsening record in the recruitment of women to academic posts (Hansard Society 1990). I can approach the subject from the point of view of people organizing within their own organization to change its practices. From this point of view I find it inappropriate to separate the narrower issues of equal opportunities policies and their implementation from the wider issues of gender differences and power relations in organizations. What I need from a psychological theory is an understanding of how these forces construct people's identities, actions and relations at work. In such a theory there could no longer be any distinction between work psychology and organizational behaviour.

I have adopted a fairly technocratic approach to equal opportunities in the recruitment of new academic staff. I have influenced the selection process at departmental level to formalize it, to try to ensure standard treatment of all candidates. I have developed a form so that judgements on candidates can be recorded according to specified job criteria, differentiated into necessary and desirable. These interventions have been accepted, and the procedures might be a little bit fairer as a result. However, I cannot help feeling sceptical about the possibility of disciplining the social judgement processes which inevitably have to be used in selection. Work psychology's attempts to influence recruitment have been based entirely on the premiss that there is such a thing as 'objective' judgement, and that a system can therefore be devised that neutrally identifies the candidate with characteristics which best fit the requirements of the job. This is a fiction. Unique qualities cannot be calibrated in this fashion. At best a standard system works more fairly because it goes in tandem with selectors who actively support equal opportunities principles. Easier said than done. These qualifications certainly suggest that wider issues of social differences in organizations, and their articulation through the dynamic, continuous and productive power relations of organizational life, must be addressed by work psychology in order to underpin attempts to change organizations. I feel that my approach was hampered, and probably rendered too technocratic, by the lack of a gender analysis of organizations, a lack which is integrated into the history of equal opportunities practices. From my own experience, the following considerations seem to be relevant.

Along with my few women colleagues, I was also raising issues which ranged from trying to change the use of sexist language in departmental documents and teaching materials, to introducing gender issues into the curriculum and starting a monthly women's lunch for all women staff. The extent to which such initiatives have a positive effect depends crucially on the good relations which can be developed with colleagues, especially including those in influential positions like chairs of committees. Different methods of influence are inseparable in practice. So, for example, I used my influence as a human resources and equal opportunities 'expert' amongst colleagues who are mainly economists. I made sure that, during the first few months of my new employment, I talked to all my (thirty plus) colleagues, so that there was no one I could not easily talk to informally. If I had not done this, their latent assumptions about feminists would probably have made their acceptance of me into decision-making on equal opportunities an impossibility.

In an organization where democratic decision-making structures operate it is necessary to be active, visible, known and have one's ideas respected, in order to be supported for election to committees, or simply to be listened to at meetings of the whole department. To do this on women's issues amongst a majority of men who consider them to be at best irrelevant and at worst dangerous to their interests, is complicated. There is a danger of having one's ideas marginalized, almost by definition. In practice, power can be exercised through groups and alliances. Other events can be drawn upon, such as the fact that an external consultant was commissioned to write a report on equal opportunities, the changing financial support for women's issues in development studies and the drive to recruit mature, notably women, students. These are some of the forces within the university which can be used in support of changing the organization and which testify to the fact that, like any organization, it is not a monolith, but a multiplicity of interests with some core purposes in common.

My gender (and this also applies to the gender or race of an applicant for a job) is not synonymous with me as an individual. It is only one feature in a complex of relational forces and can exacerbate or countervail others. It is not automatically positive or negative in a given relation, though it is never absent from relations. Any success that I have in changing my own organization is the compound product of many forces involved in power relations. In my case these are: relative hierarchical positions; length of employment; academic status, which includes the title of 'doctor'; external funding support; area of specialization in relation to the definition of the department and its history; gender, race, class and age; informal networks; visibility; reliability. None of these works in a set way and the weight of a given factor will vary considerably depending on the organization. The particular mix is always unique, and it is always mediated by others' reactions in a circular way. In summary, in the case of a professional job such as I have illustrated, working towards equal opportunities has to be understood in terms of informal as well as formal organization in which gender (or race) is but one factor in a multiplicity of forces which produce power and influence in the organization.

Sick Building Syndrome (SBS) and Stress
A problem with new potential for work psychology is only just beginning to emerge in Britain:

> Sick Building Syndrome was largely unidentified until 1980, but now four-fifths of office workers complain of it. Symptoms vary and are not easily diagnosed but include stuffy noses, dry throat, eye trouble, headaches, rashes and lethargy. Some employers blame malingerers, which is easier than blaming buildings, but the UN recognises the disease and researchers say that they have hardly begun to uncover the problem. (Nicholson-Lord 1990: 3)

Under what conditions might this become the flagship of work psychology, rather as 'fatigue' did during the First World War? Most of today's captains of industry have not got where they are by having the welfarist views of a Seebohm Rowntree (see chapter 3) and, short of a full-scale war whose efforts depended upon the productivity of office workers, the present government is unlikely to intervene with legislation against sick buildings or even support for an overstretched Health and Safety Inspectorate. Employers will be tempted to continue to 'blame malingerers', and so it is unlikely that funds will be forthcoming for research into SBS, except in small amounts from affected trade unions. And what about the conditions within work psychology? Would someone with Myers' commitment to a psycho-physiological paradigm have the theoretical tools to work in a multi-disciplinary team to understand and suggest remedies for the causes of SBS? Or has the initiative passed to ecologists, occupational health specialists and chemists (these last to try to understand the interactions produced by up to 400 chemicals in the office microclimate)? Shimmin suggests that the NIIP failed because it was too generalist in a climate where psychologists were becoming increasingly specialized (personal communication). What specialisms would serve this problem?

In fact it is from the perspective of stress that comment on SBS has been forthcoming. Stress was one of the most buoyant areas of work psychology during the 1980s and it is an area which has its origins partly in the psycho-physiological traditions of the human factors school. Cooper uses a 'total stress approach' to individuals' experience at work. He comments 'If people are showing symptoms [of SBS], I tell them to leave the building, get away from the lights, go out for twenty minutes, breathe some fresh air' (Nicholson-Lord 1990: 5). But Cooper's advice does not change any conditions, and it assumes that employees have control over their work. In the same article, a representative of a bankers' union says:

> The lower down the ladder you are, the less control you have over your work environment. Managers can stretch their legs. Clerical workers, if they are working in a data-processing centre, for example – doing entries for cheques or credit cards – are disciplined if they don't complete a given number of key strokes in an hour or a day. Half the time they don't know what they are doing. They don't see any end product. More and more clerical work has been degraded. It's hardly surprising if they keep on getting headaches. The way work is structured they would be less than human if they didn't. (Nicholson-Lord 1990: 4–5)

SBS could be the 1990s symptom of the wider ills associated with the character of work in contemporary Western societies. History suggests that work psychology has been engaged in an employers' compromise between taking no action and initiating structural change; a compromise which generates some treatment of symptoms, rather than addressing causes. For this purpose, psychology has usually been able to step in with solutions, which in this case are likely to be stress control packages.

Stress has been seen as a costly problem in many organizations for nearly a decade now.[11] Thompson and McHugh quote McKenna (1987: 403) who says 'Companies have a major stake in promoting a healthier life-style for employees, because of the potential benefits in reduced insurance costs, decreased absenteeism, improved productivity and better morale.' Psychology has provided theories purporting to predict whether individuals are stress prone, thus offering a potentially useful technique in recruitment or monitoring of employees. It has also offered stress control techniques for employees, which operate at a psychological and physiological level. By depending on levels of analysis that target the individual, even those researchers who perceive the cause of stress problems to lie in the conditions of the organization find it difficult to incorporate this into their analysis and even more difficult to address those conditions in their interventions. Psychological interventions have been popular, not least because they leave structural conditions unchallenged. But can stress control techniques at the level of the individual improve the problem sufficiently to be effective, for example in reducing absenteeism? If causes are ignored, psychology can probably only effect minor, peripheral improvements. Thompson and McHugh comment:

> The role of the organization in producing unhealthy systems and conditions of work is in danger of being ignored. In its place we get systems reinforcing the *self-attribution* of stress and anxiety as personal problems to be coped with, rather than structural issues to be contested. (1990: 324)

People tend to judge psychology in terms of how successful it is in alleviating the problem. When measured according to these same cost criteria, we are likely to find that the achievements are not dramatic. However, as Thompson and McHugh rightly suggest, psychology's main achievement lies elsewhere; in the production of knowledge which attributes responsibility for stress to the individual, rather than the organization. To the extent that individual employees are successfully positioned by such discourses, psychology is playing a powerful role in the production of subjectivity. In my view this is one of psychology's most important – and systematic – effects.

The limitations of an individual target from a management point of view are acknowledged from time to time by work psychologists. For example, Broadbent, prominent in the engineering psychology tradition, suggested two main reasons why occupational psychology and human factors have not made the impact which was hoped:

> First, we engineering psychologists took too limited a scope and did not think about jobs rather than individual displays and controls. Second, social needs have changed; it is the impact of the job on life that is now the big problem, not the efficiency of the worker. (Broadbent 1980, quoted in Shimmin and Wallis 1989: 19)[12]

Its history has certainly not prepared work psychology for the shift that Broadbent suggests is desirable. In 1913 Munsterberg articulated its purpose as 'how we can produce most completely the influences on human minds which are desired in the interest of business' (1913: 24). If, as Broadbent suggests, this is no longer 'the big problem', maybe there should be no future for work psychology as we know it.

5. A World Perspective

As the world's economics become more international and interdependent, there is pressure to reduce the cost of employment in industrialized countries to compete with the Newly Industrializing Countries (NICs) which provide cheap labour.[13] There is therefore a tie-up between the move from core to peripheral workers in Britain and the meaning of core and periphery in the international economics sense: moving jobs to the periphery, to Third World countries where labour is cheap and plentiful. If jobs remain in Britain, their cost to the firms concerned is reduced by casualizing the labour force. In non-industrialized countries the history of changes in modes of work regulation which I have documented has not occurred. Questions of self-regulation are on the agenda because of Western organizational forms and not because of indigenous historical conditions. If work psychology is to understand its applicability in this international setting, it will need to transform its outlook and pay attention to both historical differences and international economic relations between North and South ('developed' and 'developing' countries). Handy makes a similar point in arguing that 'some of our fundamental assumptions about the organization of work have feet of clay' (1979: 24). He gives the example of a lecture tour in India on his book about management of organizations: 'Gradually, as I travelled the land, I began to realise that all our assumptions about organisation were based on the belief that labour was a scarce resource and capital a plentiful one. In India the situation was reversed. My book was worthless' (Handy 1979: 24).

Universal Management Practice?

It is not only manufacturing and assembly jobs which are being transferred to the countries of the South. Organizations which are the product of centuries of development in bureaucratic and industrial forms are relatively new in the Third World, and even newer is their control by indigenous rather than expatriate personnel. In Western-style industries in sub-Saharan Africa, for example, supervisors, managers and human resource specialists are more preoccupied with timekeeping and absenteeism. The time discipline of British workers began to emerge almost 400 years ago (Thompson 1967: 80). In the early days of the British industrial revolution, labour rhythms were still irregular, depending upon whether enough money had been earned to cover necessary outgoings. Indeed keeping wages low was seen as a necessary 'preventative against idleness and it would seem to be not until the second half of the eighteenth century that "normal" capitalist wage incentives begin to become widely effective' (Thompson 1967: 81). In Rhodesia (now Zimbabwe), it was not until the late 1920s that 'a Hut Tax was imposed on the African population so that they were forced into wage labour in order to pay' (Hollway 1986: 85).

World Bank reports (for example 1989) have for some time been saying that underdeveloped human resources are one of the most critical problems of the last twenty years and they do not appear from these reports to be improving. The World Bank and many aid agencies are still putting a vast amount of funding into the development of human resources in the Third World.

Management training has been seen as a priority. For example in 1989 a grouping of aid agencies combined to launch an ambitious programme of management development in sub-Saharan Africa. In the past, management training has been a predominantly white, expatriate affair. Now indigenous management training institutes exist throughout sub-Saharan Africa and these provide the trainers, researchers and consultants for the programme. Yet, despite a nascent literature on African management,[14] there is no alternative approach to management available. Certainly management practices developed their distinct colonial character in pre-independence history, but there were no formalized discourses which were distinct from Western ones.

African managers are faced with a set of conditions, many of which are extremely difficult to operate within. Unfavourable terms of trade with the West contribute to the lack of resources for their own parastatal organizations and diminish control over the actions of multinationals (George 1989). Sub-Saharan African countries were obliged, during the 1980s, to accept the structural adjustment conditions of the World Bank and International Monetary Fund in order to secure loans.[15] As well as cutting health and social services dramatically, the loans have also resulted in holding down public sector pay to the point where employees are obliged to engage in several informal sector activities in order to sustain themselves and their families. Conditions for managers also include operating within a form of organization that is not home-grown, and that has a history of white domination over black workers which resembles the feudal type of domination based on the body which was characteristic of pre-eighteenth-century Europe. Despite policies of indigenization of management and black advancement after independence, and despite funding of training for nationals (which at senior levels takes place largely in the West), employment of expatriates was actually on the increase in Eastern and Southern Africa at the beginning of the 1980s (Hollway 1986: 92).

These are differences in conditions far greater than those which produced the quite distinct differences between British and American work psychology which have been evident in the previous chapters. In this situation, what has work psychology offered countries with such a different history of organization, industrialization and work regulation? Predictably, Western work psychology and the behavioural side of management studies have exported their preoccupations as if they were the most up-to-date universal truths established by science (which is how most Western practitioners see them). When I was in Zimbabwe, management trainers were using human relations assumptions centred on the problematic of motivation and democratic leadership, while work relations were still under the influence of colonial relations between white management and black workforce (Hollway 1986: 86ff.).

There is no off-the-shelf answer to Western assumptions in management training in the countries of the South. I have been funded by the British Overseas Development Administration to develop and run a training programme for women in management positions in the East African civil services as well as to do some research (Hollway and

Mukurasi 1990). My approach is to associate the programme as closely as possible with the women's situations at work, through pre- and post-training visits, detailed prior research, the construction of case material from their organizations and the use of methods which work from the participants' experience towards general principles and back to skills, rather than starting with (inevitably Western) management principles. I am helped in this systematic attempt to sidestep Western assumptions by the fact that the training also aims to integrate a gender analysis throughout (Hollway and Mukurasi in preparation; Hollway in preparation).

Western management principles don't exist 'out there' as a recognizable choice that one can accept or reject. Not only is my whole work experience saturated with them, but there are no prominent or systematic competing discourses. This is to some extent true for participants, despite the fact that their positions differ from those assumed by the dominant management discourse in several ways: they are from Third World countries, they work in the public sector and they are women. There will be aspects of their experience and practice which are not consistent with dominant Western management discourses. Yet, at the same time, through their training and organizational life, in an administrative system which was modelled on that of the British civil service, they too are positioned according to Western management discourse and practice and are likely to have accepted the dominant assumption of development that Western forms are superior and desirable. It is necessary to identify such contradictions and to work with them.

For myself and for the trainees, therefore, it is useful to have access to a critical historical account of the conditions which have produced work psychology and the behavioural science side of management training. Are these conditions paralleled in their organizations? If not, what do the differences indicate for workplace regulation? A deconstruction of the dominant discourse is necessary in building alternative discourse and practice. I hope that this book will provide access to these questions for other work psychologists, behavioural scientists, management consultants and trainers who work outside the range of their historical applicability, whether this is in the North or South.

In the 1990s this will not only include the Third World, but most of the Second World too. There, starting either after the Russian revolution in 1917, or after the carve-up of Europe in 1945, industrial and management history diverged from that of the First World. In the few months between the collapse of the Communist regimes of Eastern Europe and the writing of this chapter, debate in Western countries has been dominated by the assumption that Eastern Europe needs to adopt wholesale the economic and organizational forms of Western capitalism and government administration. Western government funds are being poured in to promote these ends,[16] and management training is already a popular form of intervention. The people of Eastern Europe have the right to expect from Western management consultants and trainers, and from work psychologists, an understanding of the specific conditions in Western history which produced their principles and practices. Instead, they are likely to be subjected to the ignorant vanity of a position which maintains that Western-style social relations at work, and the strategies for their management, are based on the most up-to-date and scientific knowledge about universal work behaviour. This book is an attempt to demonstrate, through detailed historical evidence, that this is not the case. I hope I have shown, rather, that the history of work psychology and related behavioural knowledge has been produced within interrelated and changing economic, technical, political, sociocultural and intellectual conditions which are specific to Western countries, and which differ between them as in the case of Britain and the United States.

I have argued that work psychology has been produced as a technology out of practical managerial need and the outcome is a non-theoretical, non-reflective discipline whose concepts have been created out of what works without asking why. If work psychology is to play a legitimate role in supporting regulation at work it must not only stay around for long enough to find out what works (which commercial consultants often do not do, especially overseas), but also it must have the analytical capacity, based on theory, which can answer the question why. Neither of these conditions will be met by commercially driven work psychology, whether this is based in consultancy firms or institutions of higher education.

6. Chances for Improvement?

My conclusions may err on the side of pessimism and I find it difficult to decide whether this is a consistent product of my analysis and, if so, whether the analytical tools are realistic. My analysis might be a product of attempting to redress the balance of the voluntarism of work psychology and of its refusal to look at the effects of power and practice on its knowledge production. None the less, it is important to look for countervailing forces. After all, according to the analysis I am using, power is not monolithic. If it consists of contradictory, colliding, *productive* forces, there must be spaces for people like me to occupy which pull in a different political direction and which exert different influences, however limited. As an academic, my primary arena is the discursive level. This book is itself an intervention. It contributes to the multiple relations of power–knowledge–practice.

The examples in this book have demonstrated that the role of knowledge is not marginal and it is not simply an effect of organizational practice which then 'acts back' on organizations in a unidimensional and politically uncomplicated way.

There is a resurgence of critical interest in work and organizations in British (and possibly American) social science, even as the fashion for organizational culture continues unabated. The conditions for this possibility seem to lie in a combination of two major factors. The first is the availability of critical perspectives which can be applied to organizational analysis by those, largely in higher education, still sufficiently independent of managerialist priorities. The second is a wider perception of the paucity of available knowledge in organizational behaviour and work psychology, yet the need for increasing sophistication of this understanding in the rapidly changing world of organizations. The first condition, many would say, is under threat,[17] and is already more undermined in American higher education as a result of the closer financial ties between business and higher education. But Western universities were built on a tradition of the independence of academic knowledge production, and there is still some space for it. The second condition ensures that alternative approaches to organizational behaviour do not just exist at the theoretical level. Organizations are not homogeneous in their requirements. There are profound differences across the range of organizations and even a variety of contradictory needs within a single organization. Paradoxically, the more managerial organizational behaviour becomes as a discipline, and the more it is limited to psychological perspectives, the more incapable it is of providing an analysis of behaviour in work organizations which can act as a reliable underpinning of practice. As I discussed above (section 4), work on stress provides an example.

Many public sector organizations in Britain, such as local government, health authorities and universities, are under heavy pressure to change their management practices in the directions of private sector priorities of efficiency, cost-saving and competition, at the expense of client service and employee welfare. Business managers from the private sector are being recruited to implement these moves. At the same time, however, people remain who have experience of, and commitment to, other priorities. If there is resistance at the level of employees in organizations, or indeed at management and senior management levels, it needs intellectual support if it is not to ossify into old patterns.

Thompson and McHugh argue that alternative management practices, and the knowledges that support them, were trapped, until recently, in a defensive reaction against anti-democratic forms of hierarchy and the 'right of management to manage'. They comment:

> Frequently they rejected any form of specialised division of labour and formal structures of decision-making, in favour of informal methods and rotation of all responsibilities. The result was seldom democratic or efficient. . . . Genuine criticisms of hierarchies and alienated work are thus lost in an attempt to put them completely into reverse. (Thompson and McHugh 1990: 365)

They quote Landry et al., who argue that the political culture from which the organizations emerged 'made it difficult to conceive of the genuine importance of skills such as financial planning . . . management and entrepreneurship' (Landry et al. 1985: 30). It is not just radical organizations which are being forced to find new accommodations to changing political and economic conditions. In Britain there are a few consultancy firms who offer experience with a critical edge for such organizations and they need knowledge which takes management issues seriously yet understands the restrictive effects of orthodox knowledge on management practices.

At the same time, organizational theory is in quite a fertile state. The 1970s and 1980s heralded major changes in the theoretical orthodoxies of social science. The epoch witnessed qualitative changes, under varying labels such as post-Marxism, post-structuralism, feminism and post-modernism. Three concerns are characteristic of these new approaches: history, meaning and subjectivity. After several decades of a pronounced ahistoricism in the social sciences, an interest in history has penetrated even into psychology and work psychology. My own interest in the history of work psychology derived from discovering the work of Michel Foucault, which was itself part of a dynamic strand of critical social science theory in the 1980s. The second concern is with meaning. Semiotics and similar traditions in theory of language stressed the production of meanings within wider social and material relations rather than in relation to objects. I have already argued that understandings of organizational culture draw on such emphases. The third concern raises new questions about subjectivity, and uses this concept to approach the traditional object of psychology, the individual, from a non-individualistic perspective, stressing power relations, language and the part played by unconscious forces. These are now being applied to the understanding of work organizations, albeit mainly by sociologists (for example Thompson and McHugh 1990 looks critically at organizational behaviour, using the perspectives I have mentioned). My own work has drawn on these traditions, and is one example of the space within the system which is conditional upon the availability of critical non-psychological theory.

Academics working in the field of work psychology and organizational behaviour have maintained almost total silence on the workings of the organizations in which they are employed: universities and other institutions of higher education. This attitude is the product of the belief that the researcher/scientist is a neutral agent of investigation, in which case her or his subjective experience has no relevance. It is also because the university has been seen as a transparent organization which facilitates, but does not affect, the production of academic knowledge. I reject both of these positions. One effect is that academics' experience as employees is absent. I have already suggested that their own professional self-regulation has encouraged researchers and consultants to assume the desirability and possibility of that position. This is made more dangerous because it is not explicit and its specificity to certain organizations and positions is not therefore examined. By using my own experience I am not suggesting that it is universal, but rather demonstrating an analysis which takes into account the specificity of a complex range of conditions. My experience is in a sector where the principle of work autonomy for academics informs organizational practice. Under present conditions, with this traditional autonomy being eroded, the experience is an interesting one in the application of self-regulation as a form of managerial control. Being an employee is a useful perspective to develop as a corrective to the managerialist traditions of work psychology and organizational behaviour.

Thompson and McHugh, in discussing alternatives in organizational behaviour, make a distinction between 'organizational change' and 'changing organizations': 'in our view, one of the tasks of analysis should be to enable those who work or are entering work, to survive, improve and transform organisations' (1990: 358).

7. Work Psychology and the Production of Worker Subjectivity

Work psychology, like psychology, takes the individual as its object. This is a point I have made continuously in this book. But what difference does it make? Psychologists, backed up by assumptions about the individual in Western societies as a whole, believe that the individual actually exists: juxtaposed to society; earning his (*sic*: this has been an assumed part of psychological models of the individual) living; less than perfectly disciplined as a result of his (*sic*) individual traits; potentially intrinsically motivated to work, but not intrinsically changed by it; the producer of ideas and language but not produced by them. If this were the case, then it wouldn't make any difference.

But who is this individual who pre-existed psychology and European history? There is no such thing, except in discourse. That individual has been produced by, among others, psychology, although the conditions of its production are very widespread. Work psychology's history is interrelated with psychology's, but not reducible to it and not dependent on it. It is conditioned by the history of the management of regulation at work. The individual at work whom work psychology is so intent on discovering (feeling that it is getting nearer to an efficacious truth as discovery succeeds discovery) is the individual that work psychology is involved, with others, in producing: the trainable hands; the fatiguable body; the individual abilities, skills and aptitudes; the sentiment; the interpersonal skills; the leadership qualities; the motivation; the boredom and satisfaction; the irrational opposition to management. This individual is all over the place, the product of diverse problems in practice, not of theory, nor even of scientific experiment. The changes in this individual over time reflect the shifting problems of regulation.

This much is amply demonstrated in the preceding chapters, I hope. The final question is: is this individual just so much talk; just discourse with no bearing on its object, those who work? My answer is no. I have elaborated elsewhere, applied to other situations than work, my argument that discourses and practices, through power relations and language, produce subjectivity (Hollway 1982, 1984b, 1989). I believe that this is the case also in work relations, which are not fundamentally different from the domestic relations on which I built my arguments. If so, work psychology not only helps to produce discourses and practices, but, through these, helps to produce subjectivity; those parts of subjectivity – all parts surely – which have something to do with work, which is so pervasive in Western culture.

Work psychology has achieved this by influencing management practice. Influence is achieved through multiple power relations, the main ones being those between management and the worker (which emerged with scientific management); those between the employer (who is likely to be a contractual entity rather than an individual) and managers who are employed to carry out the regulatory functions of the employing organization; and finally those between work psychologists (and other experts, whether as trainers, researchers or consultants) and the employing organization and its representatives. The power of work psychology is that it can reflect back the preoccupations of employers or managers in systematic, formal, apparently scientific discourses which are tied to developments in the practice of workplace regulation. These may or may not be influential; they may or may not be efficacious; they may or may not contribute to some employees' wellbeing. They are always based on that same problematic: enhancing workplace regulation; and by reflecting back this problematic as scientific, work psychology increases the legitimacy of management practices and their justifications in the workplace.

How does this influence those who work there? They are positioned in discourses, and therefore positioned in the related practices. These positions may reflect back to the occupant what is legitimate, what is normal, what is the status of their experience. However, the sum of these positions in discourses does not constitute the entire person. Whether they identify with these positions depends on a longer personal history and its relation to alternative discourses which may contest their positioning in management's or work psychology's discourses.[18] Trade unions have been of primary importance in this respect, which is one reason why they are under sustained attack. There are multiple and competing discourses which contribute to people's positioning. Work psychology and organizational behaviour have space to contribute to these alternatives, but one condition is that they recognize that the assumptions with which they work have so far been tied to the goal of regulation through management.

Notes

1. 'Black Africa . . . is the new market about to explode in the world' (Eliot Janeway, US pundit on economics, quoted in the *New York Times* and the *Guardian*, 20 March 1990).

2. Even work design became redefined through human relations in terms of job satisfaction. To say this is not to claim that psychological approaches uniformly affected the practice of work design. Engineers could rightly point out that the design of production equipment and the jobs which were thus determined continued relatively unaffected by behavioural scientists, but not unaffected by the managerial imperative to increase productivity (see the epigraph by Hackman at the top of chapter 9).

3. In the UK, alcohol dependency is a large-scale and extensive problem at all levels within work organizations. However, because of a culture which regards high levels of drinking as quite normal (particularly in men), the problem is not visible and rarely systematically addressed in organizations.

4. Thanks to Sylvia Shimmin for drawing my attention to this point.

5. In the Birkbeck College Department of Occupational Psychology, which was established in 1961 and has remained until recently the foremost institution for training postgraduate occupational psychologists, the policy was to 'give occupational psychology away', and teaching non-psychologists constituted more than half of the teaching activity. Professor Alec Rodger's reasons were pragmatic: there were just not enough positions in organizations in which trained psychologists could get employment as such.

6. The Civil Service Department had a Behavioural Sciences Division until 1972. Psychologists work in prisons under the Home Office. The Department of Employment set up Occupational Guidance Units (which owed a great deal to the vocational guidance work of the NIIP). In 1970 it was judged to be 'probably the largest employer of occupational psychologists in the United Kingdom' (White et al. 1970: 229) and this was in the field of vocational guidance. The Training Agency (until recently the Manpower

Services Commission) employs many occupational psychologists, primarily in work to do with vocational assessment and guidance. The Ministry of Defence has employed psychologists, both internal and external, ever since the First World War (see Shimmin and Wallis, forthcoming).

7. For a wide-ranging and well-documented discussion of these and other trends, see Handy (1984).

8. There are ancient precedents for the regulation of decentralized work. When Yorkshire weavers worked at home in the seventeenth and eighteenth centuries, they were paid by the length and quality of cloth they wove. They depended on that source of income. To what extent will a similar mode of regulation be reintroduced; a mode in which the worker (not necessarily an 'employee') is distanced from the organization and controlled through material and legal means?

9. Large numbers of employers, particularly in the public sector, call themselves equal opportunities employers. This is not reflected in concomitant changes in practice.

10. In the United States, equal opportunities legislation (on which the British legislation was largely modelled) had a considerable impact on psychometric testing, not only on test design, but on test theory (for example, Bray and Moses 1972). Testing became prominent during that period in a way which did not happen in Britain, where the legislation had much less impact on employment and personnel practice.

11. Lucas (1986) estimates that in excess of 40 million working days may be lost through stress-related illnesses. Many organizations offer programmes to help individuals cope with stress. Thompson and McHugh cite examples which include Pepsico's multimillion-dollar 'fitness centre', and the stress management programmes developed by the Trustee Savings Bank and Digital Equipment in the UK (Cooper 1984).

12. The extent to which individual performance preoccupies management writers like Peters is alarming. There is no hint, anywhere in his books, that people have lives outside work. The self-regulated employee stays at work until the job is complete. To hell with other commitments. (Peters does not say this but it follows from his preoccupations.) This is not just bad news for women, it is bad news for everyone.

13. The managing director of the City Shirt Company in Manchester was recently quoted as saying 'Average earnings in China are just £12 a month, whereas we pay £120 a week. Financially we just cannot compete' (*Guardian* 19 March 1990: 23).

14. Hyden (1983), Seddon (1985), Ndegwa et al. (1987), Leonard (1988), and Kiggundu (1989).

15. These conditions are now beginning to be applied to Eastern Europe.

16. 'Poland and the Soviet Union should receive about £500m from Britain's overseas aid budget, Nicholas Ridley, Secretary of State for Trade and Industry, is to tell the Cabinet' (*Independent on Sunday* 25 March 1990: 2).

17. Two important features of the tradition of independence, built into the system specifically for that purpose, were government funding of universities, administered by a body which was separated from government, and security of academic tenure, so that academics need not feel that their jobs were at risk if they said unpopular things. Both these provisions were changed under Thatcher government policy for higher education and the requirement to attract more funds from industry is predictably affecting the kind of research that can be done. Yet these changes do not mean that the tradition of independence and critical work has successfully been killed off.

18. In the early seventies, Nichols, a British sociologist, conducted research into a company which he calls 'Chemco'. At the time, ideas of job satisfaction, motivation and job redesign were very popular with management; aimed not to alter the structure of work, but to alter employees' commitment to it. On the basis of what he was told when

talking to workers, Nichols argued that the human relations discourse was inappropriate: 'The problem is not so much that Chemco workers have high expectations of work but rather that they expect so little. Accepting that they are workers, they do not expect their work to be satisfying, and they have entered into a grudging bargain with their employers. Part of just one more generation of working-class men and women well used to being denied meaning and control over their lives, like industrial whores they do enough to get enough. "It's a job", they say' (Nichols 1975: 251).

He quotes one worker's dismissal of the idea of job enrichment: 'You move from one boring, dirty, monotonous job to another boring, dirty, monotonous job. And then to another boring, dirty, monotonous job. And somehow you're supposed to come out of it all "enriched". But I never feel enriched – I just feel knackered' (Nichols 1975: 253).

References

Anthony, P.D. (1977) *The Ideology of Work*. London: Tavistock.

Argyle, M. (1953) The Relay Assembly Test Room in Retrospect, *Occupational Psychology*, 27: 98–103.

Argyris, C. (1957) *Personality and Organization: the Conflict between System and the Individual*. New York: Harper & Row.

Argyris, C. (1962) *Interpersonal Competence and Organizational Effectiveness*. London: Tavistock.

Atkins, S. (1986) The Sex Discrimination Act 1975: The End of a Decade, *Feminist Review*, 24: 57–69.

Back, K. (1973) *Beyond Words: The Story of Sensitivity Training and the Encounter Movement*. Baltimore, MD: Penguin.

Baritz, L. (1965) *Servants of Power*. Middletown, CT: Wesleyan University Press.

Bartlett, F.C. (1955) Fifty Years of Psychology, *Occupational Psychology*, 29: 23–216.

Bass, B.M. (1965) *Organizational Psychology*. Boston: Allyn & Bacon.

Bass, B.M. and Barrett G.V. (1971) An Introduction to Organizational Development.

Bayes, M. and Newton, P. (1978) Women in Authority: a Socio-psychological Analysis, *Journal of Applied Behavioural Science*: 14(1): 7–25.

Bendix, R. (1956) *Work and Authority in Industry: Ideologies of Management in the Course of Industrialization*. New York: John Wiley.

Bendix, R. and Fisher, L.N. (1949) The Perspectives of Elton Mayo, *Review of Economics and Statistics*, 31: 312–21.

Bennis, W. and Nanus, B. (1985) *Leaders*. New York: Harper & Row.

Beynon, H. (1984) *Working for Ford*. Harmondsworth: Penguin.

Bindra, D. and Scheier, I. (1954) The Relation between Psychometric and Experimental Research in Psychology, *American Psychologist*, 9: 69–71.

Bion, W. (1959) *Experiences in Groups*. London: Tavistock.

Blackler, F. and Brown, C. (1980) *Whatever Happened to Shell's New Philosophy of Management?* London: Saxon House.

Blauner, R. (1964) *Alienation and Freedom: The Factory Worker and his Industry*. Chicago: University of Chicago Press.

Blood, M. and Hulin, C. (1967) Alienation, Environmental Characteristics and Worker Responses, *Journal of Applied Psychology* 51: 284–90.

Bradford, L., Gibb, J.R. and Benne, K.D. (eds) (1964) *T-Group Theory and Laboratory Method*. New York: John Wiley.

Braverman, H. (1974) *Labour and Monopoly Capital: The Degradation of Work in the Twentieth Century*. New York: Monthly Review Press.

Bray, D.W. and Moses, J.L. (1972) Personnel Selection, *Annual Review of Psychology*, 23: 545–76.

Briggs, A. (1961) *A Study of the Work of Seebohm Rowntree 1871–1954*. London: Longman.

British Psychological Society (1960) Technical Recommendations for Psychological and Educational Tests prepared by the Committee on Test Standards of the British Psychological Society, *Bulletin of the British Psychological Society*, 13 (41): 13–17.

British Psychological Society (1965) Principles Governing the Employment of Psychological Tests and Clinical Instruments, *Bulletin of the British Psychological Society*, 18 (61): 27–8.

British Psychological Society (1969) Classification of Tests and Test Users; Courses of Training in the Use of Psychological Tests other than Degree Courses, *Bulletin of the British Psychological Society*, (22) 75: 109–11.

British Psychological Society Division of Occupational Psychology Training Committee (1986) *Developments in Occupational Psychology*. Leicester: BPS.

British Psychological Society (1988) *The Future of the Psychological Sciences: Horizons and Opportunities for British Psychology*. Leicester: BPS.

Broadbent, D. (1980) in G. Lindzey (ed.) *A History of Psychology in Autobiography, vol VII*. San Francisco: W.H. Freeman.

Buchanan, D.A. and Huczynski, A. (1985) *Organizational Behaviour: An Introductory Text*. London: Prentice-Hall.

Burns, T. and Stalker, G.M. (1961) *The Management of Innovation*. London: Tavistock.

Burrell, G. (1985) Michel Foucault and the Analysis of Organizations. University of Lancaster. Unpublished manuscript.

Burt, C. (1924) The Mental Differences between Individuals, *Journal of the National Institute of Industrial Psychology*, 11 (2): 67–74.

Burt, C. (1953) *Contribution of Psychology to Social Problems*. London: Oxford University Press (originally L.T. Hobhouse Memorial Lecture no.22).

Business Week (1980) Corporate Culture: The Hard to Change Values that Spell Success or Failure, *Business Week*, 27 October: 148–60.

Cadbury, E. (1914) Some Principles of Industrial Organisation: The case for and against Scientific Management, *Sociological Review* 7 (2): 99–117.

Cadbury, E. (1979) *Experiments in Industrial Organization*. New York: Arno Press; first published by Longman, London, 1912.

Carey, A. (1967) The Hawthorne Studies: A Radical Criticism, *American Sociological Review*, 32 (3): 403–16.

Carey, A. (1979) The Norwegian Experiments in Democracy at Work: a Critique and a Contribution to Reflexive Sociology, *Australian & New Zealand Journal of Sociology*, 15 (1): 13–23.

Cartwright, D. (1947–8) Social Psychology in the United States during the Second World War, *Human Relations*, 1: 333–52.

Chandler, A.D. (1977) *The Visible Hand: the Managerial Revolution in American Business*. Cambridge, MA: Harvard University Press.

Chapple, E.D. and Sayles, L.R. (1961) *The Measure of Management: Designing Organisations for Human Effectiveness*. New York: Macmillan.

Child, J. (1964) Quaker Employers and Industrial Relations, *Sociological Review*, 12: 293–315.

Child, J. (1969) *British Management Thought*. London: Allen & Unwin.

Clutterbuck, D. (1979) The Future of Work, *International Management*, August: 17–19.

Cooper, C.L. (1984) What's New in . . . Stress. *Personnel Management*, June: 40–4.

Cooper, R. (1974) *Job Motivation and Job Design*. London: IPM.

Cousins, M. and Hussain, A. (1984) *Michel Foucault*. London: Macmillan.

Crites, J.O. (1969) *Vocational Psychology: The Study of Vocational Behaviour and Development*. New York: McGraw Hill.

Cronbach, L. (1957) The Two Disciplines of Scientific Psychology, *American Psychologist*, 12: 671–84.

Davis, L. and Canter, R. (1956) Job Design Research, *Journal of Industrial Engineering*, 7: 275–82.

Davis, L., Canter, R. and Hoffman, J. (1955) Current Job Design Criteria, *Journal of Industrial Engineering*, 6 (2): 21–33.

Devinat, P. (1927) *Scientific Management in Europe*. Geneva: ILO.

Donzelot, J. (1979) *The Policing of Families*. London: Hutchinson.

Drucker, P. (1959) Human Relations: How Far Do We Have To Go?, *Management Record*, March.

Elson, D. and Pearson, R. (1981) Nimble Fingers Make Cheap Workers: An Analysis of Women's Employment in Third World Manufacturing, *Feminist Review*, 7: 87–107.

Emery, F. and Trist, E. (1965) The Causal Texture of Organizational Environments, *Human Relations*, 18: 21–32.

Farmer, E. and Eyre, A.B. (1922) An Investigation into the Packing of Chocolates (1), *Journal of the National Institute of Industrial Psychology*, 1(2): 12–14.

Foucault, M. (1965) *Madness and Civilisation*. New York: Random House.

Foucault, M. (1973) *The Birth of the Clinic: An Archaeology of Medical Perception*. London: Allen Lane.

Foucault, M. (1977) *Discipline and Punish*. London: Allen Lane.

Foucault, M. (1979) *History of Sexuality: An Introduction*. New York: Random House.

Fox, A. (1966a) From Welfare to Organisation, *New Society*, 9 June.

Fox, A. (1966b) Managerial Ideology and Labour Relations, *British Journal of Industrial Relations*, November: 375.

Fox, A. (1985) *Man Mismanagement*. London: Hutchinson.

French, W.O. (1978) *The Personnel Management Process*. Boston: Houghton Mifflin; first published 1970.

French, W.O. and Bell, C.H. (1973) *Organization Development: Behavioral Science Interventions for Organization Improvement*. Englewood Cliffs, NJ: Prentice-Hall.

Friedlander, F. and Brown, L.D. (1974) Organization Development, *Annual Review of Psychology*, 25: 319–41.

Garvin, D. (1983) Quality on the Line, *Harvard Business Review*, September/October.

Gellerman, S.W. (1966) *The Management of Human Relations*. Illinois: Holt, Rinehart & Winston.

George, Susan (1989) *A Fate Worse than Debt*. Harmondsworth: Penguin.

Gilbreth, F. and Gilbreth, L. (1919) *Fatigue Study: The Elimination of Humanity's Greatest Unnecessary Waste. A First Step in Motion Study*. London: Routledge.

Gilbreth, F. and Gilbreth, L. (1924) The Efficiency Engineer and the Industrial Psychologist, *Journal of the National Institute of Industrial Psychology*, 2(1): 40–5.

Goldman, P. and van Houten, D.R. (1979) Bureaucracy and Domination: Managerial Strategy in Turn-of-the-Century American Industry. In D. Dunkerley and G. Salaman (eds) *International Yearbook of Organisation Studies*. London: Routledge & Kegan Paul.

Goldsmith, W. and Clutterbuck, D. (1985) *The Winning Streak*. Harmondsworth: Penguin.

Goldthorpe, J.H., Lockwood, D., Bechofer, F. and Platt, J. (1968) *The Affluent Worker: Industrial Attitudes and Behaviour*. Cambridge University Press.

Goodman, J. and Novarra, V. (1977) The Sex Discrimination Act, 1975: A Role for Psychologists, *Bulletin of the British Psychological Society*, 30: 104–5.

Gordon, C. (ed.) (1980) *Michel Foucault: Power/Knowledge*. Brighton: Harvester.

Hackman, J.R. (1978) The Design of Work in the 1980s, *Organizational Dynamics*, 7(1): 3–17.

Hackman, J.R. and Oldham, G.R. (1980) *Work Redesign*. Reading, MA: Addison Wesley.

Halley, J.C. (1980) Management Issues of the 1980s. Unpublished topic papers produced by the *British Institute of Management*.

Hammond, V. (ed.) (1985) *Current Research in Management*. London: Pinter.

Handy, C. (1979) The Shape of Organisations to Come, *Personnel Management*, June: 24–6.

Handy, C. (1984) *The Future of Work*. Oxford: Basil Blackwell.

Hansard Society (1990) *Women at the Top*. London: Hansard Society.

Hearnshaw, L. and Winterbourn, R. (1945) *Human Welfare and Industrial Efficiency*. Wellington (NZ): Reed.

Henriques, J., Hollway, W., Urwin, C., Venn, C. and Walkerdine, V. (1984) *Changing the Subject: Psychology, Social Regulation and Subjectivity*. London: Methuen.

Herbst, P.G. (1974) *Socio-Technical Design*. London: Tavistock.

Herzberg, F. (1968) One More Time: How Do You Motivate Employees? *Harvard Business Review*, 46: 53–62.

Herzberg, F., Mausner, B., Peterson, R. and Capwell, D. (1957) *Job Attitudes: Review of Research and Opinion*. Pittsburgh, PA: Psychological Services.

Herzberg, F., Mausner, B. and Snyderman, B. (1959) *The Motivation to Work*. New York: John Wiley.

Hill, P. (1971) *Towards a New Philosophy of Management*. Farnborough: Gower.

Hobsbawm, E. (1968) *Labouring Men*. London: Weidenfeld & Nicolson.

Hobsbawm, E. (1969) *Industry and Empire*. Harmondsworth: Penguin.

Hochschild, A.R. (1983) *The Managed Heart*. Berkeley: University of California Press.

Hollway, W. (1982) Identity and Gender Difference in Adult Social Relations. PhD thesis, University of London.

Hollway, W. (1984a) Fitting Work: Psychological Assessment in Organisations. In Henriques et al., *Changing the Subject*.

Hollway, W. (1984b) Gender Difference and the Production of Subjectivity. In Henriques et al., *Changing the Subject*.

Hollway, W. (1986) Management and Labour in Transition: The Case of Zimbabwe. *International Journal of Sociology and Social Policy*, 6(2): 83–102.

Hollway, W. (1987) Psychology in Industry and Commerce. Unpublished paper presented to the Conference on the Future of the Psychological Sciences, Harrogate, February.

Hollway, W. (1989) *Subjectivity and Method in Psychology: Gender, Meaning and Science*. London: Sage.

Hollway, W. (in preparation) Power and Gender Relations in a Large Public Sector Bureaucracy: The Case of the Tanzanian Civil Service. To appear in L. Radtke and H. Stam (eds) *Gender and Power*.

Hollway, W. and Mukurasi, L. (1990) *Obstacles to Women's Progression into Senior Management in the Tanzanian Civil Service*. Unpublished Report to the Government of Tanzania and the Overseas Development Administration UK.

Hollway, W. and Mukurasi, L. (in preparation) Women Managers in the Tanzanian Civil Service. To appear in N. Adler and D. Izraeli (eds) *Women in Management Worldwide*, 2nd edn. New York: Sharpe.

House, R. and Wigdor, L. (1967) Herzberg's Dual-factor Theory of Job Satisfaction and Motivation: A Review of the Evidence and a Criticism, *Personnel Psychology*, 20: 369–89.

Hoxie, R.F. (1915) *Scientific Management and Labor*. New York: Appleton.

Hoxie, R.F. (1921) *Trade Unionism in the United States*. New York: Appleton Century.

Hyden, G. (1983) *No Shortcuts to Progress: African Development Management in Perspective*. Berkeley: University of California Press.

Industrial Health Research Board (1940) *Industrial Health in War*. Emergency Report No. 1. London: HMSO.

Jahoda, M. (1963) Some Notes on the Influence of Psychoanalytic Ideas on American Psychology, *Human Relations*, 16: 111–22.

Jaques, E. (1947a) Some Principles of Organization of a Social Therapeutic Institution, *Journal of Social Issues*, 3: 4–10.

Jaques, E. (1947b) Social Therapy: Technocracy or Collaboration?, *Journal of Social Issues*, 3: 59–66.

Jaques, E. (1947/8) On the Dynamics of Social Structure: A Contribution to the Psycho-Analytical Study of Social Phenomena, *Human Relations*, 1: 3–23.

Jaques, E. (1951) *The Changing Culture of a Factory*. London: Tavistock.

Jaques, E. (1955) Social Systems as a Defence against Persecutory and Depressive Anxiety. In M. Klein, P. Heimann and R.E. Money-Kyrle (ed.) *New Directions in Psycho-Analysis*. London: Tavistock.

JNIIP (1924–5) An American Appreciation of the NIIP, *Journal of the National Institute of Industrial Psychology*. 30: 303–4.

Kay, H. and Warr, P. (1970) Some Future Developments in Occupational Psychology, *Occupational Psychology*, 44: 293–302.

Kelly, J. (1978) A Reappraisal of Sociotechnical Systems Theory, *Human Relations*, 31 (12): 1069–99.

Kelly, J. (1985) Management's Redesign of Work: Labour Process, Labour Markets and Product Markets. In Knights et al. (eds) *Job Redesign*. Chapter 3.

Kiggundu, M. (1989) *Managing Organizations in Developing Countries*. West Hertford, CT: Kumarian Press.

Kilmann, R., Saxton, S. and Serpa, R. (eds) (1985) *Gaining Control of the Corporate Culture*. San Francisco: Jossey Bass.

King, N. (1970) Clarification and Evaluation of the Two-Factor Theory of Job Satisfaction, *Psychological Bulletin*, 74: 18–31.

Klein, L. (1976) *A Social Scientist in Industry*. Aldershot: Gower.

Knights, D., Wilmott, H. and Collinson, D. (eds) (1985) *Job Redesign: Critical Perspectives on the Labour Process*. Aldershot: Gower.

Koivisto, W.A. (1953) Value, Theory and Fact in Industrial Sociology, *American Journal of Sociology*, 58: 564–72.

Kovel, J. (1982) *Against the State of Nuclear Terror*. London: Pluto.

Lancashire, R.D. and Cohen, B.J. (1970) Developments in Vocational Guidance, *Occupational Psychology*, 44: 223–8.

Landry, C., Morley, D., Southwood, R. and Wright, P. (1985) *What a Way to Run a Railroad: An Analysis of Radical Failure*. London: Comedia.

Landsberger, H.A. (1968) *Hawthorne Revisited*. New York: Cornell University Press; first published 1958.

Lawler, E. (1969) Job Design and Employee Motivation, *Personnel Psychology*, 2: 426–35.

Lawrence, P.R. and Lorsch, J.W. (1967) *Organization and Environment*. Cambridge, MA: Harvard University Press.

Lee, J.A. (1982) The Social Science Bias in Management Research, *Business Horizons*, November/December: 21–31.

Lee, J.A. (1985) After Fads and Advocative, Ideological Social Science, Whither OD? *International Journal of Manpower*, 6(4): 11–20.

Leonard, D.K. (1988) The Secrets of African Managerial Success, *IDS Bulletin*, 19(4): 35–41.

Lewin, K., Lippitt, R. and White, R. (1939) Patterns of Aggressive Behaviour in Experimentally Created 'Social Climates', *Social Psychology*, 10: 271–99.

Likert, R. (1961) *New Patterns of Management*. New York: McGraw-Hill.

Likert, R. (1967) *The Human Organization: Its Management and Value*. New York: McGraw-Hill.

Littler, C. (1985) Taylorism, Fordism and Job Design. In Knights et al. (eds) *Job Redesign*. Chapter 2.

Lucas, M. (1986) *How to Survive the 9–5*. London: Thames Methuen.

Lupton, T. (1974) *Industrial Behaviour and Personnel Management*. London: IPM; first published 1964.

Marglin, S. (1971) *What Do Bosses Do? The Origins and Functions of Hierarchy in Capitalist Production*. Harvard Institute of Economic Research, discussion paper no. 222.

Maslow, A.H. (1943) A Theory of Human Motivation, *Psychological Review*, 50: 370–96.

Maslow, A.H. (1954) *Motivation and Personality*. New York: Harper.

Mayo, E. (1930) Changing Methods in Industry. *Personnel Journal*, 8.

Mayo, E. (1949) *The Social Problems of an Industrial Civilization*. London: Routledge & Kegan Paul.

McClelland, D. (1961) *The Achieving Society*. New York: Van Nostrand.

McDougall, W. (1914) *Psychology: The Study of Behaviour*. London: Oxford University Press.

McDougall, W. (1923) *An Outline of Psychology*. London: Methuen.

McGregor, D. (1967) *The Human Side of Enterprise*. New York: McGraw-Hill.

McKenna, E. (1987) *Psychology in Business: Theory and Applications*. London: Lawrence Erlbaum.

McNair, N. (1957) What Price Human Relations?, *Harvard Business Review*, March.

Menzies, I. (1960) A Case-Study in the Functioning of Social Systems as a Defense against Anxiety, *Human Relations*, 13: 95–121.

Metcalf, H.C. and Urwick, L. (eds) (1971) *Dynamic Administration: The Collected Papers on Mary Parker Follett*. New York: Harper; first published 1941.

Meyer, S. (1981) *The Five-Dollar Day: Labour Management and Social Control in the Ford Motor Co. 1908–1921*. New York: State University Press.

Miller, E. and Gwynne, G.V. (1972) *A Life Apart*. London: Tavistock.

Miller, E. and Rice, K. (1967) *Systems of Organisation*. London: Tavistock.

Molander, C. (ed.) (1989) *Human Resource Management*. Bromley, Kent: Chartwell Bratt.

Moore, W.E. (1965) *Industrialisation and Labor*. New York: Russell & Russell.

Moorrees, V. (1933) Industrial Psychology at Rowntree's Cocoa Works (1) The Work of the Psychological Department, *The Human Factor*, May: 159–66.

Munsterberg, H. (1913) *Psychology and Industrial Efficiency*. Boston: Houghton Mifflin.

Muscio, B. (1974) *Lectures in Industrial Psychology*. Easton: Hive; first published 1919.

Muscio, B. and Brooke, R. (1922) An Investigation into the Packing of Chocolates, 11, *Journal of the National Institute of Industrial Psychology*, 1(2): 68–75.

Myers, C.S. (1911) The Pitfalls of Mental Tests, *British Medical Journal*, January: 195–6.

Myers, C.S. (1920) *Mind and Work: The Psychological Factors in Industry and Commerce*. London: University of London Press.

Myers, C.S. (1923) The Efficiency Engineer and the Industrial Psychologist, *Journal of the National Institute of Industrial Psychology*, 1(5): 168–72.

Myers, C.S. (1926) *Industrial Psychology in Great Britain*. London: Jonathan Cape.

Myers, C.S. (1970) Autobiography, *Occupational Psychology 44*, Jubilee Volume on the NIIP.

Ndegwa, P., Mureithi, L.P. and Green, R.H. (eds) (1987) *Management for Development: Priority Themes in Africa Today*. Nairobi: Oxford University Press.

Nichols, T. (1975) The 'Socialism' of Management: Some Comments on the New 'Human Relations', *Sociological Review* 23: 245–65.

✗ Nicholson-Lord, D. (1990) Some Buildings Simply Make You Sick, *Independent on Sunday*, 25 March: 3–5.

NIIP speeches (1925) *Journal of the National Institute of Industrial Psychology*, London.

Niven, M.M. (1967) *Personnel Management 1913–1963*. London: IPM.

Northcott, C.H. (1933) Industrial Psychology at Rowntree's Cocoa Works. (2) Statistical Note upon the Results of Vocational Selection, 1923–1931, *The Human Factor*, May: 166–8.

Oldham, G., Hackman, J.R. and Pearce, J. (1976) Conditions under which Employees Respond Positively to Enriched Work, *Journal of Applied Psychology*, 61: 395–403.

Pearn, M. (1976) Race Relations Legislation and the Role of the Occupational Psychologist, *Bulletin of the British Psychological Society*, 29: 300–2.

Perrow, C. (1970) *Complex Organizations*. Chicago: Scott, Foresman.

Perrow, C. (1979) *Complex Organizations*, 2nd edn. Chicago: Scott, Foresman.

Peters, T.J. (1988) *Thriving on Chaos: A Handbook for Management Revolution*. London: Macmillan.

Peters, T.J. and Austin, N. (1985) *A Passion for Excellence*. New York: Random House.

Peters, T.J. and Waterman, R.H. (1982) *In Search of Excellence*. New York: Harper & Row.

Pollard, S. (1968) *The Genesis of Modern Management*. Harmondsworth: Penguin.

Pritchard, W. (1984) What's New in Organization Development?, *Personnel Management*, July: 30–3.

Psychological Regulations (1931) From the archives of Rowntree Mackintosh plc.

Pugh, D.S. (1969) Organizational Behaviour: An Approach from Psychology, *Human Relations*, 22(4): 345–54.

Pugh, D.S. and Hickson, D.J. (1976) *Organisation Structure in its Context: The Aston Programme 1*. London: Saxon House.

Rodger, A. (n.d.) [early 1970s?] Training and Development. Unpublished course notes of Birkbeck College, Department of Occupational Psychology.

Roethlisberger, F.J. (1949) *Management and Morale*. Cambridge, MA: Harvard University Press; first published 1941.

Roethlisberger, F.J. (1954) *Training for Human Relations*. Cambridge, MA: Harvard University Press.

Roethlisberger, F.J. and Dickson, W.J. (1970) *Management and the Worker*. Cambridge, MA: Harvard University Press; first published 1939.

Rogers, C. (1957) The Necessary and Sufficient Conditions of Therapeutic Personality Change, *Journal of Consultative Psychology*, 21: 95–103.

Rogers, C. (1965) The Characteristics of A Helping Relationship. In J.F. Adams (ed.) *Counseling and Guidance: A Summary View*. New York: Macmillan.

Roll, E. (1968) *An Early Experiment in Industrial Organisation: Being the History of the Firm of Boulton and Watt, 1775–1805*. London: Frank Cass; first published 1930.

Rose, M. (1975) *Industrial Behaviour: Theoretical Development since Taylor*. Harmondsworth: Penguin.

Rose, N. (1985) *The Psychological Complex: Psychology, Politics and Society in England, 1869–1939*. London: Routledge & Kegan Paul.

Rosenbrock, H.H. (1977) The Future of Control, *Automatica*, 13: 1–9.

Rowan, J. (1979) A Survey of Occupational Psychologists. Unpublished manuscript.

Rowlandson, P. (1984) The Oddity of OD, *Management Today*, November: 91–3.

Rowntree, B.S. (1920) The Aims and Principles of Welfare Work, *Welfare Work*, 1(2): 5 (part 1); 19 (part 2).

Rowntree, B.S. (1979) *The Human Factor in Business*. New York: Arno Press; first published by Longman, London, 1921.

Rowntree, J.S. (1923) The Scope of Vocational Selection in Industry. *Journal of the National Institute of Industrial Psychology*, 1(6): 240–5.

Salaman, G. (1981) *Class and the Corporation*. London: Collins/Fontana.

Sapienza, A.M. (1985) Believing is Seeing: How Culture Influences the Decisions Top Managers Make. In R. Kilmann, M. Saxton and R. Serpa and Associates *Gaining Control of the Corporate Culture*. San Francisco: Jossey Bass. Chapter 4.

Schein, E.H. (1985a) How Culture Forms, Develops and Changes. In R. Kilmann, M. Saxton and R. Serpa and Associates, *Gaining Control of the Corporate Culture*. San Francisco: Jossey Bass. Chapter 2.

Schein, E. (1985b) *Organizational Culture and Leadership*. San Francisco: Jossey Bass.

Schein, E. and Bennis, W.G. (1965) *Personal and Organizational Change through Group Methods: The Laboratory Approach*. New York: John Wiley.

Searle, G.R. (1971) *The Quest for National Efficiency*. Oxford: Basil Blackwell.

Seddon, J. (1985) The Development and Indigenization of Third World Business: African Values in the Workplace. In V. Hammond (ed.) *Current Research in Management*. London: Pinter. Chapter 7.

Shackel, B. and Klein, L. (1976) Esso London Airport Refuelling Control Centre Redesign – an Ergonomics Case Study, *Applied Ergonomics* 7(1): 37–45.

Sheppard, H.L. (1949) The Treatment of Unionism in 'Managerial Sociology', *American Sociology Review*, 14: 310–13.

Shimmin, S. and Wallis, D. (1989) Change and Survival in Occupational Psychology. Paper presented at the 4th West European Congress on The Psychology of Work and Organisation. Cambridge, 10–12 April.

Shimmin, S. and Wallis, D. (forthcoming) *Fifty Years of Occupational Psychology in Britain: 1939–1989. Personal Reflections*.

Sills, P. (1973) *The Behavioural Sciences*. London: IPM.

Smith, J.H. (1987) Elton Mayo and the Development of Industrial Sociology: A Problem of Historical Interpretation. Paper presented at the 6th Cheiron – Europe Conference. Cheiron, September.

Smith, M. (1952) *An Introduction to Industrial Psychology*. London: Cassell; first published in 1943.

Snell, M. (1979) The Equal Pay and Sex Discrimination Acts: Their Impact on the Workplace, *Feminist Review*, 1: 37–58.

Steiner, G. (1974) Whatever Happened to the Group in Social Psychology?, *Journal of Experimental Social Psychology*, 10: 94–8.

Stevenson, J. (1984) *British Society 1914–1945*. Harmondsworth: Penguin.

Stewart, J. (1983) Whatever Happened to the Welfare Officer?, *Personnel Management*, June: 39–41.

Taylor, F.W. (1967) *The Principles of Scientific Management*. New York: Norton; first published 1911.

Thompson, E.P. (1967) Time, Work Discipline and Industrial Capitalism, *Past and Present*, 38: 56–97.

Thompson, P. and McHugh, D. (1990) *Work Organisations: A Critical Introduction.* London: Macmillan.

Thorsrud, E. and Emery, F.E. (1976) *Democracy at Work: A Report of the Norwegian Industrial Democracy Programme.* Leiden: Martinus Nijhoff.

Tiffin, J. and McCormick, E.J. (1966) *Industrial Psychology.* London: Allen & Unwin; first published 1942.

Trist, E. (1981) The Evolution of Socio-Technical Systems. No. 2 in the series *Issues in the Quality of Working Life.* Toronto: Ontario Ministry of Labour.

Trist, E.L. and Bamforth, K.W. (1951) Some Social and Psychological Consequences of the Longwall Method of Coal-Getting, *Human Relations*, 4: 3–38.

Trist, E.L., Higgin, G., Murray, H. and Pollock, A. (1963) *Organisational Choice.* London: Tavistock.

Tunstall, W.B. (1983) Cultural Transition at AT&T, *Sloan Management Review*, 25 (1): 15–26.

Tunstall, W.B. (1985) Breakup of the Bell System: A Case Study in Cultural Transformation. In Killman, Saxton and Serpa (eds). pp. 44–65.

Turner, A.N. and Lawrence, P.R. (1965) *Industrial Jobs and the Worker.* Boston MA: Harvard University Press.

Tynan, O. (1980) *Improving the Quality of Working Life in the 1980s.* London: Work Research Unit, occasional paper no. 16.

Viteles, M.S. (1933) *Industrial Psychology.* London: Jonathan Cape.

Vroom, V.H. (1964) *Work and Motivation.* New York: Wiley.

Walker, C.R. (1950) The Problem of the Repetitive Job, *Harvard Business Review*, 58(3): 54–8.

Wallis, D. (1981) Sex Discrimination and the Law, *Bulletin of the British Psychological Society*, 33: 1–5.

Wall Street Journal (1984) AT&T Has Call for a New Company Culture, *Wall Street Journal*, 28 February: 32.

Weick, C. (1969) *The Social Psychology of Organizing.* Cambridge, MA: Addison Wesley.

Welch, H.J. and Myers, C.S. (1932) *Ten Years of Industrial Psychology.* London: Pitman.

Weld, H.P. (1928) *Psychology as Science.* New York: Henry Holt.

White, A. (1901) *Efficiency and Empire.* London: Methuen.

White, G.C. and Jessup, G. (1979) *QWL: The Development of the UK Programme.* London: Work Research Unit, occasional paper no. 14.

White, G.C., Raphael, L.H. and Crinnion, J. (1970) Vocational Guidance at the Department of Employment: the Work of Psychologists, *Occupational Psychology*, 44: 229–36.

Whitehead, N. (1937) *The Industrial Worker.* Cambridge, MA: Harvard University Press.

Whitsett, D. and Winslow, E. (1967) An Analysis of Studies Critical of the Motivator-Hygiene Theory, *Personnel Psychology*, 20: 391–415.

Wilson, A.T. (1947) Some Implications of Medical Practice and Social Case-Work for Action Research, *Journal of Social Issues*, 3: 11–28.

Woodward, J. (1958) *Management and Technology, Problems of Progress in Industry.* London: HMSO.

World Bank (1989) *From Crisis to Sustainable Growth.* Washington: World Bank.

Wundt, W. (1904) *Principles of Physiological Psychology Vol. 1.* New York: Macmillan.

Index

WORK PSYCHOLOGY AND
ORGANIZATIONAL BEHAVIOUR

05

A

A

05 A